I've Got the Music in Me

A Fan's View of
1960s and 1970s Rock and Pop Music

Written by Bruce Braine

Edited by John Lum

*****

Cover Design by Maryanne Braine

Copyright © 2017 Bruce Braine. All rights reserved.

ISBN-9781521381977

Table of Contents

Table of Contents iii

Preface 1

Acknowledgments 3

SECTION I

REELING IN THE YEARS – 1963-1976

1963 "Only the Beginning" 7

1964 "I'm Feelin' Glad All Over" 11

1965 Pt. 1 British Songs "I Believe in Yesterday" 18

1965 Pt. 2 American Songs "I've Got Sunshine on a Cloudy Day" .25

1966 Pt. 1 British Songs "Beep Beep Yeah" 32

1966 Pt. 2 American Songs "My Empty Cup Tastes as Sweet as the Punch" 40

1967 "All You Need Is Love" 54

1968 "Born to Be Wild" 63

1969 "It's the Time of the Season for Loving" 70

1970 "I've Seen Sunny Days That I Thought Would Never End" ...81

1971 Pt. 1 "Listen to the Tide Slowly Turning, Wash All Our Heartaches Away" 93

1971 Pt. 2 "All You've Got to Do Is Call" 102

1972 "It Was a Very Good Year" 112

1973 "We're An American Band" 118

1974 "You Ain't Seen Nothing Yet" 126

1975 "Thank God My Music's Still Alive" 132

1976 "Don't Go Breaking My Heart" 145

SECTION II

THE LISTS

PART 1 - FAVORITE SONG LISTS

Best Summer Songs "There Is Danger in the Summer Moon Above"
.... 161

Best Rain Songs "Listen to the Rhythm of the Falling Rain" 165

Best Christmas Songs "Santa Claus Is Coming to Town" 169

Best Comedy Singles "Please Mr. Custer, I Don't Want to Go" ... 172

My Favorite Rock Instrumentals 177

Best B-sides (ex. The Beatles) "Wham Bam Thank You Ma'am!" 181

Best Beatles B-Sides "Don't You Know It's Gonna Be Alright" ... 190

Best Long Songs "Take a Sad Song and Make It Better" 192

Best Rockin' Love Songs "And You Know You Should Be Glad" 199

Best Numeric or Alphanumeric Songs "1-2-3" 203

Best Originals/Cover Pairs "It Takes Two, Baby, Me and You" ... 211

PART 2 - FAVORITE ARTISTS AND ALBUM LISTS

My Favorite Concerts "Get Back to Where You Once Belonged" 223

Best Family Groups "It's a Family Affair" 232

Best Rock Albums "It's Only Teenage Wasteland" 236

Best Album Sides of the 1960s "With Tangerine Trees and Marmalade Skies" 245

Best Album Sides of the 1970s "Blue Jean Baby, L.A. Lady, Seamstress for the Band" 254

Appendix of Lyric Attributions 267

Bibliography 271

About the Author 273

End Notes 274

Preface

Ever since I was very young, I have always loved listening to music. Even at age three or four, when I would have terrible temper tantrums, my mother would turn to classical music to settle me down. Whether it was Beethoven, Offenbach, Tchaikovsky or Mozart, it didn't matter. Like a light switch being turned off, the tantrums would end. By age nine, I was becoming more aware of a new form of music, early rock and folk rock that I initially passively enjoyed in 1963, though show tunes and classical music remained staples in our household.

However, with The Beatles and the British Invasion of 1964-65, I became officially hooked on rock and pop music. It started with New York's WABC radio and its Top 20 survey with Dan Ingram that I religiously listened to on Tuesday afternoons after school. Soon I was buying singles and playing them on a small turntable I got for Christmas. Later, by the late 1960s-early 1970s, I was buying albums and shifting to listening to more FM radio. Everywhere, rock music was there with me. It got me through the ups and downs of junior high school, prep school and college. It put an exclamation point on my happiest days and also helped brighten my dreariest days. It was there when I fell in love, allowed me to wallow in the sadness of a breakup and then eventually energized my recovery.

This book is about rock and pop music from MY perspective paralleled with my own formative years from age 8 to 22. I am not a musician or a music critic – far from it. Of course, what I like and don't like is very subjective. I don't pretend to have the "right" opinion about whether a song or artist is good or bad.

This book is separated into two sections.

The first section is entitled "Reeling in the Years – 1963-1976". It is a year-by-year review and discussion of my favorite groups, albums and songs of that year and also includes my top 10 favorite songs along with the 10 most popular songs of the year. I found choosing my 10 favorites for a year exceedingly difficult, for most years I could easily choose 20 to 30 songs that I liked a great deal. I "cheated" somewhat in 1965, 1966 and 1971 by doing two chapters on each of these years, one for music from the U.K. and the other for American songs. This allowed me to select 10 favorite U.K. AND 10 favorite U.S. songs for these three outstanding years in rock music.

The second section is entitled "The Lists" and provides a series of lists including best album sides, best summer songs, best rain songs, best rock concerts, best B-sides, best long songs, best rock instrumentals and many others. These, of course, were my favorites and are not based on chart or popular success. Most of the songs/albums/artists are from the sixties and seventies, though in a few cases I have included songs from the late 1950s, the 1980s and even more current music.

If you like classic rock and pop music even half as much as I do, I think you will like this book. Hopefully, it brings back good memories. Enjoy!

Acknowledgments

Writing *I've Got the Music in Me* began with a series of music posts on my blog (thebrainetrust.com) that I had originally started as a public policy and economics blog. Between 2012 and 2016, I posted more than twenty blog entries on music in the 1960s and 1970s, which form much of the basis of Section I of this book. The idea to write a book became a reality after I retired from AEP in early 2016.

During the summer of 2016, I asked my longtime friend and college roommate John Lum to be my editor/publisher. John is currently retired as well, but in the past was Director of Publications at the American Stock Exchange and has significant professional editorial experience. His work and advice on this book have been invaluable and extraordinary.

I would also like to thank my friends and family who provided encouraging comments on my blogs and showed great interest in my book project. Special mention is also due to friends Neil Van Dyke and Robbie Carey. Neil first introduced me to top 40 radio in 1963 at his home and I went and saw *A Hard Day's Night* with him when it was first released during the summer of 1964. Robbie lived very nearby and I was first introduced to the music of the Doors, The Mothers of Invention (Frank Zappa), Jimi Hendrix, the Grateful Dead, Country Joe and the Fish, Jefferson Airplane and countless other rock artists during frequent visits to his home during the 1960s and 1970s.

While there are many important autobiographies and other sources that I relied on for this book, special mention is also owed to Lou Simon, host of Sirius XM Radio's *'60s Satellite Survey*. Lou is a walking encyclopedia of facts and interesting stories about the songs and artists, several of which I cite in this book. I also have had a great correspondence with Lou by email and he has even read and commented on a couple of my blogs on the 1960s that are now part of this book.

I would also like to thank my mother, Sarah Frost, who unknowingly encouraged me to become a lifelong fan of rock music by buying my first rock album (The Beatles' *Help!*) and by first lending me her transistor radio when sick so I could listen to the WABC Top 20 survey in early 1966.

Last but certainly not least, I would like to thank my loving wife, Anne, who has put up with my enjoyment of all types of trivial facts about '60s and '70s music over the years, and encouraged me to start my music blogs in the first place.

Section I

Reeling in the Years – 1963-1976

1963
"Only the Beginning"

(See Appendix for Lyric Attributions)

1963 is a year in rock/pop music that gets no respect. After all, it was before the British Invasion and "Beatlemania" dominated U.S. music in 1964. However, it is the year when I first remember hearing, though not yet listening to, popular/rock music. Granted, I was still hesitant to write about it until I realized that 1963 led to the rock tidal wave of 1964. It was what the Baroque period was to the Classical era in classical music. Some darn good music in the Baroque era (Bach and Vivaldi, most notably) and without it there would not have been the explosion of music of the Classical era (from Mozart to Beethoven and many in between). 1963 (and several years earlier) was really the rock era's Baroque period and a pretty good one at that.

Admittedly, at age nine, I wasn't listening to popular music much then. My mother listened to classical music and show tunes on her RCA Victor record player. My older sister, though three grades ahead of me in school, had relatively little interest. Nonetheless, 1963 represented some of my earliest albeit mostly subliminal memories of popular music (though I confess some of these memories may be mixed with hearing these songs as "solid gold" hits a couple of years later on WABC radio).

A big development in American rock was the California surf sound made famous by **The Beach Boys** and **Jan and Dean**. The Beach Boys first hit it big in 1963 with their second top 40 single "Surfin' U.S.A.", which rose to #3 (May). The song epitomized surf rock and was followed shortly thereafter by the slow rock ballad "Surfer Girl" (#7 Sep.) and the upbeat "Little Deuce Coupe" (#15 Sep.) as a B-side. Next, there was a third top 10 smash "Be True to Your School" (#6 Dec.) including real cheerleaders and an homage to "On Wisconsin". Finally there was the more cerebral and interesting slow-rock classic "In My Room" (#23 Dec.) that foreshadowed Brian Wilson's eventual classic album *Pet Sounds*.

Meanwhile, Jan and Dean had been a largely forgettable early rock group with "Baby Talk" of 1959 as their biggest hit. Along came Brian Wilson who collaborated with Jan Berry to write the memorable composition "Surf City" and Jan and Dean had a #1 song in July 1963.

Instrumental surf rock took a step forward with the **Rockin' Rebels'** "Wild Weekend" (#8 Mar.) released at the beginning of the year. Though a throwback to late '50s, saxophone-led, Coasters rock-'n'-roll, the song also featured the unique guitar sounds of surf rock. And by the summer of 1963, the **Surfaris** released "Wipeout" (#2 Aug.) featuring a classic rock guitar riff and drum solos that later became a staple of late '60s and early '70s rock. The song was such a big hit in 1963 that it was again released in the summer of 1966 and was among my early 45 rpm purchases that year. At the time, I just couldn't figure out why it wasn't at least a top 10 hit on WABC in 1966. I only realized later that it had been a #1 hit three years earlier.

Most Popular Hits in 1963
  1. **Sugar Shack – Jimmy Gilmer and the Fireballs**
  2. **Dominique – The Singing Nun**
  3. **Blue Velvet – Bobby Vinton**
  4. **He's So Fine – Chiffons**
  5. **Hey Paula – Paul and Paula**
  6. **Louie, Louie – Kingsmen**
  7. **Fingertips – Stevie Wonder**
  8. **I Will Follow Him – Little Peggy March**
  9. **Sukiyaki – Kyu Sakamoto**
  10. **My Boyfriend's Back – The Angels**

By the end of 1963, a new group, the **Trashmen**, ushered in the era of garage rock with "Surfin' Bird" (#4 Jan. '64), which was released in December. This was hardly a conventional surf rock song (though it stole most of its melody by combining two earlier singles, "Papa-Oom-Mow-Mow" and "The Bird is the Word" by the Rivingtons). What is notable about the song is the violent drumming which sounded eerily similar to Dave Clark Five's "Glad All Over" in 1964.

The Four Seasons were hardly new in 1963 but their sound was. In 1962, they hit it big with "Sherry" and "Big Girls Don't Cry" which owed more to doo-wop than rock for its inspiration. But in 1963, "Walk Like A Man" (#1 Mar.) *("As fast as you can")* broke new ground with its unique opening guitar riff and interesting rhythms. It is still one of my favorites of the 1960s and one of the top-selling songs of 1963.

At the same time, the girl groups (**Shirelles**, **Crystals** and **Chiffons**, etc.) were still at their peak and my favorite girl group song ever "He's So Fine" *("do lang do lang do lang")* by the Chiffons hit #1 (Apr.) just a few weeks after the Four Seasons. (And if you don't believe that this presaged 1964 rock, consider that George Harrison unintentionally plagiarized the music and harmonies in his iconic "My Sweet Lord" seven years later.) I also loved **Jimmy Gilmer and the Fireballs'** "Sugar Shack" (#1 Oct.) *("There's a crazy little shack beyond the tracks")* as much for its unique guitar and organ sound as anything else.

My Favorite Songs in 1963
 1. Walk Like a Man – Four Seasons
 2. He's So Fine – Chiffons
 3. Surfin' Bird – Trashmen
 4. Fingertips – Stevie Wonder
 5. Wipeout – Surfaris
 6. Heat Wave – Martha and the Vandellas
 7. My Boyfriend's Back – Angels
 8. Walk Right In – Rooftop Singers
 9. Blowin' in the Wind – Peter, Paul and Mary
 10. Wild Weekend – Rockin' Rebels

The Motown sound hadn't reached its peak yet. This was to come during 1964-66 with the **Supremes**, **Four Tops** and **Temptations** reaching ascendency. However, 1963 was the year when four outstanding singers/groups came to prominence and arguably led the way for Motown in the future. First, there was **Martha and the Vandellas'** "Heat Wave" (#4 Sep.) *("It's like a heat wave burning inside")*, which naturally hit it big in the summer. **Smokey Robinson and the Miracles,** after their initial success with "Shop Around" in 1961, didn't break out again until 1963 with "You've Really Got A Hold on Me" (#8 Feb.) and "Mickey's Monkey" (#8 Sep.) *("lum dee lum dee lie")*. There was the beginning of a long and storied career of **Marvin Gaye** with his hit "Pride and Joy" (#10 July). But the true artist breakout that would revolutionize music for decades to come was a 12-year-old sensation named **Stevie Wonder** who sang and played a mean harmonica in "Fingertips-Pt 2" (#1 Aug.) *("Everybody say yeah (yeah)")*.

Folk music was in full stride (later to be combined with rock by **Simon and Garfunkel**, the **Byrds** and many other groups to make American folk-rock). Hailing from New York City, the **Rooftop Singers'** "Walk Right In" *("sit right down, daddy let your mind roll on")* was a #1 hit (Jan.). **Peter Paul and Mary** scored two #2 hits with "Puff the Magic Dragon" (May) and "Blowin' in the Wind" (Aug.). Even a Catholic nun from Belgium, Sister Luc-Gabrielle, aptly named **The Singing Nun** on the record, had a French language folk hit "Dominique", which hit #1 in December. My sister bought the album (her first and only pop record purchase of the year), though I can't say I remember her playing anything but the title song.

Of course, folk's undisputed leader Robert Zimmerman a.k.a. **Bob Dylan** had his first critical and eventual commercial success with *Freewheelin' Bob Dylan* released in 1963. The album included four notable Dylan songs: "Blowin' in the Wind", "Don't Think Twice, It's Alright" (both covered by the aforementioned Peter, Paul and Mary), "Girl from the North Country", and "A Hard Rain's Gonna Fall", which later became Dylan standards.

Meanwhile, across the Atlantic, a brand new group from Liverpool had three #1 hits in the U.K.: "Please Please Me", "From Me to You", and "She Loves You". Yes, 1964 was going to be one helluva year.

1964
"I'm Feelin' Glad All Over"

In many ways, 1964 marked the beginning of rock music. It also was the true beginning of my more than 50-year interest in rock music and most popular music, even though as the year began I was just a fourth grader. My first memory of that year was early February 1964 when **The Beatles** appeared on *The Ed Sullivan Show*. I can remember watching them on TV with all the girls screaming in the audience, but really enjoying their music, though I had never heard it before. My mother, who was watching with my sister and me, actually enjoyed one song, Paul's rendition of "Til There Was You" *("There were bells on the hill but I never heard them ringing")*. Most likely, this was because it came from the musical *The Music Man*.

The Beatles!

The Beatles dominated 1964 like no artists have dominated before or after. By early April, The Beatles made history with the top five songs in one week:

The Billboard Hot 100, April 4, 1964
1. **Can't Buy Me Love**
2. **Twist and Shout**
3. **She Loves You**
4. **I Want to Hold Your Hand**
5. **Please, Please Me**

Then a week later, The Beatles set another record with 14 of the Billboard top 100 songs during the week of April 11:

The Billboard Hot 100, April 11, 1964
 1. Can't Buy Me Love
 2. Twist and Shout
 4. She Loves You
 7. I Want to Hold Your Hand
 9. Please, Please Me
 14. Do You Want to Know a Secret?
 38. I Saw Her Standing There
 48. You Can't Do That
 50. All My Loving
 52. From Me to You
 61. Thank You Girl
 74. There's a Place
 78. Roll Over Beethoven
 81. Love Me Do

In fact, during all of 1964, The Beatles had 19 songs reach the top 40 and six reach #1, a one-year feat that NO other artist has done since. While The Beatles songs would progress lyrically and musically in future years, the sound of 1964 was fresh and new. The music was a unique combination of rock-'n'-roll guitar and rhythms heavily influenced by **Chuck Berry**, **Little Richard** and **Buddy Holly**, among others. John and Paul's vocals were distinctive with Paul's leads quite varied ranging from the screaming "Long Tall Sally" to the soft "And I Love Her". The Beatles had superb harmonies in almost all their songs, borrowing heavily from Beach Boys and Four Seasons songs that preceded them.

It would require many pages to go through all the songs that I liked by The Beatles in 1964. However, five stand out in particular for me: "She Loves You" (#1 Mar.), "I Want to Hold Your Hand" (#1 Feb.), "Please Please Me" (#3 Mar.), "Twist and Shout" (#2 Apr., The Beatles' outstanding cover of the Isley Brothers' 1962 hit), and "A Hard Day's Night" (#1 Aug.). All of them featured simple but great melodies, great vocals and harmonies, and solid guitar, bass and drum lines. (Despite popular sentiment to the contrary, Ringo was a good drummer.) The epitome of The Beatles' unique style was their opening chord on "A Hard Day's Night" which was, according to Randy Bachman, "the most famous chord ever on a twelve string guitar" (For an interesting short video on this, see Randy Bachman's 2010 interview from a live CBC radio show "Guitarology 101" from http://www.youtube.com.)

A Hard Day's Night – both the movie and album – represented great memories. I first saw the movie in Livingston Manor, NY in the Catskills with my friend Neil on a visit to his parents' summer home. It was like no movie I had ever seen before and in retrospect it was perhaps the best music movie ever made and served as the beginning of the music video age some 17 years before MTV made it official. (If you don't believe me, watch the movie and pay particular attention to the opening title track and "Can't Buy Me Love"). I first remember hearing the album that year at a friend's house, Stephen White, while playing board games, listening to it over and over.

The British Invasion Begins

As dominant as The Beatles were throughout 1964, British music in general also dominated the U.S. pop charts with the beginning of the so-called British Invasion. In fact, numerous British groups first hit the U.S. charts in 1964, and many of these groups were to go on to become famous for years to follow. Most notably, **The Rolling Stones** began their unofficial reign as Britain's second best rock group by late 1964, though they were only later to dominate the U.S. charts in 1965. Interestingly, two of their first three U.S. charters were covers. The first, "It's All Over Now" (#26 Sep.) *("Because I used to love her, but it's all over now")* was originally by **The Valentinos** earlier in 1964, which the Stones heard while touring in the U.S. The second hit, "Time Is on My Side" (#6 Dec.), was originally by Mississippi soul queen **Irma Thomas** in 1963. These two covers are still among my favorite songs by the Stones. Their third American charter was "Tell Me (You're Coming Back)" (#24 Aug.), a Jagger-Richards original composition which was to become the norm in 1965. The Stones featured Keith Richards' blues-influenced, slick guitar playing and his outstanding music-writing skills, along with Mick Jagger's vocals and sneering lyrics.

Most Popular Hits in 1964
 1. I Want to Hold Your Hand – Beatles
 2. She Loves You – Beatles
 3. Hello, Dolly! – Louie Armstrong
 4. Baby Love – Supremes
 5. Where Did Our Love Go – Supremes
 6. There! I've Said it Again – Bobby Vinton
 7. Come See About Me – Supremes
 8. Can't Buy Me Love – Beatles
 9. Oh! Pretty Woman – Roy Orbison
10. Do Wah Diddy Diddy – Manfred Mann

Meanwhile, four other major British rock groups first invaded the U.S. shores in 1964 – the **Dave Clark Five**, the **Kinks**, the **Zombies**, and the **Animals**. The Dave Clark Five from London featured "hard rock" drumming with the machine-gun percussion start to their first hit, "Glad All Over" (#6 Apr.) *("You say that you love me all of the time")* and their next song "Bits and Pieces" (#4 May). (Not surprisingly, the group's leader, Dave Clark, was also its drummer.) The group also had two other top 10 hits, including a comparatively rare slow song but very tuneful "Because" (#3 Sep.) and seven top forties in total during 1964.

Also from London, the Kinks began their U.S. career with one of the greatest rock classics of all time, "You Really Got Me" (#7 Nov.) *("You got me so I can't sleep at night")* that arguably was the true beginning of "hard" rock. It was the group's guitarist, songwriter and leader Ray Davies who came up with the unforgettable guitar riff that drives the song.

From Hertfordshire, England, the Zombies started their relatively short U.S. career with one of my favorite classic rock hits, "She's Not There" (#2 Dec.) *("Well, no one told me about her, the way she lied!")*.

The Animals, from Newcastle, England, had a smash #1 hit, the controversial "House of the Rising Sun" (Sep.) *("And it's been the ruin of many a poor boy, and god, I know I'm one.")*. Eric Burdon's vocals and Alan Price's organ and the memorable opening guitar/bass arpeggio make this one of the best songs of 1964. Though not as well known, their follow-up "I'm Crying" (#19 Oct.) is another excellent example of early rock-blues fusion that was to be much of the Animals' repertoire in 1965. Other harder rock groups from Britain of note in 1964 include **Manfred Mann** with their throwback hit "Do Wah Diddy, Diddy" (#1 Oct.) and one of my favorites from the faux Southern group, the **Nashville Teens** "Tobacco Road" (#14 Oct.) *("In the middle of Tobacco Road")*. Who would've ever thought they were English?

Though harder rock was newly ascendant, several British soft/folk rock artists also had their first U.S. successes in 1964. **Herman's Hermits** had their first U.S. hit with the upbeat "I'm Into Something Good" (#13 Dec.). **Peter and Gordon**'s first hit was a chart-topper – the beautiful "A World Without Love" (#1 June) *("I don't care what they say I won't stay in a world without love")*. Their second hit was the almost as good "Nobody I Know" (#12 Aug.). Paul McCartney, who was then dating Jane Asher, composed both of these songs and gave them to Jane's brother, the "Peter" of Peter and Gordon.[1]

Chad and Jeremy, another British duo, had the poetic and beautiful "A Summer Song" (#7 Oct.) as well as a particular favorite of mine, "Yesterday's Gone" (#21 June) *("for me you were the one, but that was yesterday and yesterday's gone")*. **Gerry and the Pacemakers** scored with two top 10 hits: the cheerful "How Do You Do It" (#9 Aug.) and the beautiful but sad "Don't Let the Sun Catch You Crying" (#4 July). Not to be outdone, **Dusty Springfield** had her first solo hit, "I Only Want to Be With You" (#12 Mar.) *("It's crazy but it's true")* and later in the year "Wishin' and Hopin'" (#6 Aug.), her two best solos of her career. Finally, **Billy J. Kramer and the Dakotas** first hit it big with the double-sided hit "Little Children/Bad to Me" (#7 June/#9 June) *("they'd be sad if you're bad to me")*. "Bad to Me" was yet another Lennon-McCartney tune.

Back in the U.S.A.

Back in America, the California sound continued its dominance led by The Beach Boys and their three excellent popular hits "Fun, Fun, Fun" (#5 Mar.), "I Get Around" (#1 July), and "Dance, Dance, Dance" (#8 Dec.), which featured the group's sterling vocal harmonies, up-tempo rhythms and Brian Wilson's songwriting. The B-side of "I Get Around",

"Don't Worry Baby" (#24 July) *("Well it's been building up inside of me for I don't know how long")*, however, featured Wilson's introspective side that would blossom over the next couple of years.

Jan and Dean had another top 10 hit with the tuneful "Dead Man's Curve" (#8 May) and an even bigger hit with the equally fun "The Little Old Lady (from Pasadena)" (#3 Aug.). A brand new group, **The Rivieras,** best typified the California Sound with their rocking beach classic "California Sun" (#5 Feb.) *("We're out there having fun, in the warm California sun")*. **Lesley Gore** had her last top 10 hit in early 1964 with the haunting "You Don't Own Me" (#2 Feb.). Meanwhile, on the other coast, the "Jersey Boys" or **Four Seasons** continued to churn out hits, with seven top 40 hits in 1964 with their three best being "Dawn (Go Away)" (#3 Feb.) *("I'm no good for you")*, "Rag Doll" (#1 July), and "Save It for Me" (#10 Sep.) *("Don't let your love go astray")*.

My Favorite Songs in 1964
1. A Hard Day's Night – The Beatles
2. Oh! Pretty Woman – Roy Orbison
3. You Really Got Me – The Kinks
4. Time is on My Side – Rolling Stones
5. I Get Around – The Beach Boys
6. I Want to Hold Your Hand – The Beatles
7. Come See About Me – The Supremes
8. She Loves You – The Beatles
9. Bad to Me – Billy J. Kramer
10. A World Without Love – Peter and Gordon

Motown music was gaining popularity with several of its signature groups emerging from obscurity. **The Supremes** finally made the top 40 with their January hit, "When the Lovelight Starts Shining Through His Eyes" (#23 Jan.), and by late 1964 they had begun a record string of five #1 hits in a row with the first three from 1964 among my favorites: "Where Did Our Love Go" (#1 Aug.), "Baby Love" (#1 Nov.), and "Come See About Me" (#1 Dec.). **The Temptations** also first reached the top 40 in 1964 with their still under-appreciated "The Way You Do the Things You Do" (#11 Apr.). Meanwhile, the **Four Tops**, who had been performing since the late fifties, finally reached the top 20 with the excellent "Baby, I Need Your Lovin'" (#11 Oct.). **Mary Wells** also scored big with her only #1 hit "My Guy" (May). And a new, beautiful pop-soul voice emerged on the scene, **Dionne Warwick**, with "Anyone Who Had a Heart" (#8 Feb.) and one of her greats "Walk on By" (#6 June). And two famous jazz trumpeters, **Louie Armstrong** and **Al Hirt,** scored two of the biggest songs of the year: Armstrong's vocal hit "Hello, Dolly!" (#1 May), the title song from the popular musical, and Hirt's "Java" (#4 Feb.). The latter song was the best instrumental of the year.

Of course, as new and exciting as 1964 was, it wasn't without its disappointments for me. Many of the earlier pop artists from the early 1960s and even 1950s ranging from **Brenda Lee, Connie Francis, Andy Williams**, and **Al Martino** to **Nino Tempo and April Stevens**, were hanging on with very bland songs that still managed to chart. **Bobby Vinton**'s "Mr. Lonely" even rose to #1 (Dec.) despite it being cloying. **Elvis Presley** was still "the king" in name only after his great successes of the 1950s and early 1960s and didn't even chart in the top 10 in 1964 and didn't have a single memorable song.

But all in all, that didn't matter much in 1964, because with The Beatles, Stones, Kinks, Dave Clark Five, Animals, Peter and Gordon, Beach Boys, Four Seasons, Four Tops, Dionne Warwick, and the Temptations, to name a few, there was much to enjoy in 1964 and much to look forward to in 1965. It was hard not to feel "Glad All Over".

1965 Pt. 1 British Songs
"I Believe in Yesterday"

1965 was a magical year for rock and popular music. I say this despite the fact that I really didn't listen to music much at all on the radio (as I started to do in early 1966). In fact, I was still much more enamored with following the New York Yankees who sadly for me were to suffer their first losing season in decades in 1965, signaling the abrupt end of a baseball dynasty that had lasted more than four decades.

Musically, 1965 was a year that I remember mostly for my first record album, *Help!*, which I was allowed to play on my mother's RCA Victor as well as my second record album, *Rubber Soul,* which I bought at the end of 1965. But it wasn't long before (during 1966 and 1967) that I started catching up collecting singles and albums from 1965, which in my opinion is the best year for rock music ever. (But it's not just *my* opinion. Lou Simon of Sirius XM Radio's "'60s Satellite Survey" describes 1965 as his "favorite year" as well).

1965 was characterized by several important trends in rock/pop music. The first was the continuing dominance of The Beatles as the top group on the rock scene. The second was the continuation of the British Invasion with many 1964 groups doing well in 1965 and several notable new acts emerging. Third, it was the beginning of a new American folk-rock sound. Lastly, soul and R&B was arguably better than ever, most notably the Motown sound in 1965. In this regard, 1965 was a "classic" year with The Beatles, British Invasion, folk-rock and the Motown sound, newly ascendant or at or near its peak. Because of all the great music in 1965, I decided to split "1965" into two chapters. So here is Pt. 1, The Beatles and the British Invasion:

The Beatles

1965 began and ended with **The Beatles,** who released four albums during the year (*Beatles '65, Beatles VI, Help!* and *Rubber Soul*), though technically Beatles '65 was released on December 15, 1964, no doubt to coincide with Christmas shopping. All four albums went immediately to #1 on the charts. Similarly, the year was nicely bracketed by five outstanding Beatles singles all reaching #1: "Eight Days a Week" (Mar.), "Ticket to Ride" (May), "Help!" (Sep.), "Yesterday" (Oct.) and finishing with one of my favorite double-sided Beatles hits "We Can Work It Out/Day Tripper" (#1 Jan. '66/#5 Jan. '66) released in early December 1965. My favorite Beatles song was "Ticket to Ride" perhaps for its infectious chorus *("She's got a ticket to ride...and she don't care")* and the great Rickenbacker guitar opening riff by Paul, and I constantly sang the chorus around our apartment during 1965. But I really loved them all, from George's excellent guitar riffs of "Day Tripper" to the great vocals and harmonies in "Help!, "Eight Days a Week", and "We Can Work It Out" and finally the beautiful simplicity of "Yesterday" *("There's a shadow hanging over me")*.

Of the 1965 Beatles albums, *Help!* and *Rubber Soul* are my favorites, no doubt because they were the first albums I owned. (However, in retrospect, *Beatles '65* has many excellent songs as well including, most notably, "I'm a Loser", "No Reply", "I'll Be Back", "Baby's in Black", "I Feel Fine" (which was also a #1 single at the end of 1964/beginning of 1965), and "She's a Woman" (#4 Dec. '64).

The *Help!* album includes seven outstanding songs, all from the movie – "Help!", "Ticket to Ride", "You've Got to Hide Your Love Away", "The Night Before", "You're Gonna Lose That Girl", "Another Girl", and "I Need You". All could have been hit singles if The Beatles had chosen to release them. In fact, "You've Got to Hide Your Love Away" (#10 Nov.) became a hit single by the British group **Silkie** later in the year. The only problem with *Help!* is that it has five tracks containing soundtrack filler from the movie, and with the exception of the instrumental sitar version of *A Hard Day's Night* theme song ("Another Hard Day's Night"), these tracks are not memorable. This soundtrack filler resulted in many scratches and skips in the album as I was constantly picking up the needle to skip them.

The Beatles' *Rubber Soul* album is still one of their all-time classics. Similar to *Help!,* it features The Beatles' great songwriting, singing and harmonies. But unlike *Help!*, it contains the beginning of The Beatles' more sophisticated lyrical and musical themes, particularly John's beautiful snapshots in "Norwegian Wood" and "In My Life" as well as his complicated relationship in "Girl". And, of course, Paul had two great love songs: "Michelle" (which was later covered and charted by multiple other artists) as well as the up-tempo country and western style, acoustic "I've Just Seen a Face" which contains some fine guitar work by George. But Paul also was getting away from simple themes with his interesting and very melodic "I'm Looking Through You" *("I thought I knew you. What did I know?")*. Also, my favorite song on the album, the irresistibly catchy "You Won't See Me" *("and I will lose my mind if you won't see me")* captured Paul's desperate mood in his tenuous relationship with Jane Asher in 1965.[2]

The Rise of the Rolling Stones

However, as much as The Beatles' preeminence was an enduring characteristic of 1965, in many ways it was the emergence of **The Rolling Stones** as The Beatles' main challenger on the rock scene that characterized the year. Though the Stones didn't sell nearly as many singles or albums as The Beatles in 1965, they did have the most successful single of the year, "(I Can't Get No) Satisfaction" (#1 July). "Satisfaction" is perhaps the most famous rock anthem of the 1960s and is rightfully on many lists as the greatest rock song of all time. It had a catchy and unique guitar riff by Keith Richards that was played through a Gibson "fuzz" box in order to roughen the sound. Turns out, Keith had only intended this to be a "dub" for later use of horns in the final record. As Richards related, "Next thing I know we're listening to ourselves in Minnesota somewhere on the radio 'Hit of the Week' and we didn't even know Andrew had put the fucking thing out!".[3] And the rest was history!

Earlier in the year, the Stones had one of their first major commercial successes in the U.S. with "The Last Time" (#9 May), which features a driving guitar riff (played by Brian Jones) and was another Jagger-Richards original composition.

Later in the year, the Stones released another great rocker, "Get Off of My Cloud" (#1 Nov.), with such rapid fire vocals that Jagger managed to squeeze in the lyric *"I live on an apartment on the ninety-ninth floor of my block"* all in the first musical line of the song. The full lyrics of this song along with the aforementioned "Satisfaction" and "The Last Time" cemented the Stones' reputation as the bad boys of rock or the anti-Beatles, though of course the truth was more complicated. In December 1965, the Stones released its version of the very McCartney-like "As Tears Go By" (#6 Jan. '66) *("It is the evening of the day")*, which they had written earlier for **Marianne Faithful** in late 1964. It was a beautiful love song with the Stones arrangement including acoustic guitar and a string orchestra accompaniment very much influenced by the late 1965 success of The Beatles' "Yesterday".

British Hard Rock Rules

Though the **Dave Clark Five** had a good year in 1964 (with "Glad All Over" most notably), 1965 was their best year, starting with their excellent cover of **Chris Kenner**'s "I Like It Like That" (#7 July) and then September's very "catchy" "Catch Us If You Can" (#4 from the DC5 movie *Having a Wild Weekend*). "Catch Us If You Can" *("here they come again umm")* is the best song ever recorded by the DC5 and one of my favorites of the 1960s. Finally, DC5 ended the year with the release of "Over and Over" (#1 Dec.) *("I said over and over and over again, 'This dance is gonna be a drag'")*, their most popular and only #1 hit, and another irresistible DC5 song.

Most Popular British Hits in 1965
1. **Satisfaction – Rolling Stones**
2. **Downtown – Petula Clark**
3. **Mrs. Brown, You've Got a Lovely Daughter – Herman's Hermits**
4. **Yesterday – Beatles**
5. **Help! – Beatles**
6. **Get Off My Cloud – Rolling Stones**
7. **I'm Telling You Now – Freddie and the Dreamers**
8. **I'm Henry VIII – Herman's Hermits**
9. **Ticket to Ride – Beatles**
10. **Eight Days a Week – Beatles**

Meanwhile, **The Kinks** fed off their success in 1964 with two more great rock-'n'-roll classics. First, there was the up-tempo, guitar-infused "All Day and All of the Night" (#7 Feb.) with another unforgettable Ray Davies guitar riff and solo (much like its predecessor in 1964 "You Really Got Me"). This was followed by the slower tempo, soulful "Tired of Waiting for You" (#6 Apr.) *("But you keep me waiting all of the time, what can I do?")*. This song became the first in a long line of more introspective and lyrical Kinks songs. Ray Davies' vocal truly feels "so tired", something that John Lennon might have picked up on in The Beatles recording "I'm So Tired" three years later.

The Animals recorded some of their best songs in 1965 though they were all much less commercially successful than 1964's #1 hit "House of the Rising Sun". Their three best of the year were "Don't Let Me Be Misunderstood" (#15 Mar.), "We Gotta Get Out of This Place" (#13 Sep.), and "It's My Life" (#23 Dec.). Each featured a great tune, a great driving bass and guitar line, Eric Burdon's deep voice and occasionally Jagger-like vocals and some great lyrics such as, *"In this dirty old part of the city where the sun refuse to shine"*, *"We gotta get out of this place if it's the last thing we ever do...girl there's a better life for me and you"* and *"I'm just a soul whose intentions are good, oh lord, don't let me be misunderstood."*

My Favorite British Songs in 1965
 1. Satisfaction – Rolling Stones
 2. Ticket to Ride – The Beatles
 3. Catch Us If You Can – Dave Clark Five
 4. Get Off My Cloud – Rolling Stones
 5. It's My Life – Animals
 6. We Gotta Get Out of This Place – Animals
 7. Downtown – Petula Clark
 8. Help! – The Beatles
 9. All Day and All of the Night – Kinks
10. For Your Love – Yardbirds

A new group, the **Yardbirds,** blazed the trail for future hard rock with their first hit song in the U.S., "For Your Love" (#6 June). "For Your Love" *("I will give the stars above")* is a simple rock song with a driving beat and melody but it still stands as one of the top rock songs of the 1960s.

Interestingly, **Eric Clapton,** who had been lead guitarist for the Yardbirds since late 1963, left the group to join John Mayall's **Blues Breakers** right after the commercial success of the single, afraid the group was becoming too popular and eschewing the original group's blues roots. As he notes in his autobiography, "The truth is, I was taking myself far too seriously and becoming very critical and judgmental of anybody in music who wasn't playing just pure blues".[4] However, the Yardbirds barely missed a beat when they replaced Clapton with Jeff Beck and recorded the excellent and almost as successful "Heart Full of Soul" (#9 Sep.), which included Beck's experimental fuzz guitar sound.

British Soft Rock

A new British soft rock act, **Herman's Hermits,** invaded America at the very end of 1964, with their release of "I'm Into Something Good" (#13 Dec.). This song was the first of their SEVEN top 10 charting hits during 1965. The remaining hits included "Can't You Hear My Heartbeat" (#2 Mar.), "Mrs. Brown, You've Got a Lovely Daughter" (#1 May), "Silhouettes" (#5 May), "Wonderful World" (#4 July), "I'm Henry VIII, I Am" (#1 Aug.), and "Just a Little Bit Better" (#7 Oct.). At the time, I remember hearing "I'm Henry VIII, I Am" repeatedly while in a car (no doubt because WABC played the #1 song every hour) with my friend Neil heading up to his parents' country place in the Catskills. It was a very simple *("second verse, same as the first")*, catchy song driven by Peter Noone's excellent vocals. In retrospect, "Mrs. Brown...", the Hermits' other #1 hit, was a better song with a unique opening guitar sound and nicer tune. However, my favorite of their songs in 1965 was "Can't You Hear My Heartbeat" or as the song intones *"you're the one I love".*

Another successful "new" British act (at least on the U.S. charts) was **Petula Clark**, who scored at the beginning of the year with her best seller, and one of the top songs of 1965, "Downtown" (#1 Jan.). Petula had actually been a childhood entertainer during World War II for the British troops and a recording artist and film actress since the late 1940s. However, it took "Downtown" to make her an American singing star. The song had a great musical refrain and a wonderful musical and lyrical introduction: *"When you're alone and life is bringing you down, you can always go downtown"* led by a great piano intro and Petula's heartfelt singing. Her follow-up "I Know a Place" also sold well (#3 Apr.) and was almost as good *("a swinging place, a cellar full of noise")*. Petula had a rich and beautiful voice and finally got the song material she deserved in 1965.

Other British Invasion singles that I also enjoyed included **Wayne Fontana and the Mindbenders**' "Game of Love" (#1 Apr.), **Freddie and the Dreamers**' "I'm Telling You Now" (#1 Apr.), **Gerry and the Pacemakers**' beautiful "Ferry Across the Mersey" (#6 Mar.), the **Zombies**' excellent "Tell Her No" (#6 Feb.), and the **Fortunes**' great vocal harmonies in the impossible-not-to-sing or hum-along "You've Got Your Troubles" (#7 Oct.) *("I've got mine")*. I also enjoyed **The Moody Blues**' first U.S. hit "Go Now!" (#10 Apr.) *("We've already said, goodbye")*, though Denny Laine's tenure in the group was short-lived. The group was later transformed with his departure and the arrival of Justin Hayward and John Lodge in late 1966. And it was hard not to like **Shirley Bassey**'s only U.S. chart success with her stirring rendition of "Goldfinger" (#8 Mar.) *("He's the man, the man with the Midas touch")*. This song began a long history of excellent James Bond movie songs.

Not all British Invasion songs were good, of course, with probably my least favorites being Welshman crooner **Tom Jones**' two hits "What's New Pussycat?" (#3 July) and "It's Not Unusual" (#10 May). However, I must admit I was never a big fan of Tom Jones though I appreciated his excellent voice and understood his appeal to many fans.

But it was certainly a small quibble with an outstanding year of music from across the pond. In fact, these songs made it easy for me to *"believe in yesterday"*.

1965 Pt. 2 American Songs
"I've Got Sunshine on a Cloudy Day"

While many British hits dominated U.S. music in 1965, American music was also excellent in 1965 led by two important trends: a new fusion sound called folk-rock and the ascendancy of Motown music as well as other soul and R&B artists. In other words, there were two more reasons why 1965 is still my favorite year for rock and popular music.

The New Folk Rock Sound

Bob Dylan may have ushered in folk-rock music, but it was other artists that covered many of his songs that led to the great popularity of folk-rock in 1965. Dylan started the trend with his *Bringing It All Back Home* album released in March, which had its entire first side backed by an electric rock-'n'-roll band (a first for Dylan) including Dylan's classic songs "Subterranean Homesick Blues" (#39 May) *("Look out kid. It's something that you did. God knows when but you're doing it again")*, and "Maggie's Farm". Side 2 was more conventional for Dylan with mostly acoustic guitar and harmonica but featured two other classics: "Mr. Tambourine Man" and "It's Alright Ma, I'm Only Bleeding".

By the summer of 1965, Dylan had released another album, *Highway 61 Revisited*. The album included the ultimate electric, folk-rock song "Like a Rolling Stone" (#2 Sep.) *("How does it feel to be on your own with no direction shown, like a complete unknown")*. This is far and away my favorite Dylan song and widely considered one of the greatest rock songs of all time. The last track on the album was one of the longest, yet most interesting, folk songs (over 10 minutes) – "Desolation Row" *("And the only sound that's left after the ambulances go, is Cinderella sweeping up on Desolation Row")*. By the end of the year, Dylan released another great folk-rock single "Positively 4th Street" (#7 Oct.), which featured Dylan's characteristically biting lyrics *("You've got a lot of nerve to say you are my friend...you always seem to be on the side that's winning")*.

While Dylan technically started the folk-rock sound with his first 1965 album, it was the **Byrds** who popularized it with their first single in 1965 – the electric cover of Dylan's "Mr. Tambourine Man" (#1 June) *("Take me for a trip upon your magic, swirling ship")*. The song featured guitarist David Crosby and lead guitarist Roger McGuinn with his distinctive "jangly" electric Rickenbacker guitar sound. Gene Clark played electric bass guitar. All three were excellent lead vocalists and sang great harmonies given their experience as solo folk musicians and in folk groups (McGuinn from the **Chad Mitchell Trio** and Gene Clark from the **New Christy Minstrels**). In August, the group released another Dylan cover, "All I Really Want to Do" (#40 Aug.) *("All I really want to do is, baby, be friends with you")*, which featured great guitar and vocal harmonies. However, a "not-as-good" **Cher** version of the song did better on the charts.

Most Popular American Hits in 1965
1. You've Lost that Lovin' Feelin' – Righteous Bros.
2. I Can't Help Myself – Four Tops
3. Turn! Turn! Turn! – Byrds
4. Stop in the Name of Love – Supremes
5. Wooly Bully – Sam the Sham & The Pharaohs
6. This Diamond Ring – Gary Lewis & The Playboys
7. I Got You Babe – Sonny and Cher
8. Hang on Sloopy – McCoys
9. My Girl – Temptations
10. I Hear a Symphony – Supremes

The *Mr. Tambourine Man* album released in mid-summer was arguably the first complete folk-rock album and was by far the best individual album the Byrds ever recorded. In addition to "Mr. Tambourine Man" and "All I Really Want to Do", it also included another Dylan song, the beautifully harmonic "Chimes of Freedom" and a great cover of folk singer **Pete Seeger**'s composition "Bells of Rhymney". However, the album also featured original Byrds compositions, most notably vocalist Gene Clark's "I'll Feel a Whole Lot Better" *("when you're gone")*, another great folk-rock composition. A testament to the strength of this first Byrds album is that all five of these songs constituted almost the entire first side of the Byrds' greatest hits album released two years later, which not surprisingly was one of the first "greatest hits" albums I ever bought.

Lastly, "Turn! Turn! Turn!" (#1 Dec.) *("To everything there is a season")* was released as a single in October. This time, instead of a Dylan song, the Byrds used another Pete Seeger composition that drew its lyrics from the Bible. "Turn! Turn! Turn!" is my favorite song by the Byrds – its melody, vocal harmonies and electric guitar playing are superb – and it deservedly is the most popular song the Byrds ever released.

Following the Byrds' successes in mid-1965, another new group, **The Lovin' Spoonful** led by singer-songwriter John Sebastian, had their first hit in September – the wonderfully upbeat "Do You Believe in Magic" (#9 Oct.) followed by the excellent love song "You Didn't Have to Be So Nice" (#10 Jan. '66) in December. Meanwhile, in August, **Barry McGuire** took folk-rock in the opposite direction with the #1 hit "Eve of Destruction" (Sep.). This was the folk-rock movement's ultimate anti-war song which was even banned in Scotland and restricted in England due to its lyrics about violence and war *("the Eastern world it is exploding, violence flaring, bullets loading, you're old enough to kill but not for votin', you don't believe in war but what's that gun you're toting, and even the Jordan River's got bodies floating")*.

Michael Stewart, brother of John Stewart of the **Kingston Trio**, formed the group **We Five** and recorded the folk-rock "You Were on My Mind" (#3 Sep.) in 1965. The song's catchy melody and vocals resulted in it becoming one of the biggest hits of 1965. And another new group, the **Turtles,** had their first hit with a good folk-rock cover of Dylan's "It Ain't Me Babe" (#8 Sep.). After a few years of limited popular success (i.e., NO top 10 hits since 1961's "Hats Off to Larry"), **Del Shannon** scored with the excellent "Keep Searchin' (I'll Follow the Sun)" (#9 Jan.), one of my favorites of the year and certainly influenced by folk-rock. **The Vogues** had their first two hits in 1965 with two folk-influenced songs – "You're the One" (#4 Nov.) *("You're the one that I'm dreaming of, baby you're the one that I love")*, and "Five O'Clock World" (#4 Jan. '66), both favorites of mine. And after several years of limited commercial success, **Simon and Garfunkel** emerged on the scene with the December release of the classic folk-rock hit "Sounds of Silence" (#1 Jan. '66) *("Hello darkness my old friend")*.

The folk-rock movement also influenced music outside the U.S. **The Seekers,** hailing from Australia and featuring the beautiful voice of Judith Durham, had their first hit "I'll Never Find Another You" (#4 May) *("I still need you there beside me, no matter what I do")*, which was a superb folk song. **Donovan**, a new British artist, was also heavily influenced by Dylan and his first single "Catch the Wind" (#23 June) was a beautiful and serene folk song that was a great commercial success in the U.K., and a top 40 hit in the U.S.

The Rise of Motown

As exciting as folk-rock was in 1965, it was soul and R&B music that probably best characterized American popular music with its greatest year to date. In particular, the Motown Sound dominated the year, led by the **Supremes**.

The Supremes completed their record five #1 releases in a row with three excellent songs that charted during 1965 – "Come See About Me" (#1 Dec. '64), "Stop! In the Name of Love" (#1 Mar.), and "Back in My Arms Again" (#1 June) and then after missing #1 with "Nothing but Heartaches" (#11 Aug.), finished the year with another great tune, the #1 hit "I Hear a Symphony" (#1 Nov.) *("Whenever you're near, I hear a symphony")*. The talented songwriting team of Brian Holland, Lamont Dozier and Eddie Holland wrote all five of these songs.

My Favorite American Songs in 1965
1. Like a Rolling Stone – Bob Dylan
2. Turn! Turn! Turn! – Byrds
3. California Girls – Beach Boys
4. It's the Same Old Song – Four Tops
5. Hang on Sloopy – McCoys
6. Eve of Destruction – Barry McGuire
7. Mr. Tambourine Man – Byrds
8. Stop in the Name of Love – Supremes
9. You've Lost that Lovin' Feelin – Righteous Bros.
10. Do You Believe in Magic – Lovin Spoonful

The **Four Tops** emerged as the second most important Motown group of 1965 and my personal favorite. I loved all four of their singles in 1965. My favorite was the top 10 "It's the Same Old Song" (#5 Aug.) *("But with a different meaning since you've been gone")*, though the #1 smash "I Can't Help Myself" (#1 June) *("Sugar pie, honey bunch, you know that I love you")* was almost as infectious and was the Tops' first chart-topper. The less popular "Something About You" (#19 Dec.) was an excellent song as well and "Ask the Lonely" (#24 Mar.) showed that lead singer Levi Stubbs could belt out a slow ballad with the best of them. With the exception of "Ask the Lonely", the songs were all written by the same Holland-Dozier-Holland team.

The **Temptations** had four hits in 1965, but it was their first song, penned by Smokey Robinson and fellow Miracles member Ronnie White, that became their biggest hit to date. "My Girl" (#1 Mar.) *("I've got sunshine on a cloudy day")*. "My Girl" remains the most famous and critically acclaimed Temptations song and my favorite Motown slow ballad. Interestingly, it was also David Ruffin's first lead vocal that was followed by three other solid singles by the Temps with Ruffin also in the lead in 1965 – "It's Growing" (#18 May), "Since I Lost My Baby" (#17 Aug.), and "My Baby" (#13 Nov.). This trend would continue during the next two and a half years until mid-1968 (with Ruffin the lead or co-lead singer on virtually all of the Temps' hit songs).

Meanwhile, **Smokey Robinson and the Miracles** were having a successful year with several hit singles: "Ooo, Baby, Baby" (#16 May) (later covered successfully by **Linda Ronstadt**), "My Girl Has Gone" (#14 Nov.), and their best single to date, the beautiful "The Tracks of My Tears" (#16 Sep.) *("Well, I might be the life of the party, honey, but deep inside I'm blue")*. At the end of the year, the Miracles released their most upbeat single and my second favorite by them, "Going to a Go-Go" (#11 Feb. '66), which had a great drum opening and rhythm section throughout.

In addition to the four super Motown groups, there were several other notable soul and R&B hits. Motown solo artist **Marvin Gaye** had three top tens, "I'll Be Doggone" (#8 May), "Ain't that Peculiar" (#8 Nov.), and my favorite "How Sweet It Is to Be Loved by You" (#6 Jan.), which was later covered by **James Taylor**. The Godfather of Soul, **James Brown,** had his two most popular hits "I Got You (I Feel Good)" (#3 Dec.), and "Papa's Got a Brand New Bag" (#8 Sep.), both outstanding R&B songs. **Wilson Pickett** released the iconic "In the Midnight Hour" (Sep.), which though it only made #21, is one of the most memorable songs that many groups later covered. In fact, it seemed that at every junior high school dance I went to at the time, the local rock band would play it.

Meanwhile **Jr. Walker and the All Stars** had the rousing "Shotgun" (#4 Apr.), their first and best hit. Lead singer **Curtis Mayfield** of the **Impressions** penned the beautiful, soulful and religious "People Get Ready" (#14 Mar.), which was partly inspired by Dr. King's Civil Rights March on Washington in 1964. Finally, **Otis Redding** had his first top 40 hit with "I've Been Loving You Too Long" (#21 June) and then the single "Respect" (#35 Oct.). Both are considered among the greatest soul and R&B songs of all time, though in the latter case, it was Aretha Franklin's more famous version in 1967 that most people remember.

Other American Artists

There were also several artists that didn't fit into the new dominant trends of folk-rock or soul/R&B in the U.S. in 1965 but were excellent in 1965. This included most notably **The Beach Boys,** who had an excellent year starting with their great remake of "Do You Wanna Dance?" (#12 Mar.), "Help Me, Rhonda" (#1 May) *("Get her out of my heart")*, and finishing up with "California Girls" (#3 Aug.). The last song was a personal favorite of mine (and my Californian wife). While all three songs followed the surf sound that The Beach Boys had popularized in 1963 and 1964 (and which was the dominant U.S. rock sound in those years), "California Girls" marked a change in The Beach Boys' music, with its lengthy instrumental introduction, and a change in tempo to a slower pace than the typical Beach Boys hit. It was to presage the superb Beach Boys album *Pet Sounds* in 1966 that marked the unofficial end of the beach music era.

The **Righteous Brothers** also dominated the pop charts with their greatest song ever "You've Lost That Lovin' Feeling'" (#1 Feb.) *("You* *never close your eyes anymore when I kiss your lips")*, and in the summer with "Unchained Melody" (#4 Aug.), later featured in the 1990 movie *Ghost*. The **Four Seasons** remained a force in the pop/rock world with two big hits "Bye, Bye Baby" (#12 Feb.) and one of my personal favorites "Let's Hang On!" (#3 Dec.) *("To what we've got, don't act cuckoo we got a lot")*. Meanwhile, a brand new pop/rock group, **Gary Lewis and the Playboys,** had a very successful 1965 with five major hits, the best of the lot being "This Diamond Ring" (#1 Feb.) and "Everybody Loves a Clown" (#4 Oct.) *("So why don't you?")*.

Several individual American hits were also standouts in 1965. **Jay and the Americans** had one of their biggest hits with "Cara, Mia" (#4 July) *("Cara, Mia why, must we say goodbye"),* which featured Jay Black's outstanding voice and was easily my favorite song by the group. **Roger Miller** had the country hit of the year with the catchy "King of the Road" (#4 Mar.) *("No phone, no pool, no pets. I ain't got no cigarettes")*. The **Ramsey Lewis Trio** had the best instrumental of the year with the jazzy "The In Crowd" (#5 Nov.). **Jackie DeShannon** had the best U.S. female solo performance in 1965 with her recording of the Bacharach-David tune "What the World Needs Now is Love" (#7 July) *("It's the one thing that there's just too little of")*.

The best pure rock song from the U.S. in 1965 was the **McCoys**' "Hang on Sloopy" (#1 Sep.), which later became the official rock song of Ohio in 1985 (the McCoys were from the Dayton area) and the OSU Buckeyes. In a similar vein, I also liked the garage rock "She's About a Mover" (#13 May) by **Sir Douglas Quintet**. And for pure fun, there was the simple but catchy "Wooly Bully" (#2 June) by **Sam the Sham and the Pharaohs** (which found its way into skits on *The Sandy Becker Show*, a local kids TV program in New York), and one of the biggest hits of the year "I Got You Babe" (#1 Aug.) by **Sonny and Cher**.

No doubt I have missed some other good songs, but that's the way it was during 1965 when the music always gave you *"sunshine on a cloudy day"*.

1966 Pt. 1 British Songs "Beep Beep Yeah"

In 1966, I went from being a sixth grader in elementary school to a junior-high school student at Friends Seminary in New York City. With the doubling of class size, many new students and the end of a single-teacher system which I enjoyed in sixth grade, it was almost as if my childhood had abruptly ended in September 1966. Similarly, the country was changing with the Vietnam War no longer cloaked in anonymity. Music as always mirrored the increasing complexity of life and events during 1966.

In early 1966, I started listening to WABC music radio and their Top 20 Survey every week. In fact, 1966 was the first year that top 40 radio became a part of my daily life.

British Invasion Continues

In 1966, the volume of new artists and songs slowed from the frenetic pace of the British Invasion of 1964-65. In fact, in the U.S., American groups dominated the pop charts. Nonetheless, British music and specifically **The Beatles** continued to lead the rock music scene.

The Beatles had another strong year, but nothing like the volume of songs, singles and albums it enjoyed during 1964-1965. The Beatles released two albums in the U.S. in 1966. The first, *Yesterday and Today,* was released in June and was mainly composed of The Beatles A- and B-sides of three highly successful double-sided hits by the group during late 1965 and early 1966. This included "Yesterday/Act Naturally" (#1 Oct. '65) from late 1965, arguably Paul's best love song ever, coupled with a light-hearted Ringo cover of a country and western tune. Second, there was the outstanding double-sided hit "We Can Work It Out/Day Tripper" (#1 Jan.) released in December 1965. The third hit single from the album, "Nowhere Man" (#3 Mar.) *("Doesn't have a point of view. Knows not where he's going to. Isn't he a bit like you and me?"),* is still one of my favorites from 1966. "Nowhere Man" has it all, a great tune and chorus, wonderful harmonies and an upbeat rhythm.

"What Goes On" is only an okay B-side, though it did have the rare distinction of being co-written by Ringo.

The remaining five songs from *Yesterday and Today* are hardly album filler. In fact, several are quite notable. "Drive My Car" is a lively and catchy number which is all Paul and kicks off Side 1 with a bang – *"beep, beep yeah!"*. Side 1 also features John's interesting and edgy "I'm Only Sleeping" *("Everybody thinks I'm lazy, I don't mind I think they're crazy")*, a precursor of John's music to come and "Doctor Robert", a more conventional Beatles tune. Side 2 starts with two excellent album cuts. First, there is John's rousing "And Your Bird Can Sing" *("But you don't get me")* with wonderful guitar riffs and the second is George's contribution to the album, the excellent "If I Needed Someone" *("Carve your number on my wall and maybe you will get a call from me")*.

Most Popular British Hits in 1966
 1. **Winchester Cathedral – New Vaudeville Band**
 2. **We Can Work It Out – Beatles**
 3. **Wild Thing – Troggs**
 4. **Paint It Black – Rolling Stones**
 5. **Paperback Writer – Beatles**
 6. **Sunshine Superman – Donovan**
 7. **My Love – Petula Clark**
 8. **19th Nervous Breakdown – Rolling Stones**
 9. **Mellow Yellow – Donovan**
10. **A Groovy Kind of Love – Mindbenders**

In late June, The Beatles scored on the charts again with the single "Paperback Writer/Rain" (#1 July). I remember first hearing and enjoying "Paperback Writer" *("It's based on a novel by a man named Lear")* on the radio while at my first sleepover summer camp. (It turned out that rock/pop music was about the only positive element of my first sleepover camp experience. I apparently wrote a letter home just about every day that told my concerned mother how many days I had left until camp ended and how much I missed my brother and sister.) "Paperback Writer" was a very good song, but it was the less often played B-side, "Rain" *("I don't mind")* that was the more interesting new Beatles entry, complete with unusual rhythms and vocals recorded backwards at the end of the song.

By September, The Beatles had another double-sided hit on the charts, "Yellow Submarine/Eleanor Rigby" (#2 Sep.) but again it was the B-side that deserved more attention. "Yellow Submarine" was an excellent children's tune, complete with submarine/ship sounds and a band playing in the middle as well as Ringo's vocal and it was the first Beatles single that I bought. (It also was one of the first rock songs that I played for my daughters when they were toddlers. My oldest, Kathleen, referred to it as "yellow unterine" which is not a bad pronunciation for a two-year old.) But "Eleanor Rigby" *("all the lonely people where do they all come from")* was the more interesting and better song, the lyrics the stuff of many analyses by rock musicologists and critics since then. In addition, the string accompaniment (a string octet – complete with four violins, two violas and two cellos)[5] nicely blended with Paul's excellent singing and enhanced the beautiful melody of the song. More importantly, the song's arrangement presaged songs such as "She's Leaving Home" from the *Sgt. Pepper's* album in 1967.

The Beatles' second album in 1966 was *Revolver*. In addition to "Yellow Submarine" and "Eleanor Rigby", the album featured a number of great Beatles songs. Most notably, it was the first album that George was actually allowed to have more than one composition. On *Revolver*, Harrison had three very good tracks, the lively and guitar-laden "I Want to Tell You", the sneering and sarcastic "Taxman" and the Indian-influenced, sitar-dominated "Love You To". Of the three tracks, my favorite still is "Taxman". It is a great, lively rock song with an excellent melody and extremely clever lyrics *("Should five percent appear too small, be thankful I don't take it all")*.

McCartney had four excellent tracks that he composed and sang lead on, including the melodic and simple love song "Here, There and Everywhere", the wonderfully upbeat rocker "Good Day Sunshine" which instantly improves anyone's mood, the breakup song "For No One" *("and in her eyes you see nothing")* which was good for wallowing in a love lost, and the upbeat "Got to Get You Into My Life". (Most assumed that this was a love song about a woman, but in fact, as McCartney confirmed in 1997, it is an ode to pot).[6] This latter track and "Good Day Sunshine" are my two favorites. "Got to Get You Into My Life" probably holds some kind of chart record as the identical recording was released as a Beatles single some TEN years later (in June 1976) and managed to reach the top 10 on the U.S. Billboard charts shortly thereafter.

John Lennon had only two tracks on which he was the lead composer and the lead singer – "She Said She Said" and "Tomorrow Never Knows". The latter track was the most original piece that The Beatles had done to date "and in a sense, defined the era of music psychedelia"[7] and helped spawn psychedelic rock that was to become the rage in 1967-69. It included such groundbreaking studio techniques as reverse guitar, processed vocals, and looped tape effects.

British Rock

While The Beatles remained the dominant force from Britain, **The Rolling Stones** continued to make great rock-'n'-roll music with four more hit singles released in 1966. This began early in the year with "19th Nervous Breakdown" (#2 Mar.), followed by "Paint it Black" (#1 June) *("I see a red door and I want to paint it black"),* which became the third Stones #1 hit, the summer double-sided hit "Mother's Little Helper/Lady Jane" (#8 Aug.) and another top 10 hit "Have You Seen Your Mother, Baby, Standing in the Shadow?" (#9 Oct.) The first two songs were outstanding, hard rock-'n'-roll songs with great lead guitar and drum playing and with trademark dark and sneering Stones lyrics. "Mother's Little Helper" *("Outside the door, she took four more")* was the first song to focus on prescription drug abuse and was my favorite Stones song in 1966. "Have You Seen Your Mother, Baby" was also a good rocker and noteworthy in that it includes brass accompaniment, a first for Rolling Stones songs.

My Favorite British Songs in 1966
1. We Can Work It Out – The Beatles
2. Nowhere Man – The Beatles
3. Sunny Afternoon – The Kinks
4. Sunshine Superman – Donovan
5. Mother's Little Helper – Rolling Stones
6. Bus Stop – Hollies
7. Eleanor Rigby – Beatles
8. 19th Nervous Breakdown – Rolling Stones
9. A Well Respected Man – Kinks
10. My Love – Petula Clark

I didn't purchase any Stones albums in 1966 as this was a bit beyond my allowance budget at the time, though I did eventually buy the superlative Stones greatest hits album *High Tide and Green Grass* later in 1966, which features all the Stones' 1964-65 hits as well as "19th Nervous Breakdown" from early 1966. The 1966 album *Aftermath* included another good Stones song "Under My Thumb" which surprisingly was never released as a single.

While the Stones were still the leaders in hard rock, the **Kinks** were transforming themselves from a hard rock group with rock-'n'-roll guitar classics such as "You Really Got Me" and "All Day and All of the Night" to a more innovative group in 1966 that released very different rock music with lyrics laden with social commentary. This began in early 1966 with the release of "A Well Respected Man" (#13 Feb.), an excellent Ray Davies composition that oozed with sarcasm about the British upper class *("And he is oh so good and he is oh so fine in his body and in his mind")*. Though not as successful as "A Well Respected Man", the Kinks' next single, "Dedicated Follower of Fashion" (#36 June), is very similar in structure and sound and was almost as good a song. The target of Davies' satire was the pretentiousness and constant changeover of the latest fashions (apparently, he even got into a physical fight with one fashion designer at a party over this very issue).[8]

However, my favorite Kinks song of 1966 was "Sunny Afternoon" (#14 Sep.), which is one of the most infectious songs ever. It, too, is about wealth (and the high British progressive tax rate à la "Taxman") and speaks to the idleness and decadence of the mega-rich: *"The taxman's* taken all my dough, and left me in this stately home, lazing on a sunny afternoon. And I can't sail my yacht, he's taken everything I got. All I've got's this sunny afternoon."* It was very popular in Britain reaching #1, while managing to reach the top twenty in the U.S.

Though the **Animals** failed to match their popularity and the quality of their hits in 1964-65, they did have two very good songs in 1966. First, there was a good cover of "See See Rider" (#10 Oct.). But my favorite was the Gerry Goffin-Carole King song "Don't Bring Me Down" (#12 June) *("I beg you darling")*. Similarly, the **Yardbirds** had less success in 1966 than their breakout singles in 1965 (i.e., "For Your Love" and "Heart Full of Soul"). Nonetheless, the Yardbirds did have two interesting, high-quality songs with "Shape of Things" (#11 May) and "Over Under Sideways Down" (#13 Aug.), which featured Jeff Beck's distinctive fuzz guitar sound.

British Newcomers

The British Invasion also included one of my favorite new groups in 1966: **The Hollies**. Co-founded by Allan Clarke (the lead singer) and Graham Nash, the Hollies had their first top 40 single in the U.S. with the upbeat "Look Through Any Window" (#32 Jan.) *("What do you see? Smiling faces all around")*. The song set a pattern for the group, using a fast tempo and great tenor harmonies to drive most of their singles. The first major hit of the group, "Bus Stop" (#5 Sep.) *("Bus stop. Bus goes. She stays. Love grows. Under my umbrella")* was another up-tempo, joyful love song that always made me smile. "Stop, Stop, Stop" (#7 Dec.) *("Stop, stop, stop all the dancing give me time to breathe")* featured guitarist Tony Hicks playing a unique-sounding banjo. This is another wonderful rock-'n'-roll, dance song by the Hollies which per usual features the three-part harmonies of Hicks, Clarke and Nash.

Another relatively new artist on the singles charts, **Donovan** from Scotland, had his first big hits in 1966 beginning with the psychedelic folk/rock song "Sunshine Superman" (#1 Aug.) *("Superman or Green Lantern ain't got nothing on me")*. "Sunshine Superman" was probably the first psychedelic pop hit. In addition to being a great tune, it had a unique guitar sound played by none other than Jimmy Page (future guitarist of **Led Zeppelin**), as well as John Paul Jones (future bass player of Led Zeppelin) playing an interesting-sounding bass. "Mellow Yellow" (#2 Dec.) followed and became Donovan's second biggest hit featuring the background whispers of Paul McCartney and an infectious drumbeat.

British Pop

British pop singers continued to shine in 1966:

Petula Clark had three major song successes: "My Love" (#1 Feb.) *("is warmer than the warmest sunshine")*, "A Sign of the Times" (#11 Apr.) *("That your love for me is getting so much stronger")*, and "I Couldn't Live Without Your Love" (#9 Aug.). All three followed a familiar pattern – excellent pop tunes featuring Petula's great voice.

Dusty Springfield had her biggest solo hit with "You Don't Have to Say You Love Me" (#4 July). The song highlighted her strong voice and was her first top 40 in the U.S. since 1964's "Wishin' and Hopin'".

Peter and Gordon had two major hits: "Woman" (#14 Mar., written by Paul McCartney) and my favorite by them – the end-of-the-year, novelty hit "Lady Godiva" (#6 Dec.) *("Seventeen, a beauty queen, she made a ride that caused a scene in the town")*.

Though not able to match their enormous popularity in 1965, the **Herman's Hermits** still had five top 20 hits. The three best were "A Must to Avoid" (#8 Jan.) and "Listen People" (#3 Mar.) from early in the year and "Dandy" (#5 Nov.) *("Where you going to go now? Who you gonna run to?")* from later in the year. The last tune was my favorite 1966 song by the group and interestingly enough was written by Ray Davies of the Kinks.

Surprisingly, two of the most popular songs in the U.S. from British-born artists came from two completely new groups that were to have little success after 1966. "Winchester Cathedral" by the **New Vaudeville Band** (#1 Dec.) was the third best-selling single of 1966. However, the band was only a studio group, the creation of London-born Geoff Stephens. The song was a one-of-a-kind novelty song that featured a whistled verse and then a Rudy Vallee 1930s-style vocal arrangement as the second verse. It was catchy (I liked it at the time), but it has worn very thin over time. This was to be the one and only New Vaudeville Band top 40 single, though they did manage a follow-up single "Peek a Boo" which reached #72 on the charts in early 1967. Mercifully, the New Vaudeville Band faded into obscurity thereafter.

Meanwhile, the **Troggs**' "Wild Thing" (#1 July) peaked in the summer while I was at camp. Perhaps because it served as an important reminder of the few things I actually enjoyed at camp (i.e., 1960s rock music), I bought it when I got home in August. However, the song has also worn thin (despite its later use in the movie *Major League*) and is seldom played on oldies stations or classic rock. The Troggs quickly flamed out in the U.S., with only one other major hit record (the top 10 hit in early 1968 "Love Is All Around") and then their short-lived success was over.

One standout group in 1964 and 1965 that suffered in 1966 was the **Dave Clark Five**. They did manage a couple of decent top 40 songs with "At The Scene" (#18 Mar.) and "Try Too Hard" (#12 May), but these were nothing like the excellent hits of 1964-65 (e.g., "Glad All Over", "Bits and Pieces", "Catch Us If You Can", and "Over and Over").

Overall, 1966 was a very good albeit not a great year for British rock and pop. Meanwhile, across the Atlantic, American music was making a strong comeback, with a number of excellent new groups, and beginning to dominate rock music again.

1966 Pt. 2 American Songs "My Empty Cup Tastes as Sweet as the Punch"

In 1966, after two years of domination by British groups, American rock and pop music was making a comeback. It was a year in which a number of new or relatively new American groups were to dominate the charts during 1966 and after. 1966 was also the year that I bought my first two singles, "These Boots Are Made for Walkin'" (#1 Feb.) by **Nancy Sinatra** and "The Ballad of the Green Berets" (#1 Mar.) by **Staff Sergeant Barry Sadler**. However, my listening to music radio was on temporary hiatus in the spring of 1966 as I discovered Strat-O-Matic baseball that seemed to consume most of my spare time.

New Groups Lead the Way

While folk rock was to dominate American music in 1966, continuing **Bob Dylan** and **The Byrds**' successes in 1965, it was a series of new groups or newly popular groups that were to dominate American folk/rock/pop in 1966. Nonetheless, Bob Dylan and the Byrds were still important in 1966. Dylan released his masterpiece, the *Blonde on Blonde* album which included three particularly noteworthy songs: "I Want You" (#20 July), "Just Like a Woman" (#33 Oct.), and the rock anthem "Rainy Day Women #12 & 35" (#2 May) which urged *"everybody must get stoned!"*. But then, Dylan's recording year was cut short by a motorcycle accident. The Byrds meanwhile had their most electric hit "Eight Miles High" (#14 May) *("And when you touch down, you'll find it's stranger than known. Signs in the street that say where you're going, are somewhere just being their own.")*, a great rock song with excellent lead guitar work from Roger McGuinn. The song's chart position may have been hurt by the radio bans across several states due to the obvious drug references (though it was denied by the group at the time). Though more sedate and less popular, "Mr. Spaceman" (#36 Oct.) was also an excellent folk-rock song.

In early January 1966, **Simon and Garfunkel** had their first top 40 single reach #1 on the charts, "The Sounds of Silence" *("Hello darkness, my old friend, I've come to talk with you again")*. It was the beginning of five years of enormous commercial success for the folk-rock duo which began as Tom & Jerry with "Hey Schoolgirl" in 1957 (which peaked at #49 on the charts).

Paul Simon wrote "Sounds of Silence" in 1963. In late 1964, an acoustic version of the song was included on the duo's unsuccessful *Wednesday Morning 3 AM* album. After recording Dylan's "Like a Rolling Stone" in the studio in June 1965, Tom Wilson, who produced the original "Sounds of Silence", asked the studio musicians to lay down a new backing rhythm track with electric guitar, bass and drums. Then, he wisely remixed the original acoustic song with the new backing track later in 1965. The new electric "Sounds of Silence" was released at the end of the year reaching #1 in January 1966. The sudden success of the song in early December 1965 convinced the record company that a new album was needed PRONTO and the group quickly recorded or re-recorded a number of songs, several of which Simon had written while in England during his hiatus from 1964-65. (These were included on the *Paul Simon Songbook* released in the U.K. in August 1965).[9]

The result was the release of the *Sounds of Silence* album in late January 1966. Despite several flaws and under- production from being recorded so quickly, I always enjoyed this album for its understated folk-rock sound. In addition to the superb title track "Sounds of Silence", the album also has another up-tempo folk-rock song "I Am a Rock" (#3 June) *("A winter's day in a deep and dark December")*, the second-best song on the album. But all of the tracks are solid. My other favorites include yet another up-tempo folk rocker "We've Got a Groovy Thing Goin'" *("Bad news, bad news. I heard you're packing to leave")*, the interesting "Richard Cory" and the beautiful "April Come She Will". Interestingly, the British version of the album also has one of my favorite Simon and Garfunkel songs "Homeward Bound" (#5 Mar.), a song I would often sing to myself while waiting for the train *("I'm sitting in the railway station, got a ticket for my destination")* during my many back and forth trips between NYC and Providence in the 1970s. This beautiful song was Simon and Garfunkel's second single but was not on any U.S. album until later in 1966.

Simon and Garfunkel spent much more time on their next album *Parsley, Sage, Rosemary and Thyme*, which wasn't released until October. In addition to the aforementioned "Homeward Bound", highlights of this album include the beautifully musical and lyrical "Scarborough Fair", the simple and happy "59th Street Bridge Song, Feelin' Groovy" (later successfully covered by **Harpers Bizarre** in 1967), the achingly sad "Dangling Conversation" *("like a poem poorly written, we are verses out of rhythm, couplets out of rhyme")*, the happy/sad "Cloudy" *("sometimes I think it's hanging down on me")*, and the upbeat "Flowers Never Bend" *("so I continue to pretend my life will never end")*. Obviously, I must also include the beautiful love song "For Emily, Whenever I May Find Her" which was sung at our wedding 31 years ago!

The **Mamas and Papas** debuted in 1966 with a fresh new folk-rock sound featuring wonderful vocal harmonies, leader John Phillips' excellent songwriting and the exquisite voice of **Mama Cass**. In early 1966, the group had its first major hit with arguably their best song "California Dreamin'" (#4 Feb.) *("All the leaves are brown and the sky is gray...I'd be safe and warm if I was in L.A.")*. This song became an anthem for the hippie movement heading westward to California (including the Mamas and Papas). Shortly thereafter, the group released its first album *If You Can Believe Your Eyes and Ears*, which became one of my early album purchases. In addition to "California Dreamin", the album also included another excellent song "Monday, Monday" (#1 May) *("Can't trust that day")*, the group's most popular song. The album featured several other original Phillips songs, most notably "Go Where You Wanna Go" (later the first single by the **5th Dimension**) as well as two very good remakes: Ben E. King's "Spanish Harlem" and Lennon-McCartney's "I Call Your Name".

Most Popular American Hits in 1966
1. I'm a Believer – Monkee
2. Ballad of the Green Berets – SSgt Barry Sadler
3. Soul and Inspiration – Righteous Bros.
4. Cherish – Association
5. 96 Tears – ? and the Mysterians
6. Summer in the City – Lovin' Spoonful
7. Good Vibrations – Beach Boys
8. Last Train to Clarksville – Monkees
9. These Boots Were Made for Walkin' – Nancy Sinatra
10. Reach Out and I'll Be There – Four Tops

The group never quite topped its success either commercially or critically of early 1966, though it did have two more excellent singles in 1966. "I Saw Her Again" (#5 Aug.) *("And you know that I shouldn't have")* was another superb Phillips composition with wonderful harmonies throughout and an error by Papa Denny Doherty (who began singing the last verse too soon) that was kept in the recording to great effect. (I learned this recently from Sirius XM '60s host Lou Simon.) In December, the group released "Words of Love" (#5 Dec.) *("so soft and tender, won't win a girl's heart anymore")*, another great song that featured the soaring vocals of Mama Cass.

The **Lovin' Spoonful** first emerged in 1965 with the hit single "Do You Believe in Magic". However, in 1966, the Lovin' Spoonful had their best year commercially and musically with five top 10 hits. Once again, it was John Sebastian's songwriting and singing that led to their high-quality music. "Daydream" (#2 Apr.) is a wonderful folk rock song that masterfully conveyed a lazy but happy day *("What a day for a daydream, custom-made for a day dreaming boy")*. "Did You Ever Have to Make Up Your Mind?" (#2 June) is an excellent, lyrical song *("Did you ever have to finally decide, to say yes to one and let the other ones slide")* with Sebastian poking fun at himself and other rock stars. In December, the group released their last top 10 single "Nashville Cats" (#8 Jan. 1967) *("There's 1352 guitar pickers in Nashville and they can pick more notes than the number of ants on a Tennessee ant hill")*, a pure fun homage to country rock by Sebastian.

"Summer in the City" (#1 Aug.) is the group's most popular single and also my favorite. It was co-written by John's younger brother Mark, who had been a junior-high school classmate of my sister a couple of years earlier. Lyrically, it wonderfully conveys summer heat in New York *("Hot town summer in the city, back of neck feeling dirty and gritty...")*. Musically, it was a decidedly different turn for the group being one of the group's few more electric rock songs. So much so that when I saw John Sebastian's solo performance in Central Park in the late 1970s and yelled out to him to do "Summer in the City", he dutifully began the song, realized it wouldn't work with acoustic guitar, and then quickly morphed into "Darling Be Home Soon", a folk-rock standard for the group. The fifth and final hit for the group in 1966 was "Rain on the Roof" (#10 Nov.), a simple yet brilliant folk-rock love song which artfully conveyed being totally unfazed by being *"caught up in a summer shower, maybe it will last for hours"* with the one you love.

But the most commercially successful of the new American groups was a made-for-TV group, **The Monkees**. Beginning with the premiere of their show in September 1966, the Monkees were the best-selling music act bar none. "Last Train to Clarksville" rose to #1 in late September, followed by "I'm a Believer", which reached #1 in December. Their first album *The Monkees* spent 13 weeks at #1 and some 78 weeks on the album charts. The TV show was a major success. Both "Last Train to Clarksville" and "I'm a Believer" were good songs primarily because of outside songwriting talent – Tommy Boyce and Bobby Hart writing the former and Neil Diamond writing the latter. Mickey Dolenz had a distinctive singing voice that became the signature sound in these first two hits.

However, the Monkees were not the equals musically of so many of the other successful singer-songwriting groups such as The Beatles, Rolling Stones, Kinks, Mamas and Papas, Simon and Garfunkel and Lovin' Spoonful, to name a few. For this, they were highly criticized at the time and subject to rumors (e.g., "they don't even play their own instruments"). To be sure, the Monkees were only adequate musicians and relied heavily on studio musicians for their recordings, and did not write their own songs until guitarist Michael Nesmith emerged as a reasonably talented songwriter writing a few of the Monkees songs, and later penning "Different Drum", the first hit single of the **Stone Poneys** with lead singer Linda Ronstadt in early 1968. In fairness to the Monkees, filming a TV show in 1966 plus all the special appearances required working 12 hours a day almost seven days a week, so there was not a lot of time for practice. Even so, The Monkees were the only performers (no backup singers or musicians) on their first tour in late 1966-1967 of over 200 dates. Bizarrely enough included as the opening act on a portion of the tour in mid-1967 was the then relatively unknown guitarist Jimi Hendrix.[10]

My Favorite American Songs in 1966
 1. Cherish – Association
 2. Summer in the City – Lovin' Spoonful
 3. Good Vibrations – Beach Boys
 4. Reach Out and I'll Be There – Four Tops
 5. California Dreamin' – Mamas and Papas
 6. Sounds of Silence – Simon and Garfunkel
 7. You Can't Hurry Love – Supremes
 8. See You in September – Happenings
 9. Devil With a Blue Dress On/Good Golly Miss Molly – Mitch Ryder and the Detroit Wheels
10. Good Lovin' – Young Rascals

In addition to the Mamas and Papas, Simon and Garfunkel, Lovin' Spoonful and the Monkees, other new or relatively new folk, rock and pop groups helped lead the way in American music:

The **Association** quickly became one of my favorite groups with two excellent singles, the up-tempo "Along Comes Mary" (#7 July) *("my empty cup tastes as sweet as the punch")* and my favorite love song "Cherish" (#1 Oct.) written by group leader Terry Kirkman. I even bought their first album later in 1967, which in addition to its two hit singles included several other good songs, most notably "Enter the Young" and "Don't Blame It on Me".

The **Young Rascals** had their first hit song in 1966, the lively and utterly fun "Good Lovin'" (#1 Apr.) *("I said 'Doctor Mr. MD, can you tell me what's ailing me?'")*. The song was a cover of the Olympics' 1965 version of the song. But it was the Rascals' upbeat rendition along with a great new blue-eyed, rock-'n'-soul sound that made it the much better record. "Good Lovin" was an exception to the rule, however. Usually, the Rascals' wrote their own music, led by the prodigious songwriting team of organist and vocalist Felix Cavaliere and vocalist Eddie Brigati. This included the under-appreciated "You Better Run" (#20 July) *("Whatcha tryin' to do to my heart?")*, later covered successfully by **Pat Benatar** in 1980. 1966 was to begin a three-year run of huge commercial success for the group.

Mitch Ryder and the Detroit Wheels blasted onto the scene with the excellent single "Jenny Take A Ride" (#10 Jan.), a medley of "Jenny, Jenny" by Little Richard and ChuckWillis's "C.C. Rider". By November, the group charted with their best song, another medley, the rocking "Devil with the Blue Dress/ Good Golly Miss Molly" (#4 Nov.). Though largely only a cover band, the unique rock-blues-soul sound of the group made their renditions irresistible.

Paul Revere and the Raiders hit it big first in 1966 with their second single "Just Like Me" (#11 Jan.), but it was the group's next two singles that were perhaps their best and most memorable: "Kicks" (#4 May) and "Hungry" (#6 July). The former was an excellent Barry Mann-Cynthia Weill anti-drug composition that has stood the test of time *("Kicks keep getting harder to find...")*. "Good Thing", their last single in 1966 (and the last high-quality song by the group), entered the top 40 in mid-December and peaked at #4 in January. After a couple more successful hits in 1967, the group largely faded away (until it was reconstituted as the Raiders for the remake of "Indian Reservation" in 1971), its success limited by lack of any songwriting talent in the group or any particularly good musicianship.

Gary Lewis and the Playboys continued their commercial success in 1966 with three more top 10 hits in a row with "She's Just My Style" (#3 Feb. '66), "Sure Gonna Miss Her" (#9 May '66), and "Green Grass" (#8 July '66). This represented the end of a streak of a total of SEVEN top tens in a row. It was hard not to like the group's songs, as they were always upbeat and happy, albeit simple. My favorite in 1966 was "Green Grass" *("While the bluebirds sing their magic song, we will love the* summer long"), which was a wonderful summer song, but I also loved "She's Just My Style" *("drives me wild")* which simply conveyed the great feeling of falling in love.

Other favorites of mine from new or emerging groups or artists included:

"See You In September" – **The Happenings** (#3 Sep.) became the most popular cover group in the U.S. in 1966 when they covered the Tempos' 1959 version of "See You in September" *("I'll be alone each and every night, while you're away don't forget to write")* and turned it into their first single. The Happenings had great harmonies and falsetto vocals that made the song soar and made it one of my first single purchases.

"Red Rubber Ball" – **The Cyrkle** (#2 July) had their first single with this folk-rock song, which I found myself playing often after relationship breakups during college *("Now I know you're not the only starfish in the sea, if I never hear your name again, it's all the same to me")*. The song had a nice melody as well. The Cyrkle had a good follow-up song with "Turn Down Day" (#16 Sep.) but after that not much more.

"Elusive Butterfly" – **Bob Lind** (#5 Mar.) – Another excellent folk-rock song *("Across my dreams with nets of wonder, I chase the bright elusive butterfly of love.")*.

"Time Won't Let Me" – **The Outsiders** (#5 Apr.) *("I can't wait forever")* from Cleveland had their first and only major hit with this song. I still play this song a lot to this day. It has a great melody and upbeat tempo and seamlessly integrates brass instruments in the recording, long before Blood Sweat and Tears or Chicago did this in the late 1960s.

"Black Is Black" – **Los Bravos** (#4 Sep.) *("I want my baby back")* from Spain was one of the first Latin rock groups to hit the charts with the simple, rhythmic yet wonderful "Black Is Black". Though not technically "a one-hit wonder", the group was never again to have a top 40 single.

"Flowers on The Wall" – **Statler Brothers** (#4 Jan.) was the group's first and only top 40 hit and was an excellent pure folk song with great lyrics *("Smokin' cigarettes and watchin' Captain Kangaroo. Now don't tell me, 'I've nothing to do'").*

"I Fought the Law" – **Bobby Fuller Four** (#9 Mar.) was the first and only hit of this Texas country-rock group. This is an excellent song with an irresistible hook *("I fought the law and the law won").*

"Walk Away Renee" – **Left Banke** (#5 Oct.) *("And when I see the sign that points one way")* – a beautiful tenor love ballad by this new group from Brooklyn, NY.

Nancy Sinatra had her first hit single "These Boots Are Made for Walkin'" (#1 Feb.), which was her best. I also liked "Sugar Town" (#5 Dec.).

Several new popular groups/songs came from the "garage rock" genre. My favorites in 1966 included:

"Dirty Water" – **Standells** (#11 June) – *"I love that dirty water, oh Boston you're my town."*

"Little Girl" – **Syndicate of Sound** (#8 July) – *"Hey little girl, you don't have to hide nothin' no more."*

"96 Tears" – **? and the Mysterians** (#1 Oct.) – *"You're gonna cry ninety-six tears."*

"Psychotic Reaction" – **Count Five** (#5 Nov.) – *"I can't get your love, I can't get a fraction, oh little girl psychotic reaction."*

"Gloria" – **Shadows of Knight** (#10 May) – Good cover of the Van Morrison song.

"Lies" – **Knickerbockers** (#20 Jan.) – Though not strictly garage rock (i.e., the song included saxophone), this first single was excellent though could do no better than #20 on the charts *("Lies, lies, breaking my heart!").*

"Little Red Riding Hood" – **Sam the Sham and the Pharaohs** (#2 Aug.) – Again, not garage rock, more novelty rock, but a fun song nonetheless.

Beach Boys, Four Seasons, Rivers, Sinatra and other American Stalwarts

While new or relatively new groups were dominating American folk/rock/pop music in 1966, U.S. artists that had been around for several years or more still more than held their own. **The Beach Boys** had the best U.S. album of the year and arguably the most innovative pop song by the end of 1966. The year began inauspiciously enough for the group with their cover of the **Regents** song "Barbara Ann" (#2 Feb.). While a very good rendition, the song was more a throwback to the doo-wop era than anything innovative. However, by the spring, evidence that Brian Wilson was working on something very special arose when the single "Sloop John B" (#3 May) *("let me go home, I want to go home")*, a brilliant remake of an old nautical song featuring unique instrumentation, soared up the charts. Then, by late summer, The Beach Boys had another top 10 song, "Wouldn't It be Nice" (#8 Sep.), a unique-sounding song with an excellent tune and lyrics. The B-side, "God Only Knows" *("God only knows, what I'd be without you")*, was even better and is without question The Beach Boys' greatest love song and one of the best of the 1960s.

This double-sided hit plus "Sloop John B" fit well on the *Pet Sounds* album released in May. The album took almost a year to record, largely owing to Brian Wilson's perfectionism and the highly complex sounds and instruments (e.g., harpsichord, Electro-Theremin, dog whistles, bicycle bells, etc.) used. However, the album failed to sell as well as expected probably reflecting its deviation from past Beach Boys musical styles. In addition to the three above-noted songs, it did contain some other excellent songs, my favorites being "I Know There's an Answer", "That's Not Me", and "Caroline No" *("Where is the girl I used to know?")*, the latter a beautiful, yet scary hint to Brian Wilson's internal demons.

By the end of the year, The Beach Boys had another major hit and my favorite by the group – "Good Vibrations" (#1 Dec.) *("Good, good, good, good vibrations, bop bop, excitations")*. The song was developed during the course of the *Pet Sounds* studio work and actually took six months to record. Brian Wilson recorded the song in four separate studios, using a whole array of instruments such as cellos and string bass in the chorus and a number of exotic instruments such as the jaw harp and the electro-theremin (which produced the high-pitched "woo-hoo" sound and was first heard in the Alfred Hitchcok film *Spellbound* in 1945). Mike Love wrote the lyrics and the bass vocalizations. The song represented the pinnacle of the group's success and remains critically acclaimed as one of the best songs of the 1960s.[11]

The **Four Seasons** continued to have success in 1966 with four solid singles, three of them in the top 10. This included "Working My Way Back to You" (#9 Feb.), "Opus 17 -Don't You Worry 'Bout Me" (#13 June), "I've Got You Under My Skin" (#9 Oct.), and "Tell It to the Rain" (#10 Jan. 1967) *("And the stars that shine above, that it's me your thinking of")*. I continue to love virtually all of the Four Seasons songs (and bought both their *Gold Vault of Hits* and *Second Vault of Gold Hits* albums in early 1967). However, my favorite in 1966 was their excellent, lively rendition of "I've Got You Under My Skin", including a great musical intro and false ending.

Johnny Rivers had his best year in 1966 commercially and musically with two excellent singles: "Secret Agent Man" (#3 Apr.) *("There's a man who leads a life of danger")*, and "Poor Side of Town" (#1 Nov.) *("so welcome back baby to the poor side of town")*. The former song was the theme song from the TV series of the same name and a great, lively song with an infectious chorus. The latter song was a beautiful love ballad that featured Rivers' unique voice and vocal style.

In a similar vein, the **Righteous Brothers** released "(You're My) Soul and Inspiration" (#1 Apr.) featuring their great voices and harmonies. This song was a bit of a swan song for the duo, as they had no other top 10 songs until their comeback hit "Rock and Roll Heaven" in 1974. Meanwhile, **Lou Christie** had his best song with the excellent single "Lightning Strikes" (#1 Feb.), *("When I see lips begging to be kissed, I can't stop")*, his first charting single since "Two Faces Have I" in 1963.

Frank Sinatra was the comeback artist of the year, scoring with his first top 20 hits since "Witchcraft" (#6 Mar. '58). "Strangers in the Night" (#1

June) was Frank's biggest solo hit of the rock era and his first #1 since 1955. In addition to featuring Frank's smooth voice, it also finished with what was to become a signature *"scooby, dooby doo"*. But my favorite was "That's Life" (#4 Dec.), a more upbeat, even feisty song *("I've been a puppet, a poet, a pawn and a king; I've been up and down and over and out, and I know one thing...")*. 1966 began fittingly enough for Sinatra when in January he charted in the top 40 with another signature song, "It Was a Very Good Year" (#28 Jan.).

Soul and R&B – Motown Remains King

While U.S. folk/rock/pop had a great year, soul and R&B music was not far behind. As in 1965, it was led by the continuing success of the major Motown groups. Despite their enormous popularity in 1965, **The Supremes** were almost as popular in 1966 with four top 10 hits and two #1 hits – "My World Is Empty Without You" (#5 Feb.), "Love Is Like an Itching in My Heart" (#9 May), "You Can't Hurry Love" (#1 Sep.), and "You Keep Me Hangin' On" (#1 Nov.). The songs were all formulaic but excellent nonetheless courtesy of the songwriting talents of Brian Holland, Lamont Dozier and Eddie Holland. At the time, I was not a big Supremes fan, but that changed when I bought their *Greatest Hits* album the following summer and played it constantly.

The **Four Tops** were then and now my favorite Motown group and 1966 included my favorite Motown song, "Reach Out and I'll Be There" (#1 Oct.) *("And your life is filled with much confusion, until happiness is just an illusion")*, as well as the similar sounding but still excellent follow-up "Standing in the Shadows of Love" (#6 Dec.) *("I'm getting ready for the heartaches to come")*. In addition, there was the lively "Shake Me, Wake Me" (#18 Mar.) *("When it's over")* and "Loving You Is Sweeter Than Ever" (#45 June), which though not as popular still were very good songs. As always, the Four Tops featured the great and distinctive lead voice of Levi Stubbs as well as usually a great up-tempo instrumentation and rhythms. And of course, all of their songs were written by Holland, Dozier and Holland.

The **Temptations,** though unable to repeat the popularity of 1965's "My Girl", still had four very good singles in 1966, three of which were later covered by other artists and made even more popular. This included "Get Ready" (#29 Mar., later #4 by **Rare Earth** in 1970), "Ain't Too Proud To Beg" (#13 July, later #17 by **The Rolling Stones** in 1974), "Beauty is Only Skin Deep" (#3 Sep.) and "I Know I'm Losing You" (#8 Dec., later by Rare Earth, #7 in 1970 and by **Rod Stewart,** #24 in 1971). And with the exception of the Smokey Robinson-penned "Get Ready", the other three were written again by none other than Holland, Dozier and Holland. Wow – what a year for them!

Stevie Wonder had one of his best songs, the rockin' "Uptight" (#3 Feb.) *("Baby everything is alright")*. He finished the year with an excellent ballad "A Place in the Sun" (#9 Dec.). **The Miracles** (featuring Smokey Robinson) had the lively "Going to a Go Go" (#11 Feb.) that had one heck of a drum intro to the song. Smokey also wrote "Don't Mess with Bill" (#7 Feb.) *("Say it one more time")*, which was the **Marvelettes**' biggest hit since 1962 and arguably their best. The **Isley Brothers** had their first hit in four years also courtesy of Holland, Dozier, and Holland with the excellent "This Ole Heart of Mine" (#12 Apr.) *("Been broke a thousand times")*. **Jimmy Ruffin** (brother of lead singer **David Ruffin** of the Temptations) scored with a good tune "What Becomes of the Brokenhearted" (#7 Oct.) *("Who have loved and now departed")*.

Non-Motown soul and R&B hits included several of my favorites from the year:

"Sweet Talkin' Guy" – **Chiffons** (#10 June) *("Stay away from him")* – an excellent comeback song by this great girl group.

"Sunny" – **Bobby Hebb** (#2 Aug.) *("Yesterday my life was filled with pain")* – a great soul ballad.

"Cool Jerk" – **The Capitols** (#7 June) – The one and only hit song for the group had an infectious refrain.

The Bad and the Ugly

Not all of 1966 was good. The year represented the beginning of bubble gum music that was to become increasingly cloying over time with the

Archies in 1969 representing the worst of bubble gum. **Tommy Roe**'s "Sweet Pea" (#8 June) and **Tommy James and the Shondells**' "Hanky Panky" (#1 July) were passable but certainly not good records despite their popularity.

But the three worst songs of 1966 (which were also popular) included the horrid "The Men in My Little Girl's Life" (#6 Jan.) by talk show host **Mike Douglas**, which fortunately despite its popularity did NOT encourage Mike Douglas to have a follow-up song. In a different vein, "They're Coming to Take Me Away, Ha Ha" (#3 Aug.) by **Napoleon XIV** did well on the charts despite being banned by major radio stations such as WABC in New York for making fun of the insane. I'll admit there was some interest when I heard it the first couple of times as it was a very bizarre song, but it wore thin quickly.

But the worst of the lot was the most popular song of the year in New York, "The Ballad of the Green Berets" (#1 Feb.-Mar.), which embarrassingly enough was the first single I bought. I'll admit I liked the song early in the year, but by the end of 1966 no longer played it, as a song glorifying fighting in Vietnam was becoming increasingly hard to stomach.

However, the bad in 1966 represented only a few bumps in the road. 1966 was a year of fresh new rock/folk-rock music in America and the U.K., great Motown music and the forefront of rock music innovation. And there was the promise of more to come in 1967.

1967
"All You Need Is Love"

I originally wrote this chapter during an unusually hot Memorial Day Weekend, and it reminded me that 1967 was the "Summer of Love". Yours truly, then an admittedly somewhat nerdy 12/13-year-old, spent much of his free time listening to music on WABC radio in NYC. I also began buying and collecting numerous singles. (I was a well-known customer in a 23rd Street store called Sultan's Record Shop run by Harry Sultan, perhaps one of the original "Sultans of Swing".)

Every Tuesday afternoon, Dan Ingram of WABC presented the top 20 hits of the week (playing "super hit #1" as the second song at the top of every hour). I eagerly listened to these new WABC surveys after school keeping a written list of the top 20. This took some doing because WABC played about 3-4 commercials for every song played so I typically multi-tasked (before I knew what that was!) and did my math homework at the same time. Though popular music was decidedly moving towards more sexually explicit lyrics along with hidden and not-so-hidden drug references, I was mostly blithely unaware of all this at the time.

I also played Strat-O-Matic baseball almost obsessively, calculating the batting averages and ERAs for the shortened AL "season" that I played (to those who don't know about Strat-O-Matic, it is a board game played with dice and individual player cards based on the actual statistics of the players). I supplemented this with the occasional game of stick-ball, punchball and wiffle ball, though usually only when my mother yelled at me to go outside and play. This occurred typically when my brother, my friends and I started playing indoor baseball, basketball and hockey, which could become rather rough – and particularly rough on the furniture, walls and the built-in wooden closets.

It was a great summer to follow Major League Baseball both live (75 cents for a bleacher seat, $1.50 for a grandstand seat) and on TV even though my favorite team, the New York Yankees, were last most of the year. 1967 featured an incredible AL pennant race between the Red Sox,

Tigers, Twins and White Sox with all four in the race coming into the final weekend of the season. I got caught up in the race plus Carl Yastrzemski's pursuit of the triple crown and even rooted for him to achieve the feat as well as his team to achieve The Impossible Dream from ninth the previous season (only two games out of last) to first in the AL. (This in spite of the fact that in later years, the Red Sox became my "Darth Vader" as a fan.)

British Music Still Ascendant

But as exciting as 1967 was for baseball fans, it also featured many new and exciting rock music developments. There were the **Spencer Davis Group**'s first and only two top 40 hits "Gimme Some Lovin'" (#7 Feb.) and "I'm a Man" (#10 Apr.). The group featured an 18-yr-old **Steve Winwood**, born in South Wales. At age 14, Steve had formed the group in Birmingham, England with brother Muff (bass) and Peter York (drums) and brought out the unique sounds of the Hammond organ as well as being an excellent lead guitarist and lead vocalist. (One actually wonders why the group wasn't called the "Steve Winwood Group" even back then.) This marked the beginning of Steve Winwood's legendary and lengthy career which has spanned Spencer Davis, **Traffic**, **Blind Faith**, Traffic again and a very successful solo career that continues to this day. Winwood, whom I saw several years ago in concert with Eric Clapton, still is among my favorite artists of all time.

Disraeli Gears by the trio **Cream** – Jack Bruce (bass), Ginger Baker (drums) and Eric Clapton (guitar) – was released in England in 1967 and at the end of 1967 in the U.S. It was the best album by **Cream** and featured the iconic songs "Sunshine of Your Love", "Strange Brew" *("killed what's inside of you")* and "Tales of Brave Ulysses" *("and the sirens sweetly singing")*. It was also the breakout album success for the lead guitarist **Eric Clapton**.

The Beatles had an eventful year with the March release of the double-sided hit "Penny Lane/Strawberry Fields Forever" (#1 Mar.) simultaneously with two separate promotional videos. These were among the first "music videos" in which musicians weren't just performing and predated MTV by almost 15 years. "Strawberry Fields" is one of the earliest and probably defining works of the psychedelic rock genre. In addition to unique instrumentation and lyrics and Lennon's extraordinary vocals *("let me take you down, cause I'm going to Strawberry Fields, nothing is real")*, the song featured a dramatic shift in musical tempo and key midway through, which creates a very unique effect. In fact, this all happened by accident as two separate versions of the song (that John had created) were melded together by the production genius of George Martin.[12]

Of course, The Beatles were only beginning in 1967 and followed up with the early summer release of *Sgt. Pepper's Lonely Hearts Club Band,* which is considered by many (e.g., *Rolling Stone*) as the greatest rock album of all time. It was hard to disagree even after repeated listenings that virtually every song on the album was great and blended together nicely from the "Sgt. Peppers/With a Little Help from My Friends" intro to the "Sgt. Peppers (reprise)/ A Day in the Life" finale. In between were several very unique songs: the psychedelic brilliance of "Lucy in the Sky with Diamonds", the jarring yet upbeat "Getting Better", the bizarre, circus-sounding "Being for the Benefit of Mr. Kite", and the interesting-sounding rockers "Lovely Rita" and "Good Morning".

Later in the summer and fall, The Beatles had two new singles, "All You Need Is Love" (#1 Aug.), the unofficial anthem of the Summer of Love, and "Hello Goodbye/I Am The Walrus" (#1 Dec.). The latter two-sided single included as the A-side, "Hello Goodbye", which was the fitting opening song of McCartney's solo concert that I saw performed in 2002. The B-side, "I Am the Walrus", was a great Lennon-inspired hit that took psychedelic rock to newer and even more avant-garde directions *("Yellow mother custard, dripping from a dead dog's eye...")*.

Though not one of their better years, **The Rolling Stones** weren't silent either in a 1967 that featured an outstanding two-sided hit "Ruby Tuesday/Let's Spend the Night Together" (#1 Mar.) and later in the year "Dandelion" (#14 Oct.) *("Tell me if she laughs or cries, blow away dandelion")*. Being a naive seventh grader, I had assumed that "Ruby Tuesday" *("Yesterday don't matter if it's gone...no one knows she comes and goes")* was about the day "Tuesday" rather than Linda Keith, who had a love relationship with Keith Richards. Richards notes that "Linda Keith was the one that first broke my heart" and "Basically, Linda is 'Ruby Tuesday'".[13]

Back in the U.S.A.

In 1967, American born **Jimi Hendrix** had his first popular success in the U.K. as he formed the **Jimi Hendrix Experience** and released several singles before releasing his first, and in my opinion, "best" album *Are You Experienced*. (Hendrix had spent several years prior in the U.S. recording and touring with various acts including the **Isley Brothers**, **Joey Dee and the Starlighters** and **Little Richard**, to name a few.) The first album included such great songs as "Purple Haze" (#65 Sep.) *("Purple haze, all in my brain, lately things, they don't seem the same")*, "Foxey Lady" (#67 Jan. 1968), "Hey Joe", "Fire", and the title track from the album "Are You Experienced" and gives a good indication of why Hendrix is considered the best rock guitarist in history by many.

Meanwhile from LA, the **Doors** burst onto the scene with their first album, *The Doors,* released in January that fittingly included "Break on Through (To the Other Side)" as its first track. The album features one of the greatest rock songs of all time, "Light My Fire" (#1 Aug.), in its seven-minute version, as opposed to the three-minute version that AM radio played and made popular during the summer. (This marked the first divide between AM and FM radio as FM was just beginning to play album music, including all seven minutes of songs like "Light My Fire".) The album, which is considered one of the best albums in rock history, also features "The Crystal Ship" *("Before you slip into unconsciousness, I'd like to have another kiss")*, "Back Door Man", and "Twentieth Century Fox", among other iconic songs. The album finishes up with "The End", an 11-minute FM classic that it is truly unforgettable for those who remember the opening credits to the movie *Apocalypse Now*.

Most Popular Hits in 1967
1. To Sir With Love – Lulu
2. Ode to Billie Joe – Bobby Gentry
3. The Letter – Box Tops
4. Groovin' – Young Rascals
5. Daydream Believer – Monkees
6. Happy Together – Turtles
7. Windy – Association
8. Light My Fire – Doors
9. Something Stupid – Nancy and Frank Sinatra
10. Hello Goodbye – Beatles

Up north in San Francisco, **Jefferson Airplane,** originally formed in 1966, decided to add a new, then unknown female lead vocalist, **Grace Slick**, who had been singing and writing with the group **The Great Society**, for their second album *Surrealistic Pillow* in 1967. In addition to her rather extraordinary rock voice, Grace penned two songs on the album that were path-breaking – "Somebody to Love" (#5 June) and "White Rabbit" (#8 Aug.) *("One pill makes you larger and one pill makes you small")*. At the same time, to memorialize the San Francisco rock and love scene, there were two popular hits, **Eric Burdon and the Animals**' "San Franciscan Nights" (#9 Sep.) *("It's an American dream includes Indians too")* and **Scott McKenzie**'s "San Francisco" (#4 July) *("be sure to wear some flowers in your hair")*.

Buffalo Springfield hit its peak in 1967 with "For What It's Worth" (#7 Mar.) *("Paranoia strikes deep into your life it will creep")*, its highest-charting single and what was to become a political anthem of the 1960s. Later that same year, the group released its best album *Buffalo Springfield Again* that included three other classics: "Bluebird" (#58 Aug.), "Mr. Soul", and "Broken Arrow". The group featured **Stephen Stills** and **Neil Young** who in a couple of years made up half of the highly successful **Crosby, Stills, Nash & Young**.

The other half of the future CSNY – the **Byrds' David Crosby** and the **Hollies' Graham Nash** – were also active. The Byrds had an excellent album and two very good songs: Bob Dylan's "My Back Pages" (#30 May) and the satiric "So You Want to Be a Rock N Roll Star" (#29 Feb.) *("Just get an electric guitar and take some time to learn how to play")*.

Both songs were from their fourth album *Younger than Yesterday* early in the year. However, by the end of the year, Crosby had been "fired" by the other group members due to his highly egotistical, erratic and contentious nature.[14]

Meanwhile, Graham Nash left the Hollies on a high note after finishing the recording of the colorful "On a Carousel" (#11 May) *("Riding along on a carousel, got to catch up to you")*. Both Crosby and Nash teamed up with Stills to start CSN in late 1967.

My Favorite Songs in 1967
 1. Light My Fire – Doors
 2. Happy Together – Turtles
 3. Gimme Some Lovin' – Spencer Davis Group
 4. Ruby Tuesday – Rolling Stones
 5. All You Need is Love – Beatles
 6. White Rabbit – Jefferson Airplane
 7. Can't Take My Eyes Off You – Frankie Valli
 8. Friday on My Mind – Easybeats
 9. Windy – The Association
10. Sunshine of Your Love – Cream

There are many other great individual rock songs and memories for me in 1967, including:

I first saw **The Turtles**' "Happy Together" (#1 Apr.) *("Imagine me and you I do")* performed on TV during *The Smothers Brothers Comedy Hour* (before the show was cancelled because of their anti-war/anti-police skits in 1968).

"Windy" (#1 July) by **The Association**, which much later became one of the earliest songs my eldest daughter Kathleen at age 2 could remember. (This dad made sure to play and educate his daughters about 1960s music!)

The Easybeats' "Friday on My Mind" (#16 May) included lyrics that I found very relatable even in junior high school. *"Monday morning seems so bad. Everybody seems to nag me."*

"Good Thing" (#4 Jan.) by **Paul Revere and the Raiders** (I can still remember trying to count how many times they repeat "Good Thing" in the song).

Other songs that evoked positive memories:

Procol Harum's first hit "Whiter Shade of Pale" (#5 Aug.) *("Skipped the last fandango. Turned cartwheels across the floor")* had very unique lyrics and stately organ playing.

"I Think We're Alone Now" (#4 Apr.) *("There doesn't seem to be anyone around")* by **Tommy James and the Shondells** – This very catchy tune was one of my first single purchases of 1967.

"The Letter" (#1 Sep.) by **The Box Tops** was one of the liveliest hits of the year (love that opening "popping" drum sequence) and the first hit by this Memphis blue-eyed soul group. But "The Letter" was almost over before it started, checking in at only 1 min. 58 sec. on my copy of the single.

"We Ain't Got Nothin' Yet" (#7 Feb.) by the **Blues Magoos** was the first and only top 40 hit by this Bronx group and evoked memories of the garage rock sound.

"Sock It to Me Baby" (#6 Mar.) by **Mitch Ryder and the Detroit Wheels** was another enjoyable Mitch Ryder rocker.

"Kind of a Drag" (#1 Feb.) by the **Buckinghams** was the first hit by this group as well as by any "Chicago" group that featured brass instruments.

Frankie Valli's "Can't Take My Eyes Off You" (#2 July) *("You're just too good to be true")* was the best slow ballad of the year.

The Mamas and the Papas had their last two top 20 songs "Dedicated to the One I Love" (#2 Mar.) and "Creeque Alley" (#5 May) *("And no one's getting fat except Mama Cass")*. The former song is a beautiful cover of the Shirelles song from the early 1960s. The latter song is a nice autobiographical tune about the group's early years, a memoir of sorts in light of their fall from popularity shortly thereafter.

Likewise, the **Lovin' Spoonful** had their last two top 20 hits – "Darling Be Home Soon" (#15 Mar.) *("For the great relief of having you to talk too")* and "Six O'clock" (#18 June) *("There's something special about six o'clock")*. Both were excellent Sebastian compositions.

1967 also marked the height of the **Monkees**' popularity, which really only lasted for the two years of their very popular TV show from fall 1966 to summer 1968. At the time, I cringed at the fact that the group didn't even play on much of their first two albums, relying instead on session musicians. However, several of their songs from 1967 have endured the test of time, largely benefitting from excellent songwriting from the likes of **Carole King** ("Pleasant Valley Sunday", #3 Aug.), **Neil Diamond** ("A Little Bit Me, A Little Bit You", #2 Apr.), and "I'm a Believer", #1 Jan.), and **John Stewart** of the **Kingston Trio** ("Daydream Believer", #1 Dec.).

In addition, two of my favorite female vocalists near the end of their popular careers – **Petula Clark** and **Lesley Gore** – hit it big with "Don't Sleep in the Subway" (#5 July) *("Don't stand in the pouring rain")*, and "California Nights" (#16 Mar.), respectively. (In the latter case, Lesley sang this song while appearing as one of Catwoman's sidekicks in an episode of *Batman*.) Sixteen-year-old **Janis Ian** had her first hit with the beautiful and socially conscious "Society's Child" (#14 July) *("I can't see you anymore, baby")*, a song she had written at age 14. Another outstanding female vocalist, **Dionne Warwick,** had a big hit with "I Say a Little Prayer" (#4 Dec.) *("The moment I wake up before I put on my makeup")*.

Meanwhile, Motown and other soul and R&B hits were excellent. The most famous and long-lasting hit was **Aretha Franklin**'s "Respect" (#1 June) *("All I'm asking for is a little respect")*. However, the year also featured:

The **Supremes**' "The Happening" (#1 May) *("It happened to me and it can happen to you")* and "Reflections" (#2 Sep.) *("Reflections of the way life used to be")*. Both songs were outstanding and written by Holland-Dozier-Holland, though "Reflections" broke a streak of four #1 hits in a row for the Supremes.

The **Four Tops**' "Bernadette" (#4 Apr.) *("I want you cause I need you to live!")*, and "7 Rooms of Gloom" (#14 June) *("I see a house of stone, a lonely house cause now you're gone")* were both irresistible hit songs by my favorite Motown group.

Other excellent Motown hits included **Stevie Wonder**'s "I Was Made to Love Her" (#2 Aug.), **Smokey Robinson and the Miracles**' "I Second that Emotion" (#4 Dec.) *("But if you feel like loving me, if you got the notion, I second that emotion")*, the **Temptations**' "You're My Everything" (#6 Sep.), **Sam and Dave**'s "Soul Man" (#2 Nov.), **Arthur Conley**'s "Sweet Soul Music" (#2 May) *("Do you like good music? Yeh, Yeh.")* and **Gladys Knight and the Pips**' "I Heard It Through the Grapevine" (#2 Dec.) *("Bet you're wondering how I knew")*.

Last but not least was the unforgettable "(Your Love Keeps Lifting Me) Higher and Higher" (#6 Sep.) *("Than I've ever been lifted before")* by **Jackie Wilson**, an always inspiring love song, which was a featured opening song that I played on my tape deck for my friend Jonathan's wedding more than three decades later.

*****

Though not quite as good a year as 1965 and 1966, 1967 was still a very good year. And though 1967 was mostly about psychedelic and folk rock (e.g., Beatles, Stones, Byrds, Buffalo Springfield, Cream, Jimi Hendrix, Mamas and Papas, Lovin' Spoonful, etc.), there were signs of the emerging hard rock boom that was to start in 1968.

1968
"Born to Be Wild"

1968 was an interesting and tumultuous year for American politics, music and for me personally. It was the end of my last year of junior high at Friends Seminary in NYC, and the beginning of living away from home at Taft School in Connecticut. In the political world, there was greater violence with the assassinations of Martin Luther King, Jr. and Robert Kennedy, inner city riots, and a violent end to the Democratic National Convention on the Chicago streets. Change and conflict were hallmarks of 1968.

The Death of Soft Rock/Folk Rock?

1968 was also an important year of change for rock music. **The Byrds, Mamas and Papas, Frankie Valli and The Four Seasons, Association,** the **Seekers, Herman's Hermits, Hollies, Gary Lewis and the Playboys, Lovin' Spoonful, Peter and Gordon, Johnny Rivers,** and **Petula Clark** and their folk-rock or softer-rock sound of the mid-sixties had largely disappeared from the pop charts by 1968. Three excellent soft rock songs proved to be exceptions to that trend – the Association's "Everything that Touches You" (#9 Mar.), the Four Seasons' cover of "Will You Love Me Tomorrow" (#24 Mar.), and **Mama Cass'** solo of "Dream a Little Dream of Me" (#12 Aug.) *("Birds singing in a sycamore tree")*.

The **Beach Boys'** surf rock sound, which had been a staple from 1962-67, was no longer in vogue although The Beach Boys did have an *excellent* single "Do It Again" (#20 Aug.) that spoke longingly about the group's past. In fact, "Do It Again" *("Let's get back together and do it again")* was a bit of a throwback even for The Beach Boys which had strayed far from their original sound with Brian Wilson's complex and very different "Heroes and Villains" single and *Smiley Smile* album of 1967.

The Monkees' pop-rock sound and TV show had dominated the popular music scene in 1966-67 courtesy of the excellent songwriting skills of Carole King, Neil Diamond and Tommy Boyce-Bobby Hart. However, in early 1968, the group had its last top 10 hit "Valleri" (#3 Mar.) and its TV show was cancelled in the spring. The group released a movie later in 1968 entitled *Head*, which was bizarre (to put it mildly) and was ostensibly about the death of the Monkees. It was directed by a new up-and-comer in Hollywood – Jack Nicholson.

There were a number of exceptions to this trend away from soft/folk rock. This included, most notably, **Simon and Garfunkel**'s superb *Bookends* album with the hits "Mrs. Robinson" (#1 June) *("Where have you gone, Joe DiMaggio?")*, "At the Zoo" (#16 Aug. 1967) *("Someone told me it's all happening at the zoo")*, and "Fakin' It" (#23 Aug. '67) *("Girl does what she wants to do")*, and the lyrically and musically beautiful "America" *("counting the cars on the New Jersey turnpike")*. **The Turtles** scored with one of my favorite melodies "Elenore" (#6 Oct.), which poked fun at themselves with lyrics such as, *"I really think you're groovy, let's go out to a movie"*. **The Rascals**' upbeat "A Beautiful Morning" (#3 May) *("I think I'll go outside for awhile and just smile")* and the up-tempo "People Got to be Free" (#1 Aug.) *("People everywhere just wanna be free")* kept the group at the top of the charts. Frenchman **Paul Mauriat** had the instrumental top seller of the year with the soothing "Love Is Blue" (#1 Feb.). However, my two favorite instrumentals in 1968 were "Classical Gas" by **Mason Williams** (#2 Aug.), featuring great acoustic guitar work and orchestration by this *Smothers Brothers Comedy Hour* writer, and the eerie "The Good, the Bad and the Ugly" (#2 May) by **Hugo Montenegro**. Other soft rock vocal favorites of mine for the year included **Merilee Rush** with "Angel of the Morning" (#7 June), **The 5th Dimension** with "Stoned Soul Picnic" (#3 July) *("Come along and surry")*, **Judy Collins**' hit version of Joni Mitchell's "Both Sides Now" (#8 Dec.), and **Mary Hopkin** with "Those Were the Days" (#2 Nov.).

Most Popular Hits in 1968
1. Hey Jude – Beatles
2. I Heard It Thru the Grapevine – Marvin Gaye
3. Love Is Blue – Paul Mauriat
4. People Got to Be Free – Rascals
5. Dock of the Bay – Otis Redding
6. Honey – Bobby Goldsboro
7. Love Child – Diana Ross & The Supremes
8. This Guy's in Love With You – Herb Alpert
9. Mrs. Robinson – Simon and Garfunkel
10. Judy in Disguise – John Fred & His Playboy Band

Hard Rock On the Ascent

However, a harder rock, more electric sound was on the rise particularly in Great Britain. **The Who** had their first American top 10 single in late 1967-early 1968 with "I Can See for Miles" (#9 Dec. '67) *("I know you've deceived me now here's a surprise")* that begins with an unforgettable electric guitar riff and later followed it with "Magic Bus" (#9 Sep.). **The Rolling Stones** had experimented with a softer, flower power sound ("Ruby Tuesday" and "Dandelion" in 1967) and imitated The Beatles' *Sgt. Pepper's* with the psychedelic album *Her Satanic Majesty's Request* released in late 1967, which included the early 1968 psychedelic hit "She's a Rainbow" (#25 Jan.) *("She comes in colors everywhere, she combs her hair")*, and the interesting space song "2000 Light Years from Home" which was the B-side. However, by mid-1968, they had returned to their hard rock roots with one of the greatest rock songs ever, "Jumpin' Jack Flash" (#3 July) *("I was born in a cross-fire hurricane")* with Keith Richards' guitar driving the song.

Jimi Hendrix followed up his album success of *Are You Experienced* with *Axis: Bold As Love* in 1968 and its hard rock version of Dylan's "All Along the Watchtower" (#20 Oct.) *("'There must be some kind of way out of here', said a joker to the thief")*. And the two hard rocking singles from *Are You Experienced* in 1967, "Purple Haze" and "Foxey Lady", became a staple on the newly emerging rock-oriented FM radio during 1968. A new British group, **Deep Purple,** produced a hard-rock classic "Hush" (#4 Sep.). A one-hit wonder from Chilton, England, the

Crazy World of Arthur Brown released the bizarre and combustible "Fire" (#2 Oct.) *("You're gonna burn")*.

Back in the U.S., **Big Brother and the Holding Company** burst onto the scene with their album *Cheap Thrills* and the hits "Piece of My Heart" (#12 Oct.) from the album as well as "Down on Me" (#43 Oct.). Their lead singer, **Janis Joplin**, introduced the world to an extraordinary female hard-rock voice. Another new group, **Steppenwolf,** had two huge hits: "Born to Be Wild" (#2 Aug.) *("Get your motor running, head out on the highway")* and "Magic Carpet Ride" (#3 Nov.) *("Why don't you come with me little girl on a magic carpet ride")*, as well as the song "The Pusher" *("I say 'God damn the pusher'")*, that was featured at the beginning of the movie *Easy Rider*. Steppenwolf's "driving" electric guitars perhaps best epitomized the new hard rock sound in the U.S. Even **Tommy James and the Shondells** moved away from its pop sound in 1967 to the rock classic "Mony, Mony" (#3 June).

Hard rock jams and long songs were also relatively new in 1968. On the FM dial, **Cream** led this new trend with their double album *Wheels of Fire* and its hit "White Room" (#6 Nov.) *("In a white room, with black curtains at the station")* and the lengthy jams "Traintime", "Crossroads" *("I went down to the crossroads, fell down on my knees")*, and "Toad", the latter two being over 16 minutes in length. However, Cream's biggest hit of the year was the rerelease of the much shorter "Sunshine of Your Love" (#5 Aug.). Another new rock group, **Iron Butterfly,** took long songs to an excessive level with its 17-minute, interminably repetitive "In-a-Gadda-da-Vida". The **Chambers Brothers** had both an AM radio version of "Time Has Come Today" (#11 Sep.) *("Young hearts can go their way. Can't put it off another day")*, one of my favorites of the year, and a very long 11-minute version of the song on their album which later became part of the soundtrack of the Jane Fonda/Jon Voight movie *Coming Home* in 1978. **Creedence Clearwater Revival** had their first hit song with "Suzie Q Part I" (#11 Oct.), but the whole song is over eight minutes long and was featured on their first album.

Of course, the leader of these new trends was **The Beatles**. After the 1967 "thematic" and "psychedelic" albums, *Sgt. Pepper's* and *Magical Mystery Tour*, The Beatles moved to a simpler, often harder rock and less ornate sound. This started with the rockin' piano in McCartney's "Lady Madonna" (#4 Apr.) in the spring and then was followed by the extraordinary two-sided hit "Hey Jude/Revolution" (#1 Oct.). "Hey Jude" is still one of my favorite songs of all time and was the first very long song (e.g., seven minutes) to be played regularly on top-40 radio. But it was "Revolution" in particular that best epitomized the hard rock trend (with some ferocious guitar playing) while lyrically symbolizing the 1968 tensions between the peace movement and the newly emerging, more violent protests *("But when you talk about destruction, you know that you can count me out")*.

My Favorite Songs in 1968
1. **Hey Jude – Beatles**
2. **Jumpin' Jack Flash – Rolling Stones**
3. **I Heard It Thru the Grapevine – Marvin Gaye**
4. **Time Has Come Today – Chambers Bros.**
5. **Mrs. Robinson – Simon and Garfunkel**
6. **Dock of the Bay – Otis Redding**
7. **For Once in My Life – Stevie Wonder**
8. **Dance to the Music – Sly and the Family Stone**
9. **Magic Carpet Ride – Steppenwolf**
10. **Hush – Deep Purple**

The Beatles (often referred to as the *White Album*), despite less critical acclaim than *Sgt. Pepper's*, was clearly album of the year and in my opinion, one of The Beatles' best accomplishments. Unlike *Sgt. Pepper's*, there was far less collaboration in songwriting BUT it remains an extraordinary showcase of the three singer-songwriters of The Beatles. George Harrison had "Savoy Truffle", "Long, Long, Long", "Piggies", and perhaps his best single composition, "While My Guitar Gently Weeps", which featured Eric Clapton on lead guitar. (Uncredited on the *White Album*, Clapton came to sessions under the alias Eddie Clayton.) Harrison showed his appreciation for Clapton's stellar guitar work by later co-writing "Badge" *("Thinking about the times you drove in my car")*, one of Clapton's best songs.[15]

John Lennon also had several excellent compositions, most notably "Happiness Is a Warm Gun" *("She's not a girl who misses* much"), "Glass Onion", the slower-paced "Revolution #1", "Dear Prudence", "Sexy Sadie", "Julia", and "Cry Baby Cry".

Paul McCartney's compositions were outstanding, ranging from (1) the soft ballads of "Blackbird" *("Take these broken wings and learn to fly")*, "Mother Nature's Son", "I Will", and "Martha My Dear"; (2) the country-and-western-inspired "Rocky Raccoon"; to (3) the hard-rockin' "Back in the U.S.S.R.", "Helter Skelter", and "Birthday". While not every one of the 30 tracks was good (I ALWAYS skipped the Yoko Ono-inspired "Revolution #9" on side 4), there were only a few that were not up to The Beatles' usual standards.

Motown and soul music continued to shine. **Sly and the Family Stone** burst on the scene with the energetic and catchy "Dance to the Music" (#8 Apr.) *("All we need is a drummer for people who only need a beat")*, which remains their best single ever. Though not as successful as in the prior four years, the **Supremes** still had two excellent records with "Love Child" (#1 Nov.) *("Never meant to be, love child, born in poverty")* and "I'm Gonna Make You Love Me" (#2 Jan. '69) *("Every minute every hour I'm gonna shower you with love and affection")*. The latter song was recorded as a duet with the **Temptations** in late 1968.

The Temptations showcased David Ruffin's vocal talents in the beautiful, soulful ballad "I Wish It Would Rain" (#4 Feb.) *("Sunshine blue skies please go away")*. However, they soon showed the world they didn't need Ruffin. The Temps unanimously forced Ruffin out of the group due to his drug abuse (cocaine and sedatives) and perennially showing up late or not at all. Then they recorded near the end of the year, the up-tempo soul rocker "Cloud Nine" (#6 Dec.) *("I'm doing fine on cloud nine")*, which featured all the Temps as vocalists.[16]

Stevie Wonder had a minor hit earlier in the year with "Shoo-Be-Doo-Be-Doo-Da-Day" (#9 May), the first song he wrote in his career, then capped the year off with one of my favorite upbeat songs ever, "For Once in My Life" (#2 Dec.) *("I have someone who needs me, someone I needed so long")*. **Marvin Gaye & Tammi Terrell** had two excellent top 10 hits "Ain't Nothing Like the Real Thing" (#8 May) and "You're All I Need To Get By" (#7 Sep.). Marvin then finished the year with the great solo, "I Heard It Through the Grapevine" (#1 Dec.) covering **Gladys Knight and the Pips**' hit of a year earlier.

Aretha Franklin recorded three great R&B songs with "Chain of Fools" (# 2 Jan.), "Since You've Been Gone" (#5 Mar.), and "Think" (#7 June) *("You'd better think, think about what you're trying to do to me")*. Later, Aretha reprised "Think" while appearing in 1980's *The Blues Brothers* movie. However, the soul song of the year was the posthumous "Dock of the Bay" (#1 Mar.) by **Otis Redding** (he had died in a plane crash in December 1967). Unlike the rest of the year, this song was for relaxing.

All in all, it was a good year in music to *"get your motor running"*.

1969
"It's the Time of the Season for Loving"

In 1969, rock music entered a great divide that would only widen in the 1970s. It was a time of greater distinction between the FM and AM radio dials. AM continued to feature the top 40 popular hits, which included some mainstream rock but "only the hits". FM began to feature "progressive rock", which still included the most popular rock groups (e.g., Beatles, Rolling Stones, Creedence, etc.) but also newer or less well-known groups who weren't played or seldom played on AM (e.g., the Grateful Dead, The Band, Mountain, Country Joe and the Fish, etc.). FM increasingly became album rock where multiple album cuts were played.

Music on the radio was the only allowable source of entertainment in the first half of 1969 during the end of my lower-middle year (i.e., freshman year) at Taft School, though by the summer when I was back home in New York City, my collecting and playing of singles and record albums began anew. Fortunately, by the fall of 1969, Taft had liberalized its rules and record players were allowed in the dorm rooms. Because progressive stations were only just getting started in 1969 in Connecticut, AM radio was my main staple in early 1969.

Hair and Woodstock

Rock and popular music in 1969 were perhaps best characterized by two important events in the world of music. The rock musical *Hair* moved to Broadway in late 1968 and the cast album soared to the top of the album charts during the spring of 1969. *Hair* was about sex, love, drugs, and hippy communes, which was to become a dominant musical theme throughout 1969. As popular as the album was across the nation and at my prep school (imagine the utter glee of a group of 14/15-year-old boys listening to some of the sexually explicit lyrics of the *Hair* album), perhaps more significantly, it spurred four distinctly different "covers" by popular groups:

The **5th Dimension**'s "Aquarius/Let the Sun Shine In" (#1 Apr.) turned two "Hair" songs into a beautiful medley (featuring Marilyn

McCoo's gorgeous voice), which ended up being the best-selling single of the year.

The **Cowsills** did a surprisingly good version of "Hair" (#2 May) *("Oh say can you see my eyes, if you can then my hair's too short")*.

Oliver recorded "Good Morning Starshine" (#3 July) *("The earth says 'hello', you twinkle above us, we twinkle below")*, which became very popular in the summer and was my favorite uplifting song of the year.

Finally, a new group, **Three Dog Night**, which had its first major hit in the summer with the excellent, tuneful and rollicking "One" (#5 June), had its second major hit with its version of "Easy to be Hard" (#4 Sep.) *("How can people be so heartless?")* from *Hair*.

The second major music event of 1969 was the Woodstock music festival in August. Woodstock was the largest outdoor concert ever up until that time (400,000+ people) and was a showcase of many of the major (and minor) folk/rock groups of the time. This included in order of appearance: **Richie Havens, Country Joe and the Fish, Sweetwater, Incredible String Band, Bert Sommer, Tim Hardin, Ravi Shankar, Melanie, Arlo Guthrie, Joan Baez, Quill, Santana, John Sebastian, Keef Hartley Band, Canned Heat, Grateful Dead, Mountain, Creedence Clearwater Revival, Sly and the Family Stone, Janis Joplin, The Who, Jefferson Airplane, Joe Cocker, Ten Years After, The Band, Blood Sweat and Tears, Johnny Winter** (and **Edgar Winter**), **Crosby, Stills & Nash, Paul Butterfield Blues Band, Sha-Na-Na,** and **Jimi Hendrix.**

Most Popular Hits in 1969
1. Aquarius/Let the Sunshine In – Fifth Dimension
2. Sugar, Sugar – Archies
3. Honky Tonk Women – Rolling Stones
4. Everyday People – Sly and the Family Stone
5. In the Year 2525 – Zager and Evans
6. Get Back – Beatles
7. Crimson and Clover – Tommy James
8. Dizzy – Tommy Roe
9. Leaving on a Jet Plane – Peter, Paul and Mary
10. Wedding Bell Blues – Fifth Dimension

Several of the acts had very long sets. **The Who** performed almost their entire brand-new double album *Tommy*; **Crosby, Stills & Nash** performed 16 songs including almost all their first album. The music went from Friday, August 15 to Monday morning the 18th. (Interestingly, **Jimi Hendrix** insisted on being the last act and ended up playing Monday at 9am to dwindling crowds.) While many major acts appeared, it was also interesting how many major groups turned the event down because they didn't understand how big it was to be, including **Led Zeppelin**, the **Doors** and the **Byrds**. My favorite reason was **Tommy James** turning it down because he was told by his secretary "there's this pig farmer in upstate New York who wants you to play in his field".[17]

Woodstock was well documented through a movie released a year later and two subsequent albums (a triple and a double album) of concert music and sounds. It served to cement and expand the popularity of relatively new rock groups and artists. Most notably, this included **Jimi Hendrix, Creedence Clearwater Revival**, and **Sly and the Family Stone,** who all had their first records in either 1967 or 1968.

Woodstock also introduced most of the U.S. to a new Latin-rock fusion band, **Santana**, which released its first album and its catchy single "Evil Ways" (#9 Mar.) early that year *("You've got to change those evil ways, baby")*. Another Woodstock group, **The Band** Dylan's touring rock band, had actually settled in Woodstock, New York before releasing their excellent first album *Music from Big Pink* in 1968 featuring the songs "The Weight" *("Take a load off Fanny, take a load for free...and you put* *the load right on me")* and Dylan's "I Shall Be Released". They became even more popular due to their Woodstock appearance and their first top 40 hit the superb "Up on Cripple Creek" (#25 Nov.) *("A drunkard's dream if I ever did see one")* followed shortly thereafter. I was definitely too young to attend Woodstock, though one of my prep school classmates did and described in detail the lovemaking and drug-taking that took place all around him.

Rock Albums Rule!

Rock albums in 1969 were better than ever. **The Rolling Stones** released *Let It Bleed*, which is my favorite Stones album and most notably includes three of their rock anthems: "Gimme Shelter", "Midnight Rambler", and my favorite "You Can't Always Get What You Want". Interestingly, "Honky Tonk Women" (#1 Aug.) *("Give me the honky tonk blues")*, another outstanding Rolling Stones song, was #1 for four weeks in the summer of 1969 but was NOT on the album. Instead, *Let It Bleed* had the original version of the song, "Country Honk", a distinct country-style song featuring fiddles instead of electric guitar.

The Beatles released *Abbey Road* in the fall of 1969 featuring a free-flowing and beautifully paced Side 2 that starts with George Harrison's best Beatles song, "Here Comes the Sun" and ends fittingly and compellingly with the rock-'n'-roll "The End" including rotating guitar solos from Paul, George and John (though technically McCartney's short ditty "Her Majesty" is actually the last track). Side 1 was almost as good with the two-sided hit single "Come Together" and "Something" starting the album and the side finishing with the infectious and electric "I Want You (She's So Heavy)", which abruptly ends as if the plug was pulled. Though it is hard to beat *Sgt. Pepper's* among Beatles albums, *Abbey Road* is my favorite.

The Beatles also had a great hard-rocking single in the spring of 1969, "Get Back" (#1 May), which featured Billy Preston on organ (Preston has the distinction of being the only non-Beatles artist to ever be "credited" on a Beatles single). In addition, the group released an animated movie and an accompanying album, *Yellow Submarine*. The album only had four new songs, most notably the catchy "All Together

Now", and "Hey Bulldog" *("Sheepdog standing in the rain. Bullfrog. Doing it again")*. The latter song was another excellent Lennon hard rock composition featuring great guitar and bass playing. Lastly, The Beatles released "The Ballad of John and Yoko" (#8 July), a good rocker about John and Yoko's public stay-in-bed peace demonstration. The song managed to get banned from many AM radio stations (most notably WABC in New York) because of the lyrics *("Christ, you know it ain't easy you know how hard it can be, the way things are going they're going to crucify me")*, which was a thinly veiled comparison to Jesus Christ (and, given John's statement a few years earlier that The Beatles were "more popular than Jesus Christ", probably made the stations extra sensitive).

My third favorite album of the year was **The Who**'s *Tommy*. The rock opera *Tommy* was unique in rock music history. It was the first rock opera ever recorded, taking off from The Beatles' *Sgt. Pepper's* and The Moody Blues' *Days of Future Passed* concept albums in 1967. However, it was also musically brilliant largely due to the extraordinary songwriting and guitar playing of Pete Townshend, Roger Daltry's powerful singing and John Entwistle's bass and Keith Moon's superb and often manic drumming. The album is nicely bookended by the tuneful "Overture" and "We're Not Gonna Take It" *("See me, feel me, touch me, heal me")*, which are also my two favorite tracks on the album. In between, there are the two popular singles from the album – "I'm Free" (#37 Aug.) and, most notably, "Pinball Wizard" (#19 May), in which Townshend excellently combines acoustic and electric guitar playing into a great hook line.

Two of my other favorite albums from the year were from new groups that were formed from mid-'60s groups. *Blind Faith* combined Eric Clapton (guitar) and Ginger Baker (drums), both formerly of **Cream,** with Steve Winwood (keyboards and guitar) from **Traffic**, and Rick Grech (bass) from **Family**. With the exception of the overly long "Do What You Like", the album was excellent musically. In fact, three of the songs have become rock standards: Winwood's beautiful "Sea of Joy" *("Waiting in our boats to set sail")* and "Can't Find My Way Home" *("Come down off your throne and leave your body alone")* and

Clapton's guitar-infused "Presence of the Lord". In many respects, Winwood dominated the album, in terms of songwriting, singing (his haunting voice is prominent throughout) and even playing (he played keyboards, guitar and harmonica). The group was short-lived (lasting only seven months), as Winwood went back to Traffic and Clapton went on to a solo career.

Lastly, the Band released their best album *The Band* featuring the aforementioned "Up on Cripple Creek" and "The Night They Drove Old Dixie Down" which was to become Joan Baez's biggest hit in 1971.

My Favorite Songs in 1969
1. **Here Comes the Sun – Beatles**
2. **You Can't Always Get What You Want – Rolling Stones**
3. **Honky Tonk Women – Rolling Stones**
4. **Everyday People – Sly and the Family Stone**
5. **Suite Judy Blue Eyes – CSN**
6. **Get Back – Beatles**
7. **Bad Moon Rising – CCR**
8. **Down by the River – Neil Young**
9. **Overture from Tommy – The Who**
10. **Sea of Joy – Blind Faith**

Another new group, **Crosby, Stills & Nash** (CSN), was formed in late 1968 by David Crosby from the **Byrds**, Stephen Stills from **Buffalo Springfield**, and Graham Nash from the **Hollies**. CSN released their first album in mid-1969, *Crosby, Stills & Nash*. The album has wonderful vocal harmonies and several excellent songs, including the singles "Marrakesh Express" (#28 Aug.) and "Suite: Judy Blue Eyes" (#21 Nov.) *("It's getting to the point, where I can't go on anymore, I am sorry. Sometimes it hurts so badly, I must cry out loud.")*. The latter song was written by Stills about his love interest Judy Collins. The album also featured four other favorites of mine – "Wooden Ships", "Long Time Gone", "You Don't Have to Cry", and "Helplessly Hoping".

Meanwhile, Neil Young, also from Buffalo Springfield, released his first solo album, *Everybody Knows This Is Nowhere,* backed by the group **Crazy Horse**. I didn't discover and buy this album until 1972 when I discovered I loved Neil Young (due to his *Harvest* album release that year). Yet, this first solo album contains perhaps three of classic rock's finest songs: "Cinnamon Girl" (#55 July '70) *("I wanna live with a cinnamon girl")* and the long, guitar-jam-infused songs "Down by the River" *("I shot my lady. Shot her dead ooh shot her dead"),* and "Cowgirl in the Sand". This was the harder side of Neil Young with prominent electric guitar playing throughout (using his 1952 Gibson Les Paul model he dubbed "Old Black").[18] The album sharply contrasted with the largely acoustic folk sound in Neil's next two albums.

Other Rock Singles

After their initial success with "Suzie Q" in 1968, **Creedence Clearwater Revival** (CCR) emerged in 1969 as both a highly popular AM group and highly respected FM progressive rock group. Featuring a country-rock, rockabilly throwback sound, CCR had four excellent hits in a row: "Proud Mary" (#2 Mar.), "Bad Moon Rising" (#2 June), "Green River" (#2 Sep.), and "Down on the Corner" (#3 Dec.) and three top 10 albums during 1969. However, unlike most rock groups who used B-sides of singles for throwaway songs, Creedence had four excellent songs on the B-sides of these hits, three of which charted: "Lodi", "Commotion", and most notably "Fortunate Son", which was CCR's most blatant anti-war song and perhaps its best overall composition of the year.

Several other popular rock favorites of mine included the **Zombies**' "Time of the Season" (#3 Mar.), featuring an interesting and infectious repeating four-note rhythm. The song was actually recorded two years earlier right before the group disbanded. I also enjoyed the incredibly catchy "The River Is Wide" (#31 May) *("The river gets long now, the water runs deep...")* by the **Grassroots**, and to a lesser extent "I'd Wait a Million Years" (#15 Sep.). Meanwhile, **The Guess Who** from Winnipeg, Canada first had major success in the U.S. in 1969 with the hit single "These Eyes" (#6 May) and the double-sided hit "Laughing/Undun" (#10 Aug.). In many ways, the understated "Undun" was perhaps my favorite of the three, though **Burton Cummings**' vocals really shine in both "Laughing" and "These Eyes". Two of the most uplifting pop songs in 1969 included "More Today than Yesterday" (#12 June) by the **Spiral Starecase** *("but not half as much as tomorrow"!)* and the inspiring

"Hooked on a Feeling" (#5 Jan.) *("I'm high on believing that you're in love with me")* by **B.J. Thomas**.

Soft pop-rock favorites included **Jackie DeShannon**'s "Put a Little Love in Your Heart" (#4 Aug.), later featured in the uproarious Bill Murray movie *Scrooged* and the late 1969 hit "Leaving on a Jet Plane" (#1 Dec.), performed by **Peter, Paul and Mary** and penned by **John Denver**. I was also a sucker for **Johnny Maestro**'s comeback record with the "Worst that Could Happen" (#3 Feb.) *("Girl, I heard you're getting married")* by the **Brooklyn Bridge**. (Johnny was the lead singer for the doo-wop group, **The Crests**, best known for their late '50s hit "Sixteen Candles".)

However, the epitome of soft rock was the revamped **Blood, Sweat and Tears** (enter **David Clayton Thomas,** exit **Al Kooper**), which released its self-titled second album in early 1969. The album was highlighted by the beautiful "You've Made Me So Very Happy" (#2 Apr.), as well as some other very good songs such as "Spinning Wheel" (#2 July) *("What goes up must come down")*, "And When I Die" (#2 Nov.), "Sometimes in Winter", and "God Bless the Child", though I confess that I quickly tired of Thomas' vocal style after this BS&T album. And, of course, **Bob Dylan**'s "Lay Lady Lay" (#7 Sep.) is a slow rock classic (as well as much of the rest of his country inspired *Nashville Skyline* album). However, by far my favorite soft-rock song of the year was the classic "Get Together" (#5 Aug.) *("Come on people now smile on your brother")* by **The Youngbloods**, which has the unique distinction of being the only secular song sung by the congregation at my wedding 31 years ago.

Just like fine wine, **Neil Diamond** tunes have grown on me with age. 1969 was a pretty good year for Neil with the smash hits "Holly Holy" (#6 Dec.) and "Sweet Caroline" (#4 Aug.) though the latter hit was spoiled for me when the Red Sox adopted it as their seventh inning stretch song several years ago. However, by far Neil's best composition in 1969 was the less popular but thoroughly enjoyable "Brother Love's Traveling Salvation Show" (#22 Apr.) *("Hot August night and the leaves hanging down and the grass on the ground smelling sweet")*. Meanwhile, 1969 was a comeback year for **Elvis Presley,** who scored with "In the Ghetto" (#3 June) and with my favorite Elvis song since the

1950s, "Suspicious Minds" (#1 Oct.) *("We can't go on together with suspicious minds")*.

Perhaps to avoid the bubblegum pop/rock label, **Tommy James** turned to "psychedelic" rock songs in 1969 with "Crimson and Clover" (#1 Feb.), "Crystal Blue Persuasion" (#2 July), and "Sweet Cherry Wine" (#7 May). These songs were hopelessly overplayed *("Crimson and clover, over and over")*, leading to my general dismissal of them as good music at the time. However, with time and age, I find I really like these songs, particularly "Crimson and Clover", which has been covered by many artists, most notably Joan Jett in a great version in 1982.

It's hard to talk about 1969 without touching on perhaps the two most interesting and enjoyable songs (but for completely different reasons): "A Boy named Sue" (#2 Aug.) by **Johnny Cash** and "Atlantis" (#7 May) by **Donovan**. The former was written so beautifully by Shel Silverstein that it seemed that Johnny Cash was telling his own story as he described his fight *("kicking and gouging in the mud and the blood and the beer")*. "Atlantis" was pure, probably unintended comedy with Donovan reverently describing *"the antediluvian kings"* and exhorting us in the chorus *"way down below the ocean where I wanna be"*. But both songs had nice melodies and were utter fun.

On the soul and R&B side, **The Temptations** led the way with their outstanding smash hit "I Can't Get Next to You" (#1 Oct.) and the lesser known but still excellent "Runaway Child, Running Wild" (#6 Mar.). Former Temptation **David Ruffin** had his best solo song, "My Whole World Ended" (#9 Mar.) *("The moment you left me")*, which sounded, of course, much like a Temptations song from 1967. **Sonny James and the Checkmates** had the great throwback soul hit "Black Pearl" (#13 June) *("Precious little girl, let me put you up where you belong")* and the **Edwin Hawkins Singers** had a surprise hit with the gospel song "Oh Happy Day" (#4 May). **The Foundations** had the highly successful and catchy "Build Me Up Buttercup" (#3 Feb.) *("Don't break my heart")* and **Edwin Starr**'s "25 Miles" (#6 Apr.) and its refrain *"Got to keep on WALKING"* had us all moving in 1969. **The Isley Brothers** had a huge R&B comeback hit with the lively "It's Your Thing" (#2 May) *("Do what you wanna do")*.

Marvin Gaye, though missing his collaborations with the very ill **Tammi Terrell** (who was diagnosed with a brain tumor in October 1967), still had two soul classics: "Too Busy Thinking About My Baby" (#4 June) and "That's the Way Love Is" (#7 Oct.). However, **Sly and the Family Stone** were clearly the kings of R&B with two of the best-selling and best songs of the year, the upbeat soul ballad "Everyday People" (#1 Feb.) *("Different strokes for different folks")*, and the silky smooth and soulful "Hot Fun in the Summertime" (#2 Oct.) *("End of the spring and here she comes back. Hi hi hi hi!")*.

Even instrumentals were pretty darn good in 1969. There was the fittingly emotional "Love Theme from Romeo and Juliet" by **Henry Mancini**, which went very well with the Oscar-winning movie that year. There was perhaps TV's greatest theme song "Hawaii Five-O" by **The Ventures** (#4 May) and two top-flight songs by **Booker T and the MGs:** "Time is Tight" (#6 Mar.) and "Hang 'Em High" (#9 Feb.).

The Bad

1969 was not all good, of course. Regrettably, **Bobby Sherman** decided to branch out from his TV role in *Here Come the Brides* and sing the vacuous "Little Woman" (#3 Sep.). The two-dimensional group **The Archies** (Ron Dante being the studio singer behind the cartoon) scored with the second most popular song of 1969, "Sugar, Sugar" (#1 Sep.), which also had the distinction of making my top 10 WORST singles list of ALL TIME back in 1979 in an article I wrote for the Stanford Graduate School of Business *Reporter*. Other bubblegum music lived on with the **1910 Fruitgum Co.** hitting it big with what now would be the very politically incorrect "Indian Giver" (#5 Mar.).

Finally, 1969 was a bad year for several notable groups. It was the beginning of the end for **The Supremes,** who had no major hits or good songs except for "I'm Livin' in Shame" (#10 Feb.) and "Someday We'll Be Together" (#1 Sep.) *("Yes we will, yes we will")*. These two hits were actually **Diana Ross** solo efforts backed by the **Andantes**. This was a direct reflection of the loss of Holland, Dozier, and Holland as Motown songwriters in early 1968 and the obvious fracturing of the group. Likewise, **The Four Tops** had little success or good songs in 1969 due to the aforementioned loss of the HDH songwriting team. **The Rascals,** after dominating the charts from 1966-68, had much less to offer in 1969 as their career spiraled downward. And though I liked **The Doors'** single "Touch Me" (#3 Feb.) *("Come on, come on now touch me babe"),* even the Doors had an off-year, with their 1969 album *Soft Parade* not nearly as good as their first two albums (*The Doors* and *Strange Days*) or as good as 1968's *Waiting for the Sun*. Lastly, largely unknown to all of us at the time, **The Beatles** as a group were falling apart at the seams (Lennon formed the **Plastic Ono Band** in 1969 and recorded "Give Peace a Chance" (#14 Nov.), which was one clear sign). This, of course, was the worst of possible news for most rock fans.

*****

Though 1969 wasn't the best of years for rock/popular music, it was an important change year that gave us the first rock opera, first rock musical and an epic three-day rock concert. Rock music was maturing, boding well for the coming decade. The 1970s were going to be an exciting time for rock-'n'-roll.

1970
"I've Seen Sunny Days That I Thought Would Never End"

1970 was a year of contrasts for me. The early winter/spring was the end of my middle year (sophomore year) at Taft School where I suffered through some bullying and medical ailments including a bad case of bronchitis at the end of the school year. The second half of the year was quite different. I had a great summer working for my dad's investment counseling firm as a messenger and then returned to Taft for my junior year with my best roommate at Taft (Eric Kitchen) and discovered a new passion (bridge playing) and of course, rock music.

The Beatles Before and After

When it came to rock music in 1970, the year was also divided into two parts – Pre- and Post-Beatles breakup. Though John Lennon privately informed the other Beatles in the fall of 1969 that he would be leaving the group, the official break-up occurred on April 10, 1970, when Paul McCartney publicly announced his departure. Shortly thereafter in May, the *Let It Be* album was released, but strangely most of the album was actually recorded in early 1969, BEFORE The Beatles recorded *Abbey Road*. (This probably meant that it was not a coincidence that the last full musical track on *Abbey Road* was called "The End".) Produced originally by Glyn Johns, The Beatles were unhappy with *Let It Be* and shelved the project in mid-1969. Eventually in the winter of 1969-70, Phil Spector was hired to remix the tapes and complete the album with its release in 1970. The album was only mediocre by Beatles standards and many critics panned it at the time, but even a mediocre Beatles record is still very good by other groups' standards!

The strengths of the album include the singles "Let It Be" (#1 Apr. '70 but recorded in early 1969) and "Get Back" (#1 May) released in early 1969, which were among the best recordings The Beatles ever made. Other very good songs from the album include Lennon's "Across the Universe" *("Pools of sorrow, waves of joy are drifting thru my open mind, possessing and caressing me")* and McCartney's simple, childlike but beautiful "Two of Us". Unfortunately, an excellent tune, "The Long and Winding Road" (#1 June) was diminished ironically by Spector's overproduction.

Other tracks largely credited to Lennon and Harrison on the album ("I Dig a Pony", "One After 909", "I Me Mine", and "For You Blue") paled in comparison to their contributions on *Abbey Road* (e.g., "Come Together", "I Want You", "Sun King", "Something", and the outstanding "Here Comes the Sun"). Nonetheless, it didn't stop me from running out and buying the album and playing it constantly when I finished my middle year at Taft in late May.

By the second half of 1970, the post-Beatles era had begun. All four Beatles released their first solo albums starting with *McCartney* in May. (Even **Ringo** released TWO albums in 1970, and while they were okay efforts, I bought neither so won't have anything to say about them.) Though critically panned at the time, *McCartney* was a respectable first effort and included some good songs: "That Would Be Something", "Every Night" *("But tonight I just want to stay and be with you")*, "Junk", and "Teddy Boy", as well as Paul's best post-Beatles song EVER, "Maybe I'm Amazed" *("The way you love me all the time")*. Paul McCartney played ALL the instruments on the album and fortunately Linda only joined in as a backup singer on a few of the songs. The album was less rock-oriented and more soft rock than anything The Beatles had ever done, or for that matter many of Paul's recent Beatles songs. Furthermore, the album definitely suffered from the unfinished nature of many of the tracks. In fact, this under-production was quite intentional as Paul was reacting to his intense displeasure with Phil Spector's overproduction of the *Let It Be* album and particularly the song "The Long and Winding Road". (Paul commented that he "couldn't believe it" that his simple acoustic track now included "harps, horns, an orchestra and a women's choir".).[19]

John Lennon released his first album *Plastic Ono Band,* which contrasted sharply with *McCartney*. This was John Lennon engaging in "primal scream" therapy, dealing with all of his inner emotions such as his rift with McCartney and his feelings about his fame as a Beatle ("Working Class Hero") *("is something to be")*, his relationship with Yoko ("God"), or his childhood anger of losing his mother at an early age ("Mother")

("Mama don't go, daddy come home"). It is a brilliant album with great lyrics and fitting music and vocals. However, while I bought it eventually, I didn't play it a lot, perhaps because it was very dark and depressing. In contrast, Lennon also had an excellent rousing and far more upbeat single, "Instant Karma" (#3 Mar.) *("Gonna get you")* released prior to the official Beatles breakup under the **Plastic Ono Band**. He also had an interesting single "Cold Turkey" (#30 Dec. '69) *("has got me on the run")*, the only single I can remember that said "PLAY LOUD" on the disc and featured sharp and yes LOUD guitar work from Eric Clapton.

Last but not least, **George Harrison** released *All Things Must Pass* at the end of 1970, an ambitious triple album. This was actually Harrison's second solo album (he released an experimental, instrumental-only album in 1968 called *Wonderwall Music*) and it benefits greatly from George's pent-up supply of songs that he wrote, but The Beatles did not record, during the 1967-70 period. However, like most triple albums (let alone double albums), the album would have been much better (and less expensive) if it had been a double album. Nonetheless, it contains a number of songs that rank as George's best of his solo career, including "My Sweet Lord" (#1 Dec.), (despite the unintentional plagiarism of the Chiffons' "He's So Fine"), "What is Life" (#10 Mar. 1971), "Isn't It a Pity" *("Isn't it a shame, how we break each other's hearts")*, the wonderful guitar playing of "Wah Wah", the two excellent collaborations with Dylan "If Not for You" and "I'd Have You Anytime", and the brilliant finality of "All Things Must Pass".

Simon And Garfunkel and Folk-Rock/ Soft Rock

Early 1970 also marked the release of the last studio album by **Simon and Garfunkel** – *Bridge Over Troubled Water*. The title song was arguably their best song ever and quickly went to the top of the U.S. charts. But the album had much more, including the beautiful 1969 single "The Boxer" (#7 May '69) *("By the light, by the li-li-li-li-light")* and the cheery and funny "Cecilia" (#4 May) *("I got up to wash my face, when I come back to bed, someone's taken my place")*. Other tracks were also very good: the classical-sounding "El Condor Pasa" (#18 Oct.) *("I'd rather be a sparrow than a snail")*, the upbeat and rousing "Baby

Driver" and "Keep the Customer Satisfied", and a great live remake of the Everly Brothers "Bye Bye Love". While the duo did not split officially until 1971, the album was their last real collaboration. Fortunately, it was the best album of 1970 and certainly the most acclaimed (with the album and title song winning multiple Grammys in 1971). It was another of my immediate buys when I got home in May.

In addition to Simon and Garfunkel's final album, rock music in 1970 was decidedly folk-rock oriented. With no new studio material from **The Rolling Stones** or **The Who**, no popular songs from the **Doors** (though still some excellent recordings such as the album *Morrison Hotel*), and the fading fortunes of **Steppenwolf** and **Deep Purple**, there was a dearth of hard rock songs, so folk-rock and softer rock were king. My favorite albums and songs followed this pattern in 1970.

Most Popular Hits in 1970
 1. I'll Be There – Jackson 5
 2. Raindrops Keep Fallin' on My Head – BJ Thomas
 3. My Sweet Lord – George Harrison
 4. ABC – Jackson 5
 5. I Think I Love You – Partridge Family
 6. Venus – Shocking Blue
 7. Let It Be – Beatles
 8. Spirit in the Sky – Norman Greenbaum
 9. Bridge Over Troubled Water – Simon & Garfunkel
 10. The Tears of a Clown – Smoky Robinson & The Miracles

Crosby, Stills & Nash followed up their huge success in 1969 by adding former Stills band mate **Neil Young** to the mix and releasing CSNY's first album *Déjà Vu* in March 1970. This included three excellent singles: "Woodstock" (#11 May), a rock cover of the Joni Mitchell folk ballad about the event, "Teach Your Children" (#16 July), and "Our House" (#30 Oct.) *("is a very very very fine house")*, the latter two compositions by Graham Nash. It also included even better contributions from Stills ("Carry On") and Neil Young ("Helpless" and "Country Girl"). In fact, this is one of those rare albums where all the songs were very good.

By the end of the year, despite the rousing success of their collaboration and their subsequent summer tour, the group had imploded. In fact, all four came out with solo albums during late-1970/early-1971. I bought both the *Stephen Stills* solo album and Neil Young's *After the Gold Rush*. However, I barely listened to the Stills album other than the first song on Side 1, the very catchy hit single "Love the One You're With" (#14 Jan. '71) *("and if you can't be with the one you love")*, which is why most everyone else bought the album, as well as the first track on Side 2, "Sit Yourself Down".

In contrast, *After the Gold Rush* included some of Young's best songs ever such as "Southern Man", "Only Love Can Break Your Heart" (#33 Dec.) *("When you were young and on your own, how did it feel to be alone?")*, "Tell Me Why", and "When You Dance" (#93 Apr. '71) *("Ooh, I can really love")*. Neil Young also penned one of the best songs of the year, "Ohio" (#14 Aug.) *("Tin soldiers and Nixon coming, we're finally on our own. This summer I hear the drumming, four dead in Ohio!")*. CSNY quickly recorded this song after the Kent State shootings.

Folk rock came from a new direction with the release of **James Taylor**'s second album, *Sweet Baby James,* which was his first commercial success. My sister Bonnie bought the album in mid-1970 after hearing Taylor at her first Brown spring weekend as a freshman and during the summer months, I started playing the album more than she did. It is without question Taylor's best album, including the beautiful hit song "Fire and Rain" (#3 Oct.) *("Just yesterday morning they let me know you were gone")* and some excellent folk tunes such as "Sunny Skies", "Blossom", and "Sweet Baby James" *("Goodnight you moonlight ladies, rock-a-bye sweet baby Jame*s*")*, though my favorite song was "Country Road", which I couldn't help but hum/sing when I was *"walking on a country road"*. In addition, Taylor's first single, the beautiful "Carolina in My Mind" (#67 Dec.) *("Can't you see the sunshine, can't you feel the moon shine")*, which was taken from his first album, finally cracked the top 100 after being released in February, no doubt because of the success of his second album.

My Favorite Songs in 1970
1. Bridge Over Troubled Water – Simon and Garfunkel
2. Ride Captain Ride – Blues Image
3. 25 or 6 to 4 – Chicago
4. Who'll Stop the Rain – CCR
5. I'm Your Captain – Grand Funk Railroad
6. Let It Be – Beatles
7. Question – Moody Blues
8. Celebrate – Three Dog Night
9. Green Eyed Lady – Sugarloaf
10. My Sweet Lord – George Harrison

Several other soft rock/pop groups included the new group **Bread** that began a string of top 10 hits with two solid entries: "Make It With You" (#1 Aug.) and my favorite by them, "It Don't Matter to Me" (#10 Nov.) *("You need some time to be free")*. **Neil Diamond** had two good songs with "Solitary Man" (#21 Sep.) and "Cracklin' Rosie" (#1 Oct.) though the latter suffered from overexposure on top 40 radio. Even **Ray Stevens** took time away from his mostly dumb, novelty-song career (which was only to get worse with "The Streak" a few years later) and charted the very successful and beautiful pop tune "Everything Is Beautiful" (#1 May) *("like a starry summer night or a snow covered winter's day")*.

Three Dog Night had great commercial success with conventional rock songs: "Mama Told Me" (#1 July) and "One Man Band" (#19 Dec.), two reasonably good efforts. But it was the softer rock sound of "Celebrate" (#15 Mar.) and the acoustic "Out in the Country" (#15 Oct.) *("before the breathing air is gone")* that remain my two favorites by the group that year. **The Hollies** had their first hit single in about three years with the irresistible "He Ain't Heavy, He's My Brother" (#7 Mar.) *("The road is long with many a winding turn")*.

Meanwhile, the summer of 1970 was when I discovered **The Moody Blues**. Working as a messenger on Wall Street, I would hear the song "Question" (#21 June) *("Why do we never get an answer when we're knocking at the door, with a thousand million questions about hate and death and war?")* playing on radios in stores and buildings and in the street. I found the song very catchy and soon bought the album *A Question of Balance* and absolutely loved it. Songs such as "It's Up to

You", "Dawning Is the Day", and "As the Tide Rushes In" were beautiful ballads and "Bet You Feel Small" and "The Tortoise and the Hare" were pure fun rock songs. Were The Moody Blues "pretentious"? Sure, songs like "The Balance", which included drummer Graeme Edge's voiceover, were a bit ridiculous. BUT, to all those critics who dislike the Moodies (and have kept them out of the Rock and Roll Hall of Fame), I say they have forgotten what rock music was all about, which was good music, good singing and simple, pure fun.

Another discovery for me in 1970 was the group **Chicago** and their superb hit singles "Make Me Smile" (#9 June) and "25 or 6 to 4" (#4 Sep.), which featured a new brass, rock and jazz fusion sound that was both unique and irresistible. I liked "Make Me Smile" *("I'm so happy that you love me")* when it came out in the spring of 1970 but really loved "25 or 6 to 4" *("Waiting for the break of day")*, which had both a catchy guitar and brass riff, as well as an excellent guitar solo from Terry Kath and certainly qualified as one of the best rock songs of the year. I eventually bought the album *Chicago,* which was actually Chicago's second album and one of many double albums for the group. And though it was a good double album, it would have been an outstanding single album!

I found myself listening almost exclusively to Sides 2 and 3, which featured several excellent songs written by keyboardist Robert Lamm: "Fancy Colours", "Wake Up Sunshine", and "25 or 6 to 4" as well as the outstanding 13-minute "Ballet for a Girl in Buchannon" written by trombonist James Pankow. This latter composition was actually a compendium of seven songs that flowed smoothly together: "Make Me Smile", "So Much to Say, So Much to Give", two instrumentals ("Anxiety's Moment" and "West Virginia Fantasies"), "Colour My World", "To Be Free" (another short instrumental), and the finale "Now More Than Ever", which was the last verse of the single version of "Make Me Smile". Chicago, which I have since seen live in concert four times (twice in a fairly intimate nightclub setting in Las Vegas), did a wonderful job playing the "Ballet for a Girl in Buchannon" to open one of these concerts.

In October, Chicago released "Does Anybody Know What Time It Is?" (#7 Dec.), from their first album, *Chicago Transit Authority,* released in 1969. Another great Chicago song, this was to become their third top 10 of 1970.

Hard Rock is NOT Dead

The more conventional, hard rock sound that had ruled the airwaves in the late 1960s was by no means "dead" though it was evolving. In the U.S., **Creedence Clearwater Revival** remained dominant in 1970 and continued their pattern of releasing successful two-sided hits beginning with "Travelling Band/Who'll Stop the Rain" (#2 Mar.), "Up Around The Bend/Run Through the Jungle" (#4 May), and finally "Looking Out My Back Door/Long as I Can See the Light" (#2 Sep.). *Cosmo's Factory,* released in July, was the group's best and most successful album. In addition to the six double-sided hit songs of 1970, the album included a great 11-minute cover of "I Heard It Through the Grapevine". My two favorite CCR songs of the year were first and foremost the outstanding "Who'll Stop the Rain" *("and I wonder still I wonder who'll stop the rain")*, which provided John Fogerty's recollections of Woodstock, but resonates with anyone who is tired of rain. Second, there was the musically and lyrically fun "Looking Out My Back Door" *("Tambourines and elephants are playing in the band. Won't you take a ride on the flying spoon?")*. The latter song features Fogerty's often-underrated guitar playing.

Santana released *Abraxas,* which highlighted the group's unique fusion of blues, jazz, Latin and rock music and most notably Carlos Santana's distinctive and superb guitar playing. The album included two outstanding songs/jams: "Black Magic Woman/Gypsy Queen" (#4 Dec.) and "Oyo Como Va" (#13 Mar. '71) and three excellent instrumental songs, most notably "Samba Pa Ti". But the album cover actually resulted in one fellow student being expelled from Taft, as he plagiarized, for his "original" poetry project, quotations on the back of the album from Hermann Hesse's "Demian". This might be the dumbest expulsion story ever, since our English teacher had used "Demian" in his course previously and also owned the *Abraxas* album!

Several relatively new American groups also released some excellent rock songs in 1970. This included "Ride Captain Ride" (#4 July) by **Blues Image**, another very catchy song I remember hearing as I was delivering messages on Wall Street.

Meanwhile, **Grand Funk Railroad** released the album *Closer to Home*, highlighted by the 10-minute song "I'm Your Captain (Closer to Home)" (#22 Oct.). The second half of the song became a single in the fall of 1970, though the whole song was played constantly on FM progressive radio and eventually ranked as one of the top 100 rock songs by several major progressive radio stations. I loved the whole song particularly the bass playing that linked the two parts of the song, and definitely bought the album in 1971 because of it.

Other very good rock songs included **Norman Greenbaum**'s "Spirit in the Sky" (#3 Apr.), a stark contrast to **John Lennon**'s anti-religious "God", and "All Right Now" (#4 Oct.) by **Free** (with a great guitar "hook"). The latter song was to become the Stanford University marching band's theme song at football games (much to my delight when I attended games in 1978-79). Canadian group **The Guess Who** had the excellent "No Time" (#5 Feb.) and the outstanding double-sided hit "American Woman/Undun" (#1 May). "American Woman" had the highly recognizable guitar riff that **Randy Bachman** developed quite by accident while messing around after a concert playing guitar variations of Led Zeppelin's "Whole Lotta Love".[20] Notably, the group's output suffered after Randy Bachman parted ways with the group eventually to form **Bachman-Turner Overdrive**.

From across the pond, **Eric Clapton** was without a group in 1970, but still had a good solo rock composition, "After Midnight" (#18 Dec.) *("We're gonna let it all hang down")*. Meanwhile, **Joe Cocker**, fresh off his newfound success at Woodstock, hit it big with three excellent rock covers: "She Came in Through the Bathroom Window" (#30 Jan.), "Cry Me A River" (#11 Nov.), and "The Letter" (#7 May). Though I wasn't yet a big fan of **Led Zeppelin**'s music, it was hard not to enjoy the ultimate hard rocker "The Immigrant Song" (#16 Jan. '71) *("Ah-ah ah. We come from the land of the ice and snow from the midnight sun where* *the hot springs flow")* that was from *Led Zeppelin III* released at the end of the year.

Last but certainly not least, the **Kinks** had two excellent songs in 1970 with "Apeman" (Feb. '71) *("Cos compared to the flowers and the birds and the trees, I am an apeman")*, released at the end of the year (which was **Ray Davies**' first "environmental" song) and the totally unique and brilliant "Lola" (#9 Oct.). Lyrics such as *"Well, I'm not dumb but I can't understand why she walks like a woman and talks like a man"* and *"girls will boys and boys will be girls, it's a mixed-up, muddled-up, shook-up world"* certainly cemented Davies' reputation as an extraordinary rock lyricist willing even to take on transvestite/transsexual issues. Musically, the song was equally brilliant with excellent guitar work and a great tune. Further, the song had wonderful pacing that changed from simple acoustic guitar and solo singing in the innocent portion of the song, to louder rock vocals and electric guitar as Lola's true nature is revealed.

Motown, Soul and R&B

It was a solid year for soul music led per usual by Motown. **The Temptations** emerged as the top Motown group (with the **Supremes** having lost **Diana Ross**) and continued their success with two great singles: "Psychedelic Shack" (#7 Feb.) and "Ball of Confusion" (#3 June). I particularly liked the latter song, as it combined wonderful vocals from the Temps, a driving beat, an excellent tune and the first Temptations song with an overtly social and political message:

"Evolution, revolution, gun control, sound of soul
Shooting rockets to the moon, kids growing up too soon
Politicians say more taxes will solve everything
And the band played on…
Eve of destruction, tax deduction, city inspectors, bill collectors
Mod clothes in demand, population out of hand, suicide, too many bills, hippies moving to the hills.
People all over the world are shouting 'End the war' and the band played on"

Diana Ross, having recently left the **Supremes**, had a great cover of "Ain't No Mountain High Enough" (#1 Sep.). Meanwhile, the Supremes, with new lead singer **Jean Terrell**, had two top 10 hits with "Up the Ladder to the Roof" (#10 Apr.) and the infectious "Stoned Love" (#7 Dec.). **Smokey Robinson and the Miracles** had the excellent #1 smash "Tears of a Clown" (#1 Dec.) with lyrics by Smokey and music co-written by **Stevie Wonder**. But perhaps the biggest Motown song of the year was from relatively unheralded **Edwin Starr** (who had only one previous hit, "Twenty Five Miles") with his outstanding vocal on "War" (#1 Sep.). The record has stood the test of time, being part of a gag on a Seinfeld episode more than 20 years later when Elaine tried to convince an aspiring Russian author that the original title of Tolstoy's "War and Peace" was actually *"War What Is It Good For (ABSOLUTELY NOTHING)!"*.

The Jackson 5 dominated the charts with three top sellers in 1970: "ABC" (#1 Apr.), "The Love You Save" (#1 June), and "I'll Be There" (#1 Oct.). I will admit that I didn't like the juvenile sound of the group and particularly could not tolerate Michael's vocal in the massively over-played "I'll Be There", but in retrospect, Jackson 5 songs such as "The Love You Save" were very good pop records.

Stevie Wonder had begun writing or co-writing his own songs and also produced his first record, "Signed, Sealed, Delivered" (#3 Aug.) in 1970, an excellent soul/rocker. Stevie also produced the **Spinners**' first big hit, "It's a Shame" (#14 Oct.) *("The way you mess around with your man. It's a shame the way you hurt me.")*, another personal favorite of mine in 1970. **Rare Earth**, Motown's only white group and one of its few rock groups, had considerable success during the year with two Temptations rock song remakes: "Get Ready" (#4 June) and "I Know I'm Losing You" (#7 Sep.).

Outside of Motown, soul R&B and the newly emerging funk was spearheaded by San Francisco's **Sly and the Family Stone**. Sly had two excellent hits: "Thank You (Falettinme Be Mice Elf Agin)" (#1 Feb.) and the almost as good B-side "Everybody Is a Star". Other good R&B songs included "Gimme Just a Little More Time" (#3 Mar.) by the **Chairmen of the Board**, "Love on a Two Way Street" (#3 May) by the

Moments, "Love or Let Me Be Lonely" by **Friends of Distinction** (#6 Apr.), and another of my favorites, "Didn't I Blow Your Mind" (#10 Mar.) by **The Delfonics** *("I gave my heart and soul to you")*.

*****

1970 wasn't all good. There were two huge hits by **The Carpenters**: "Close to You" (#1 Aug.) and "We've Only Just Begun" (#2 Nov.), which drove me crazy due to their saccharine sweetness, their incessant airplay and their "wah wah" and "la la" choruses. (In retrospect, I will note that Karen Carpenter had a gorgeous voice and the songs were good, so perhaps if they had toned down the overproduction, I might have had a different opinion.) Similarly, **Tony Orlando and Dawn**'s two big hits, "Candida" (#3 Oct.) and "Knock Three Times" (#1 Jan. '71) were just horrid. And there was the silly, cloying inanity of **The Partridge Family**'s "I Think I Love You" (#1 Nov.) and **The Poppy Family** (Terry and Susan Jacks) doing "Which Way You Goin' Billy?" (#2 June). And last but certainly not least, there was the awful **Bobby Sherman** doing "Julie, Julie, Do You Love Me?" (#5 Sep.) and though not his last big hit, perhaps his most prescient, "Easy Come, Easy Go" (#9 Apr.).

1970 also was a year that saw us lose two major groups, **The Beatles** and **Simon and Garfunkel**, and a year when the **Supremes** saw their last major successes.

Conversely, there were many new artists or artists that were hitting their peak by 1970 (who I would enjoy for many years to come) such as **Chicago, The Moody Blues, James Taylor, The Spinners** and the **Delfonics,** as well as the individual Beatles as solo artists. And 1971 was around the corner, with the return of **The Rolling Stones** and **The Who** with some of their best material by far. It was the beginning of *"sunny days I thought would never end"*.

1971 Pt. 1
"Listen to the Tide Slowly Turning, Wash All Our Heartaches Away"

1971 was a great year for rock/pop music. It was a year of excellent rock albums particularly from the U.K. This completed a conversion begun in the late 1960s, with the rock/popular LP album supplanting the single in terms of sales and popularity. In my own case, it was also a great year. Prep school actually was fun as I began to engage in all types of extracurricular activities (enough said) and increasingly began to branch out from my studies. I visited colleges that summer including Dartmouth and Middlebury with my friend Neil, and Brown with my sister (who was already attending). Meanwhile, my own record-buying habits were mimicking the trends in the industry, with my album purchases exceeding singles.

British Rock Albums Rule!

In 1971, a wealth of British artists released rock albums that were the best or near the best that they ever produced. This included **The Rolling Stones, The Who, Yes, Jethro Tull, Rod Stewart, Elton John, Cat Stevens, Moody Blues, Derek and the Dominoes, John Lennon** and **Paul McCartney**.

My favorite rock album in 1971 was *Who's Next* by **The Who,** released in August. Notably, it contains three Who songs that have emerged as standards – and still played in virtually every concert by the group today – "Behind Blue Eyes", "Baba O'Riley", and "Won't Get Fooled Again". The last of the three, "Won't Get Fooled Again" (#15 Sep.) *("We'll be fighting in the street, with our children at our feet")*, remains my favorite song by the group, so much so that I bought it as a single in August before the album had even been released. Little did I know that the single version at four minutes pales in comparison to the eight-minute version on the LP.

"Behind Blue Eyes" *("no one knows what it's like to be the bad man, to be the sad man")* was also a single (#34 Dec.) that nicely alternated between a beautiful acoustic guitar ballad and great hard rocker. "Baba

O'Riley" is the most interesting Who song on the album and also one of my favorites. It starts with a great synthesizer melody (which continues throughout), builds with opening piano chords, drums, guitar and then vocals *("Teenage wasteland, it's only teenage wasteland")*.

But all the songs on the album are excellent. From the upbeat "Gettin' in Tune", "Goin' Mobile", and "Bargain" to the humorous, semi-autobiographical (for John Entwistle) "My Wife" and the very sad "The Song is Over". The musical quality on ALL the songs is unbelievably good, including seamless use of synthesizer, keyboards, and other instruments. In addition, there is Pete Townshend's usual fine guitar work, John Entwistle's great bass playing, Keith Moon's energetic drumming and Roger Daltrey's soaring vocals.

Most Popular British Hits in 1971
  1. **Maggie Mae – Rod Stewart**
  2. **How Can You Mend a Broken Heart – Bee Gees**
  3. **She's a Lady – Tom Jones**
  4. **It Don't Come Easy – Ringo Starr**
  5. **Brown Sugar – Rolling Stones**
  6. **Uncle Albert/Admiral Halsey – Paul McCartney**
  7. **Lonely Days – Bee Gees**
  8. **Imagine – John Lennon**
  9. **I Hear You Knocking – David Edmunds**
10. **Peace Train – Cat Stevens**

The Rolling Stones released *Sticky Fingers* in April and it remains one of the best Stones albums. It begins with two excellent singles "Brown Sugar" (#1 May) and the often underrated, rock'n'bluesy "Wild Horses" (#28 July) *("couldn't drag me away")* sandwiching the slow rocker "Sway" on Side 1. But it also features one of the best Stones album cuts EVER: "Can't You Hear Me Knocking", a six-minute tour-de-force that ends with a wonderful saxophone solo. Side 2 is good, featuring songs such as "Bitch" and "Dead Flowers". The former could easily have been a hit single but was relegated to the B-side of "Brown Sugar".

Rod Stewart's *Every Picture Tells a Story* was his third album and by far his best. Released in May, it peaked in popularity in October 1971 (at the same time "Maggie Mae" was #1 on the charts). It seemed like everyone I knew at Taft school in September owned this album. Side 2 was superb. It featured the mega-hit "Maggie Mae" complete with a nice Renaissance-style guitar intro, and Rod's wonderful singing and lyrics *("you turned into a lover, but mother what a lover, you wore me out...you laughed at all of my jokes")*. "Maggie Mae" was followed by the slow ballad "Mandolin Wind", featuring Ron Wood's mandolin and guitar playing. The third track was the up-tempo, rock-'n'-roll extraordinaire version of the Temps' "I (Know) I'm Losing You" (#24 Dec.). The final track, "Reason to Believe", featured Stewart's great vocals on this **Tim Hardin** song *("knowing that you lied straight-faced while I cried, still I look to find a reason to believe...")*. The autobiographical title cut, "Every Picture Tells a Story", gets Side 1 off to a rollicking start, an excellent rock song chock full of wonderful lyrical imagery *("Shanghai Lil never used the pill, she claimed it 'just ain't natural', she took me up on deck and bit my neck...")*. The rest of Side 1 is not nearly as good, though Stewart's cover of "That's All Right" (Presley's first single that was released in 1954) is excellent.

Madman Across the Water by **Elton John** was released in November 1971. It was a Christmas Day 1971 gift along with a pair of new headphones. And what a great gift! The album remains one of my favorites. Side 1 is particularly strong with the first two cuts, "Tiny Dancer" (#41 Apr. '72) and "Levon" (#24 Jan. '72), two of John's best compositions. What makes this album so great is the seamless integration of orchestration along with Elton's piano and backing guitar and bass. This is probably most evident with the final cut on Side 1, "Madman Across the Water" *("I can see very well, there is a boat on a reef with a broken back")*, an excellent song made even better with the sweeping feel of a full orchestra and Elton's great emotionally charged vocals. But Side 2 is pretty good too, with "Holiday Inn" as my favorite, but "Rotten Peaches" and "All the Nasties" also standouts. Even the slower paced "Indian Sunset" is quite good and very interesting after several listenings.

Elton John, Elton's first album, was released at the end of 1970, but for all practical purposes became popular in early 1971 with Elton's first top 10 single "Your Song" (#8 Jan.), a beautiful love song. The album was almost the equal of *Madman*... with brilliant songs such as "Sixty Years On", *("Who'll walk me down to church when I'm sixty years of age?")*, "The King Must Die" and "Take Me to the Pilot". Elton had two more album releases in 1971 but neither of these was as good as his first or his last album of the year.

The Yes Album was released by **Yes** in February 1971. Though the third album by the group, this was their first commercially successful album. The album is built around four long songs, almost mini rock symphonies. Side 1 includes "Yours Is No Disgrace" *("On a sailing ship to nowhere, leaving any place, if the summer change to winter, yours is no disgrace")* and "Starship Trooper" *("Sister bluebird, flying high above")*, both nearly 10 minutes long, that showcase the group's musical strengths – Steve Howe's guitar, Chris Squire's bass guitar, Bill Bruford's drums, Tony Kaye's keyboards, and Jon Anderson's vocals. (In between the two long songs is sandwiched "The Clap", a short yet excellent acoustic guitar solo by Steve Howe.) Side 2 has the best song on the album, "I've Seen All Good People", which has two parts: "Your Move" (#40 Nov.) *("move me on to any black square")*, a gorgeous tune sung very well by Anderson and the rocking chant "All Good People". "Perpetual Change", the last of the four major songs of the album, is almost as good as the other three. In listening to this album MANY times, I am fascinated not just by the great basic melodies, verses and bridges but the intricacy of the different musical lines of the songs from Howe's multiple guitar chord progressions and Chris Squire's very distinctive bass lines. All four long songs are incredibly catchy. I defy anyone to listen to them several times and not get sucked into the music. And for that reason every time I listen, I find myself wishing the songs would never end. This was one of only a few albums that I literally wore out and had to replace several years later.

My Favorite British Songs in 1971
1. Won't Get Fooled Again – The Who
2. Layla – Derek and the Dominos
3. Maggie Mae – Rod Stewart
4. Story in Your Eyes – Moody Blues
5. Uncle Albert/Admiral Halsey – Paul McCartney
6. I've Seen All Good People – Yes
7. Baba O'Riley – The Who
8. Tiny Dancer – Elton John
9. I'd Love to Change the World – Ten Years After
10. Simple Sister – Procol Harem

By now, it will come as no surprise that one of my favorite albums of 1971 was *Every Good Boy Deserves Favour* by **The Moody Blues**. The album begins with the intro song "Procession" which nicely segues into the guitar intro of "The Story in Your Eyes" (#23 Sep.) *("Listen to the tide slowly turning, wash all our heartaches away")*, which was one of my favorite songs of the year. But all the songs on the album are very good with particular highlights including "Our Guessing Game", "One More Time to Live" *("Look out of my window, see the world passing by")* and "You Can Never Go Home". While rock critics often denounced The Moody Blues for their pretentiousness, there is little question that they wrote great melodies (most notably Justin Hayward) and sang and played them well. There was strong evidence of this on EGBDF.

Folk rocker **Cat Stevens** (nee Steven Georgiou in London) had his first major successes in 1971 with the albums *Tea for the Tillerman* (released at the end of 1970 and peaking in the spring of 1971) and *Teaser and the Firecat,* released in the fall of 1971. Of the two albums, *Tea...* was my favorite with Cat's first single "Wild World" (#11 Apr.), *("It's hard to get by just upon a smile")*, the best song on the album. The album was also loaded with many other excellent songs, including a father and son talking past one another in a great tune "Father and Son" *("find a girl, settle down if you want you can marry, look at me I am old but I'm happy")*, the brilliant and spirited "Miles from Nowhere" *("guess I'll take my time")*, and three other beautiful songs: "On the Road to Find Out", "Hard Headed Woman", and "Where Do the Children Play?" *("I *know we've come a long way, we're changing day-to-day but tell me...").* In fact, there is not a weak cut on the album. *Teaser and the Firecat* is not as consistent but was the source of three beautiful songs: "Moon Shadow" (#30 Aug.) *("I'm being followed by a moon shadow")*, "Peace Train" (#7 Oct.), and "Morning Has Broken" (#6 May '72).

In hindsight, *Aqualung,* released in April 1971, was **Jethro Tull** at its best. Though I enjoyed it and bought it when it came out, I gravitated towards *Thick as a Brick,* released in 1972, which I passed out listening to on headphones on more than a few occasions during freshman year in college. However, *Aqualung* has stood the test of time much better. The album is excellent from the opening title track, which remains the best known, to the last track "Wind Up". It has a nice mix of acoustic guitar, piano, electric guitar and Ian Anderson's ever-present flute. In addition to the title track, my favorites on the album include "Locomotive Breath" *("in the suffering madness of the locomotive breath")*, "My God", "Hymn 43" *("And Jesus saves, well he better save himself")*, and "Cross Eyed Mary".

Layla and Other Assorted Love Songs by **Derek and the Dominoes** was released in November 1970, but only began to receive U.S. airplay in 1971. The group was formed during the summer of 1970 and included Eric Clapton (guitar), Bobby Whitlock (keyboards), Jim Gordon (drums and piano on "Layla"), and Carl Radle (bass). Notably, Duane Allman played slide guitar on most of the tracks of the album. I can remember enjoying hearing the shorter, single version of "Layla" (#51 May) on the radio in the spring of 1971. But this joy turned into rapture when I discovered the seven-minute album version including Jim Gordon's piano, which dominates the second half of the song. Eventually, "Layla" would be released as a seven-minute single in early 1972 and it would not only become the centerpiece of the album, but one of rock's most famous songs.

But the *Layla* album had much more, which I only appreciated with the passage of time. For one, Clapton wrote most of the album's songs during an "incredibly creative time". Clapton noted that he was "driven by my obsession with Pattie" (Pattie Boyd was his friend George Harrison's wife). "All the songs I wrote for the Dominoes' first album are really about her and our relationship." "Layla" is the prime example, where Clapton wanted Pattie to move in with him so he wrote, *"What'll you do when you get lonely?"* This love affair is evident lyrically and vocally throughout most of the other songs of the double album as well. Musically, in addition to the fine guitar and keyboard playing, the songs "Tell the Truth" *("Who's been fooling who?")*, "Bell Bottom Blues" *("If I could choose a place to die it would be in your arms")*, "Keep on Growing", "Key to the Highway", "Why Does Love Got to Be So Sad", and a cover of Hendrix's "Little Wing" are all standouts on the album.[21]

Last but certainly not least, **John Lennon** and **Paul McCartney** produced their second solo albums in 1971. Perhaps it was a sign of the strength of British rock music generally that neither had the same reception as their first solo efforts in 1970. Nonetheless, they were solid if not spectacular albums. Lennon's *Imagine* featured the title track "Imagine" (#3 Nov. '71), arguably Lennon's best solo effort but there were other very good songs on the album ranging from the self-aware "Jealous Guy", to the vitriolic "How Do You Sleep?" *("A pretty face may last a year or two, but pretty soon they'll see what you can do")*, aimed at Paul, the political "Gimme Some Truth", the love song "Oh My Love" and the happy and upbeat "Oh Yoko" *("In the middle of the night I call your name")*. Though arguably not as good overall, the album was much more polished than Lennon's outstanding, raw "primal scream" therapy, first album.

McCartney's second album *Ram* was released in the early summer. The album was critically panned at the time (unfairly in my view) though it was viewed more favorably with the passage of time. The album includes one of my favorite post-Beatles singles by Paul McCartney, "Uncle Albert/Admiral Halsey" (#1 Sep.) *("We're so sorry Uncle Albert")*, which like many McCartney singles has meaningless lyrics, but has an outstanding melody and vocals by Paul.

But *Ram* also has several other very good songs. I really liked the interesting love song "Back Seat of My Car" *("But listen to her daddy's song, don't stay out too long")* and the country rock "Heart of the Country". "Too Many People" is a more up-tempo rocker that has several slights that John took personally *("Too many people preaching practices, don't let them tell you what want to be...")*. (John, who was then recording his album, retaliated with the song "How Do You Sleep?")[22] "Monkberry Moon Delight" is a hard-rocking drug song featuring McCartney's "rough" voice, which has grown on me over the years. And Linda's backing vocals are strong for a change. McCartney started the year with his first solo single, "Another Day" (#5 Apr.), a very enjoyable soft rock-pop song, which would have fit perfectly both musically and lyrically on *Ram*, but for unknown reasons was not on the album or any album until a *Greatest Hits* collection much later. McCartney was repeating a pattern very prevalent with **The Beatles,** with singles such as "Paperback Writer" and "Hey Jude" that were not on any album, until later greatest hit collections.

More British Hits

In addition to the supergroups and stars noted above, other British artists produced some other very good songs and singles:

Procol Harum released the album *Barricades* with its highlight song "Simple Sister" *("Got whooping cough. Have to burn her toys")*, a brilliant, long instrumental-infused rocker featuring Robin Trower at his best (his last album with the group) with excellent guitar licks throughout.

"I'd Love to Change the World" (#40 Oct.) by **Ten Years After** was one of my favorite singles of the year. It is a wonderful hard rocker with Albin Lee playing a great lead guitar, but lyrically might be quite politically incorrect these days *("Everywhere there's freaks and hairies, dykes and fairies tell me where there's sanity")*. (Some said they were being "ironic" since they were long hairs; however, I wonder how much that would matter these days, irony being lost in the "gotcha", internet environment.)

Ringo Starr had his first post-Beatles top-forty song, "It Don't Come Easy" (#4 June), an excellent rocker, ably assisted by the backing vocals of **Badfinger**. This has always been my favorite Ringo solo song.

Though I was never much of an **Emerson, Lake and Palmer** fan, it was hard not to notice the artistic cover (white dove on a green background) of the group's first album *Emerson, Lake and Palmer*. Particularly noteworthy was the best song the group ever produced and the album's only single, "Lucky Man" (#48 but on the charts for 19 weeks) *("He had white horses, and ladies by the score all dressed in satin and waiting by the door")*.

"I Hear You Knocking" (#4 Feb.) *("You went away and left me long time ago, and now you're knocking on my door")* by Welshman **Dave Edmunds** is an interesting rock rendition of an old R&B song by **Smiley Lewis** from 1954. The guitar sound is a unique twangy sound that permeated **T. Rex** songs like "Bang a Gong" two years later.

"How Can You Mend a Broken Heart" (#1 Aug.) by the **Bee Gees** represented the pinnacle of their success as soft rock balladeers. I always liked the tune and rendition, although it is admittedly very schmaltzy. Earlier in the year, the group scored with another good song, "Lonely Days" (#3 Jan.) *("Where would I be without my woman?")*, but it wasn't until 1975 when the Bee Gees shifted to disco that they were to have another top 10 song.

"Here Comes That Rainy Day Feeling" (#15 July) *("And soon my tears they will be falling like rain")* by the **Fortunes** was the group's first big hit since "You've Got Your Troubles" six years earlier and it was to be their last. I love this song for its cheery, upbeat melody and tempo even though it is about depression of all things!

*****

All and all, 1971 was an amazing year for British rock, but across the Atlantic, rock music was far from dead.

1971 Pt. 2
"All You've Got to Do Is Call"

While music from the U.K. dominated the rock scene in 1971, there was also important American music particularly in the folk-rock and R&B genres. To be sure, my album collection swelled in 1971 largely because of British artists such as **Yes, The Who, The Moody Blues, McCartney, Lennon, ELP, Jethro Tull** and **The Rolling Stones**. However, I also enjoyed a number of American albums and singles as well.

Folk-Rock and Soft Rock Remain Dominant

Folk-rock morphed into soft rock in 1971 and became the dominant form of American rock music.

The U.S. album of the year was from singer-songwriter **Carole King**, who released *Tapestry* in early 1971, her second solo album and by far and away her best. The album features the two-sided hit "It's Too Late/I Feel the Earth Move" (#1 June) as well as the beautiful and mournful "So Far Away" (#14 Oct.) *("Doesn't anyone stay in one place anymore...")*. But the album had much more – two outstanding sides of music and no weak tracks. Side 1 not only features King's newer solo hit songs (e.g., "It's Too Late", "I Feel the Earth Move", "So Far Away") but also new songs such as "Beautiful", a song that I still find very inspiring on depressing days: *"You've got to get up every morning with a smile on your face and show the world all the love in your heart, and people gonna treat you better, they're gonna find...that you're as beautiful as you feel"*. Side 2 is dominated by her old 1960s standards made famous by **Aretha Franklin** ("A Natural Woman"), the **Shirelles** ("Will You Love Me Tomorrow") and her friend **James Taylor** ("You've Got A Friend") but all sung and performed adeptly by Carole. Side 2 also includes the excellent tune "Where You Lead" which is noteworthy for its inclusion as the theme song in the hit TV series *Gilmore Girls*, a show I used to enjoy watching with my daughters. (Carole also appears as a record store owner during one episode with her hit song written for the Monkees "Pleasant Valley Sunday" playing in the background. Naturally, I couldn't help but notice the intentional coincidence!)

James Taylor released his third solo album, *Mud Slide Slim* but it wasn't nearly as good an album as his second, *Sweet Baby James*. However, it did feature one outstanding song, Taylor's beautiful version of "You've Got a Friend" (#1 July). This was to be Taylor's only #1 hit on the charts during his entire, still ongoing career. "Long Ago and Far Away" was also an album highlight and managed to chart in the top 40 in November. Both songs were enhanced considerably by backing vocals from **Joni Mitchell**. While I am not a fan of most of Joni Mitchell's music, I also must acknowledge the release of Joni's *Blue* album in 1971, which is critically acclaimed as one of the best albums of all time. My favorite songs on this album are "California" and "Case of You".

Likewise, I am not a **John Denver** fan, but I did enjoy his music during 1971-72. In 1971, he released his first single, "Take Me Home, Country Roads" (#2 June), which along with "Rocky Mountain High" (#9 Feb. '73) *("The Colorado Rocky Mountain high, I've seen it rainin' fire in the sky"),* recorded at the end of 1972, are the two best songs he ever recorded.

Chicago III was a disappointment after **Chicago**'s very strong first two albums. It did feature two pretty good songs: "Free" (#20 Mar.) and "Lowdown" (#35 June). However, the highlight of the year for Chicago was the release of two excellent double-sided hit singles excerpted from Chicago's first two albums: "Beginnings/Colour My World" (#7 Aug.) and "Questions 67 and 68/I'm A Man" (#24 Nov.).

Most Popular American Hits in 1971
1. Joy to the World – Three Dog Night
2. Knock Three Times – Dawn
3. Brand New Key – Melanie
4. Family Affair – Sly and the Family Stone
5. Theme from Shaft – Isaac Hayes
6. One Bad Apple – Osmonds
7. It's Too Late – Carole King
8. Never Can Say Goodbye – Jackson 5
9. Indian Reservation – Raiders
10. Gypsys, Tramps and Thieves – Cher

It was also hard to ignore the **Grateful Dead,** who received significant FM airplay during 1971 (but no top 40 radio airplay) due to the critical success of two of their best albums released during the latter half of 1970: *Workingman's Dead* (June 1970) and *American Beauty* (Nov. 1970). I first discovered the Dead hearing the song "Truckin'" (#64 Dec.) *("Lately, it occurs to me what a long strange trip it's been")* being played on the radio at our snack shop at Taft School in the early fall of 1971. While I never became a big fan or a Dead Head and never owned any of their albums, I grew to like many of their classic songs, particularly from these two albums. In addition to "Truckin'", this included "Sugar Magnolia", "Friend of the Devil", "Casey Jones" *("riding that train, out of cocaine, Casey Jones you better watch your speed")* and my favorite by them, "Uncle John's Band" (#69 Sep. 1970) *("Come hear Uncle John's band by the riverside")*. At their best, the Dead reminded me of an advanced form of electric folk-rock à la the **Byrds**, which is no small compliment.

Singer-songwriter **Harry Nilsson** released the album *Nilsson Schmilsson* in November. The album included his best-selling single and one of his best songs, "Without You" (#1 Feb. '72) *("I can't live if living is without you")*, which was written by Pete Ham and Tom Evans of **Badfinger**. The album included two other interesting singles that became hits in 1972: "Coconut" (#8 Aug. '72) *("you put the lime in the coconut")* and "Jump in the Fire" (#9 Apr. '72).

Other good soft-rock/pop singles included:

Neil Diamond – "I Am, I Said" (#4 May)

Canadian **Gordon Lightfoot** – "If You Could Read My Mind" (#5 Feb.) *("What a tale my thoughts could tell")*

Richie Havens – "Here Comes the Sun" (#16 May) was an excellent cover of this George Harrison song and was Havens' only chart success. Havens was first discovered by most music fans at Woodstock "strumming holy hell out of his E-chord open-tuned acoustic guitar and bellowing, entranced like a shaman". Havens was aptly described by Rolling Stone as "a black singer with a percussive, strummed guitar style" and fittingly began this song with a lengthy acoustic guitar intro.[23]

Three Dog Night – "Joy to the World" (#1 Apr.). Despite being overplayed on the radio, I still enjoy it to this day. I also liked the Paul Williams composition "Old Fashioned Love Song" (#4 Dec.) *("Playing on the radio")*.

Brewer and Shipley – "One Toke Over the Line" (#10 Mar.) *("Sitting down south on a railway station")* with an assist from the Dead's **Jerry Garcia,** who played steel guitar.

Stampeders – "Sweet City Woman" (#8 Oct.) This Canadian group, fittingly from Calgary, had their only top 40 hit in 1971. I like this song for its banjo lead and a nice tune. *"Bon c'est bon, bon c'est bon..."*

5th Dimension – "Light Sings" (#45 June). Okay, I admit this is a strange and obscure one. However, it is on the list because it became a sort of theme song during a June 1971 four-day hiking trip in the Adirondacks. My friend Jonathan had brought along a radio and during a day of rain and thunderstorms when we remained in our lean-to, we kept hearing this song on the local station (which makes you wonder about that radio station's playlist). However, dampened by the rain and storms, we thought the 5th Dimension was singing, "Lightning all over the world".

The Carpenters – "For All We Know" (#3 Mar.), "Rainy Days and Mondays" (#2 June) and "Superstar" (#2 Oct.). The Carpenters remained the most successful duo in 1971. As I have noted before in an earlier chapter about 1970, I was never a fan because I found the production of their songs simply too saccharine. But Karen Carpenter had an exquisite voice and her rendition of "Rainy Days and Mondays" was outstanding and eerily prescient given her later affliction with anorexia/depression and her eventual, premature death. *"Hangin' around, nothin' to do but frown, rainy days and Mondays always get me down."*

"Rockin' in the U.S.A."

Hard rock was still alive and well in the U.S. though three rock mainstays of the late 1960s were to have their lives ended in their twenties between September 1970 and July 1971. In addition, a major supergroup was to have its last commercial successes in 1971 and disband in 1972.

The Doors' last album with **Jim Morrison**, *L.A. Woman*, was released on April 19, 1971 (coincidentally on the same day of our wedding which was exactly 15 years later – not sure what this says about our marriage!). Morrison died three months later in July. The album is uneven but did have three of the best songs the group ever recorded. This included the singles "Love Her Madly" (#11 May) *("Don't you love her as she's walking out the door")* and "Riders on the Storm" (#14 Aug.) *("Like a dog without a bone, and actor without a loan")*, though in the latter case the album included the much better, seven-minute version of the song with Ray Manzarek's excellent keyboard solo. The title cut from the album, "L.A. Woman", is vintage Doors and was largely written by all the Doors members jamming together. The result was nearly an eight-minute, rock masterpiece, best known for its oft-repeated, drug reference *"mojo rising"*. I did like several other cuts on the album, but these three are far and away the highlights.

Janis Joplin had her last album overall and second solo album *Pearl,* which was released posthumously in January 1971 (Joplin died on October 4, 1970 of a heroin overdose). The album was by far her best (including those that she did as the lead singer for **Big Brother and the**

Holding Company). It features three superb songs: "Move Over", "Cry Baby" (#42 June), and best of all "Me and Bobby McGee" (#1 Mar.) *("Busted flat in Baton Rouge, waiting for a train and I'm feeling near as faded as my jeans")*. It was a unique album full of blues and country influences and of course, Joplin's raspy and distinctive voice.

Only a few weeks earlier, **Jimi Hendrix** had died of a drug overdose on September 18, 1970 at the age of 27. But it seemed thereafter that FM radio stations were paying homage for the remainder of 1970 and most of 1971, constantly playing Hendrix songs from all his albums.

My Favorite American Songs in 1971
1. Riders on the Storm – Doors
2. Theme from Shaft – Isaac Hayes
3. It's Too Late – Carole King
4. You've Got a Friend – James Taylor
5. Beginnings – Chicago
6. Sooner or Later – Grass Roots
7. What's Going On – Marvin Gaye
8. Have You Ever Seen the Rain? – CCR
9. If You Could Read Mind – Gordon Lightfoot
10. Smiling Faces Sometimes – Undisputed Truth

1971 was to prove to be the last full year **Creedence Clearwater Revival** was together as a group. It was also the last time that they were to reach the top 10 singles chart with the double-sided hit "Have You Ever Seen the Rain/Hey Tonight" (#8 Mar.) and "Sweet Hitchhiker" (#6 Aug.). All three of these songs were from the *Pendulum* album released in December 1970. "Sweet Hitchhiker" and "Hey Tonight" were excellent rockers, featuring some fine guitar playing by John Fogerty and brother Tom. "Have You Ever Seen the Rain" was a country-rock ballad and a great tune with John Fogerty's excellent vocals. The official swan song of the group was "Someday Never Comes" (#25 June '72). It was their last single as a group from their final sub-par album *Mardi Gras*. The group officially disbanded in October 1972.

With the success of the *Abraxas* album, **Santana** released several singles from the album (see chapter on 1970) and then followed with the *Santana III* album in 1971. While I did not own it, I do remember liking three songs from this 1971 album: "Everybody's Everything" (#12 Nov.) was a spirited, fully orchestrated tune; "No One to Depend On" (#36 Mar. '72) was more typical of Santana – a Latin rocker sound that intoned *"I AIN'T got nobody that I can depend on"*; and "Everything's Coming Our Way" was a more sedate song featuring Carlos Santana both singing AND playing the high notes.

There were several other harder rock/pop singles that I enjoyed in 1971:

The Five Man Electrical Band from Ontario, Canada released "Signs" (#3 Aug.). How can you not love a song with lyrics such as, *"And the sign said 'Long Haired Freaky People Need Not Apply'"*?

"Superstar" – **Murray Head** (#14 on charts for 24 weeks from January to June) was the highlight song of the Broadway musical *Jesus Christ Superstar* and certainly my favorite. (Australian **Helen Reddy** had her first single, "I Don't Know How to Love Him" (#13 June) taken from the score of *Jesus Christ Superstar* as well.)

The Grass Roots had three formulaic hits: "Temptation Eyes" (#15 Mar.), "Sooner or Later" (#9 July), and "Two Divided by Love" (#16 Nov.), which all seem to have their roots from the earlier hit "Midnight Confessions". Nonetheless, the formula was excellent and I enjoyed all three, though particularly the upbeat *"Sooner or later, love is gonna get you, it's just a matter of time..."*

Alice Cooper – "Eighteen" (#21 Apr.) was the band's first single and an excellent rock song. I liked the song even more about one year later when I turned 18. *"I'm eighteen and I like it."*

Soul and R&B

Soul and R&B music was excellent in 1971, but it was no longer the **Supremes** that dominated as in the late 1960s. The king of soul and of Motown in 1971 was **Marvin Gaye,** who had an outstanding album in *What's Going On* and three excellent singles/songs from the album. "What's Going On" (#2 Apr.) *("Don't punish me with brutality. Talk to me so you can see what's going on")* is the best. But I also really like

"Mercy, Mercy Me (The Ecology)" (#4 Aug.), and "Inner City Blues (Makes Me Wanna Holler)" (#9 Nov.).

Stevie Wonder had two great songs in 1971. The first, "We Can Work It Out" (#13 Apr.), is THE BEST COVER of a Beatles song ever. Stevie took a soft rock song sung by McCartney and turned it into an R&B classic. The second, "If You Really Love Me" (#8 Oct.) *("Won't you tell me")*, was co-written by Stevie Wonder and his first wife Syreeta Wright and is another excellent Wonder tune.

The Temptations had their first #1 hit in two years, "Just My Imagination" (#1 in Mar./Apr.) The song is a beautiful soul ballad written by Whitfield/Strong (who wrote most of the Temptations songs during the '60s and early '70s) with a stellar lead vocal by Eddie Kendricks. The Temps also had a good song at the end of the year with "Superstar (Remember How You Got Where You Are)" (#18 Dec.).

Outside of Motown, **Aretha Franklin** had a strong comeback year and had her first top 10 hit since 1968. The undisputed "Queen of Soul" had two highly successful covers: first with Simon and Garfunkel's "Bridge Over Troubled Water" (#6 June) and second with Ben E. King's "Spanish Harlem" (#2 Sep.). The latter song is one of my favorite remakes and one of Aretha's best. Aretha finished up the year with the excellent "Rock Steady" (#9 Nov.).

But outside of the perennial R&B hit makers, there were several soul and R&B songs I really enjoyed:

The heavily instrumental "Theme from Shaft" (#1 Nov.), written and performed by **Isaac Hayes,** won the Oscar for best song with Isaac's soulful performance and the great musical production at the ceremony bringing the house down. This was to be Hayes' only top 20 song of his career and one of my favorites of 1971. *"They say this cat Shaft is a bad mother f...(shut your mouth!). But I'm talking about Shaft (but we can dig it)."*

Another #1 song, "Family Affair" (#1 Dec.), followed Isaac Hayes at the top of the charts. It was the last top-ten song for **Sly and the Family**

Stone. The song is unique among the group's compositions with a much funkier sound.

One of the best covers of the rock era was **Ike and Tina Turner**'s "Proud Mary" (#4 Mar.). This was to be the most successful single and by far and away the best song by this duo. What I loved about this song is the way they slowed the CCR version of the song's tempo down in the first half and used Ike's slow bass voice to great effect "roll-ing-on-a-riv-er" and then sped it up to faster than anything John Fogerty had ever imagined with Tina Turner's amazing voice powering the song. Wow!

Undisputed Truth – "Smiling Faces" (#3 Sep.) was the first single and only top 40 hit by this R&B trio from Detroit. *"Beware of the pat on the back..."*

Another new artist, **Bill Withers,** scored with the soulful "Ain't No Sunshine" (#3 Sep.). This was the first single for the West Virginia R&B singer-songwriter with his best yet to come. *"And I know, I know, I know, I know..."*

And I would be remiss if I didn't mention the **Jackson 5**, who had continued success with "Mama's Pearl" (#2 Feb.) and one of the biggest hits of the year, "Never Can Say Goodbye" (#2 May). I didn't care for either very much but if you like child voices, **Michael Jackson** at 12-13 years old is probably the best you will ever hear.

The Bad and Ugly

American music in 1971 was not all good. For one, there was the loss of three major American artists during late 1970-early 1971: **Jimi Hendrix, Janis Joplin** and **Jim Morrison**. It was also the practical end of two major supergroups: **Creedence Clearwater Revival** and **Sly and the Family Stone**.

And some of the groups and songs were annoying and atrocious and in a few cases both. The **Osmonds**, an attempted white Mormon clone of the **Jackson 5**, were horrible. "One Bad Apple" (#1 Feb.) *("Don't spoil the whole bunch, girl")* was the epitome of the group, and despite being the #6 ranked song of the year was extremely difficult to listen to unless you like pre-pubescent screeching. As if this wasn't enough, lead singer **Donny Osmond**'s solo hit "Sweet and Innocent" (#7 May) takes the saccharine sweetness and the singing (?) a step further.

Likewise, the **Partridge Family**'s "I'll Meet You Halfway" (#6 June) and "Doesn't Somebody Want to Be Wanted" (#9 Mar.) was TV's way of copying a successful concept and a reasonably good family singing group – **The Cowsills** – and turning it into something much worse.

And in the category of not really awful, but just downright annoying were **Melanie**'s "Brand New Key" (#1 Dec.) *("I got a brand new pair of roller skates, you got a brand new key...)* and **Cher**'s "Gypsy's Tramps and Thieves" (#1 Nov.). After hearing these songs enough times on the radio, I wanted Melanie to break her neck roller skating and Cher to be hauled away by the gypsies, tramps and thieves!

*****

But more than in almost any other year, the good in 1971 far outweighed the bad and 1971 was one of the most exciting years for rock. *"All you've got to do is call."*

1972
"It Was a Very Good Year"

1972 was an excellent year for rock music AND for me personally. I graduated from prep school (Taft School) in June and began my freshman year at Brown University in September. Not to diminish my high school graduation or my freshman year at Brown, but 1972 was a huge year for rock, one in which several new groups burst onto the scene and many existing groups had their musical "tour de force".

In early 1972, the rock group **Yes** emerged from relative obscurity with their album *Fragile* and their first hit single "Roundabout" (#13 Apr.) *("In and around the lake, mountains come out of the sky, they stand there")*, which is one of my all-time favorites. (They later followed this up with the musically superb *Close to the Edge* late in 1972.)

Meanwhile, **Led Zeppelin** came out with their *Untitled Led Zeppelin IV* (released in late 1971) that included perhaps the most famous song in rock history, "Stairway to Heaven" (that interestingly enough was NEVER released as a single). This was the first time, in my opinion, that Led Zeppelin had released a full album of excellent songs. These ranged from outstanding rockers such as "Black Dog" (#15 Feb.) *("Hey mama, said the way you move, gonna make you sweat gonna make you groove")* and "Rock'N'Roll" (#47 Apr.) *("Been a long time since I rock n rolled")* to more lengthy ballads like "Going to California", "Battle of Evermore", and of course "Stairway". *Led Zeppelin IV* remains one of the most popular rock albums of all time to this day.

Neil Young released his *Harvest* album, his greatest single achievement and perhaps the greatest folk-rock album ever with stellar songs such as "Heart of Gold" (#1 Mar.) *("Keeps me searching for a heart of gold, and I'm getting old")*, "Old Man" *("Take a look at my life, 24 and there is so much more")*, "Out On The Weekend", "Alabama" *("Your Cadillac has got a wheel in the ditch and a wheel on the track")*, and the "Needle and the Damage Done".

A new group, **America**, issued their first album (and what turned out to be their best album) with its iconic drug culture single "A Horse with No Name" (#1 Mar.) *("In the desert you can't remember your name")*, which included "I Need You" (#9 June) and one of my favorite folk-rock jam songs "Sandman" *("Ain't it foggy outside, all the planes have been grounded")*.

And that all happened by the spring of 1972!

In May 1972, the **Hollies** (minus **Graham Nash**) released their best single (and one of the best rock-'n'-roll songs ever), "Long Cool Woman in a Black Dress" (#2 Sep.) *("Just one look I was a bad mess. Cause that long cool woman had it all")*. This was followed by a less popular but still compelling "Long Dark Road" (#26 Dec.) *("and you know, I love you")*.

In June, another new group, the **Eagles**, released their first album and their first hit single, "Take It Easy" (#12 July), a unique-sounding Western folk-rocker if there ever was one.

The fall of 1972 featured the increased airplay and huge popularity of a **Kenny Loggins with Jim Messina** *Sittin' In* album, which was originally released at the end of 1971. The album included a wonderful merge of folk, rock, and country sounds as well as elaborate instrumentation with flutes, violins and horns. Songs such as "Trilogy", "Nobody But You" (#86 June), "House at Pooh Corner" *("count all the bees in the hive")*, "A Love Song", "Danny's Song", "Back to Georgia", and "Vahevala" (#84 May) *("homeward sailor")* were frequently played and later covered by several artists. Originally intended to be the first album for Kenny Loggins, with Messina as just a producer, this album launched a duo career of several years and the album became known as *Sittin' In*.

I admit I am a bit biased when it comes to *Sittin' In* (and their second album *Loggins and Messina* released at the end of 1972, which included "Your Mama Don't Dance" (#4 Jan. '73) *("and your daddy don't rock n roll")*, "Thinking of You" (#18 May '73), and a 10-minute version of "Angry Eyes"). However, Loggins and Messina was the first rock group

I ever saw in concert. It was in March 1973 in a University of Rhode Island gym (of all places) and included a virtual unknown then as the opening act: **Jim Croce**!

Most Popular Hits in 1972
 1. **American Pie – Don McLean**
 2. **Alone Again Naturally – Gilbert O'Sullivan**
 3. **First Time Ever I Saw Your Face – Roberta Flack**
 4. **Let's Stay Together – Al Green**
 5. **Rockin' Robin – Michael Jackson**
 6. **Me and Mrs. Jones – Billy Paul**
 7. **Brandy – Looking Glass**
 8. **Without You – Nilsson**
 9. **A Horse With No Name – America**
 10. **Heart of Gold – Neil Young**

The fall of 1972 also featured the release of **The Moody Blues**' seventh album fittingly titled *Seventh Sojourn*. This was technically the group's eighth album if you count the *Magnificent Moodies* as their first. The *Magnificent Moodies* was released during future **Wings** member **Denny Laine**'s heyday with the group and BEFORE the arrival of **Justin Hayward** and **John Lodge** (in 1967). Hayward and Lodge proved to be the group's most prolific singers and songwriters. *Seventh Sojourn* was an excellent album and was the Moodies' first to top the U.S. album charts. 1972 proved to be a big year for The Moody Blues and their music with substantial FM (and even AM) radio airplay of ALL their previous six albums and their biggest single ever, "Nights in White Satin" (#2 Oct.).

At the same time, the rerelease of "Nights in White Satin" in 1972 spurred even greater popularity for the album *Days of Future Passed* such that it became one of the staples among album collections that fall at Brown. *Days of Future Passed* (originally released in late 1967), was the second rock "concept" album in history (coming out after the summer 1967 release of *Sgt. Pepper's*). Though the album occasionally meandered and was unusually pretentious on Side 1 (which covered the sunrise, morning and lunch hour), Side 2 is one of the greatest album "sides" and features Justin Hayward's singer-songwriter skills extraordinaire in "Tuesday Afternoon" (#24 Sep. '68) *("I'm looking at myself, reflections of my mind"*) and "Nights in White Satin" *("Never reaching the end, letters I've written never meaning to send").*

Of course, I haven't forgotten about **The Rolling Stones**, who released a double album *Exile on Main Street* in 1972, which many fans and critics consider the best among Stones albums and that *Rolling Stone Magazine* ranked as the #3 rock album between 1967 and 1987. My own opinion is that it doesn't compare with either *Let It Bleed* or *Sticky Fingers*, which are both outstanding single albums, BUT I will grant that there are 10-12 very good songs on the *Exile* album including most notably "Rocks Off", "Happy" (#22 Aug.) *("I need a love to keep me happy")*, "Tumbling Dice" (#7 May) *("you got me rollin")*, "All Down the Line", "Soul Survivor", "Ventilator Blues", "Rip This Joint", and "Sweet Black Angel".

There were many other important albums in 1972. **Jethro Tull** released the first truly rock concept album, *Thick as a Brick*, which really was one continuous song. (This album was panned by most critics, but is still one of my favorites.) **Elton John** released a very good album, *Honky Chateau*, which included several very good songs e.g. "Honky Cat" (#8 Sep.) *("Get back honky cat")*, "Mona Lisa and Mad Hattters", "Mellow" and one outstanding song, "Rocket Man" (#6 July) *("And I think it's gonna be a long long time")*, which spoke as much about isolation and loneliness on earth as it did in space. "Rocket Man" harkened back to **David Bowie**'s well-crafted "Space Oddity" (#15 Mar. 1973) *("ground control to Major Tom")* released in the U.K. in 1969 but popularized in the U.S. at the end of 1972.

My Favorite Songs in 1972
  1. **Stairway to Heaven – Led Zeppelin**
  2. **American Pie – Don McLean**
  3. **Roundabout – Yes**
  4. **Rocket Man – Elton John**
  5. **Nights in White Satin – Moody Blues**
  6. **Long Cool Woman in a Black Dress – Hollies**
  7. **Garden Party – Rick Nelson**
  8. **Taxi – Harry Chapin**
  9. **Go All the Way – Raspberries**
  10. **Heart of Gold – Neil Young**

1972 also featured a lot of good songs/singles. **Don McLean**'s "American Pie" (#1 Jan.) *("I met a girl who sang the blues and asked her for some happy news but she just smiled and turned away")* was not only a great song, but interpreting its lyrics was the source of considerable entertainment for many of us during early 1972. (Hey, there wasn't that much to do at prep school!) Interestingly, Don McLean was the first artist my daughter Kathleen ever saw "officially" (she was all of 6 months old and in a baby carriage at the time) as Anne and I saw him performing at the Montgomery County Fair (MD) in 1989.

"Taxi" (#24 May) by **Harry Chapin** was a lyrical masterpiece that spoke to the awkwardness and indignities of a brief reunion of former lovers. No one who knows this song can ever forget the lines, *"So she handed me $20 for a two-fifty fare and said 'Harry, keep the change'. Another man might have been angry, another man might have been hurt, but another man would've never let her go, I stuffed the bill in my shirt."*

Carly Simon's "Anticipation" (#13 Feb.) *("These are the good old days")* was a great pop song that got knocked down a peg when Heinz later used the chorus to advertise its ketchup. Meanwhile **Todd Rundgren**'s second top 40 single "I Saw the Light" (#16 June) was excellent.

Jackson Browne launched his popular career with "Doctor My Eyes" (#8 Apr.) *("Doctor, my eyes have seen the years and the slow parade of tears")*. His first album also included another great song, "Rock Me on the Water" (#48 Sep.) *("Sister will you soothe my fevered brow")*. Likewise, the **Raspberries**' first top 40 was the upbeat rock classic "Go All the Way" (#5 Sep.). **Billy Preston** showed off his keyboard talents in his first solo instrumental hit, "Outa-Space" (#2 July). A British group **T. Rex** had the extremely catchy and interesting rock hit "Bang a Gong (Get it On)" (#10 Mar.) *("You're dirty and sweet oh yea")*.

Rick Nelson had his comeback hit with "Garden Party" (#6 Oct.) *("See, you can't please everyone, so you got to please yourself")*, his best song ever. "Garden Party" is a wonderful lyrical song about how Nelson got booed at a Madison Square Garden concert for playing new songs instead of his old hits from the late '50s-early '60s. Then, there was another great cover by **Johnny Rivers** with "Rockin' Pneumonia and the Boogie Woogie Flu" (#6 Dec.) his first top 10 song in five years.

The Bad

1972 wasn't all good. While there was much that was new and exciting, there were some big gaps left behind as many top 1960s and early 1970s artists faded into oblivion (e.g., **Creedence Clearwater Revival, The Rascals, The Beach Boys, Blood Sweat and Tears**, to name a few) or died before they got old. **The Who** took a year off from recording after the great success of *Who's Next* in 1971 and before their critically acclaimed *Quadrophenia* in 1973. **The Doors** were no more after **Jim Morrison** died in June 1971 and their last album hit it big that fall. **The Beatles**' solo incarnations proved a woeful substitute in 1972. **John Lennon** and **George Harrison** recorded nothing new in 1972 after very good albums during 1970-71. **Paul McCartney** had only the very bland album *Wild Life* (Dec. 1971).

In addition, there were several very annoying singles that made it to the top of the charts and thus were played constantly. For example, who can forget "The Candy Man" (#1 June) by **Sammy Davis Jr.** or **Michael Jackson**'s homage to a rat "Ben" (#1 Oct.) or the thoroughly ridiculous instrumental "Popcorn" (#9 Oct.) by **Hot Butter**? And shouldn't **Chuck Berry** have just rereleased one of his many outstanding 1950s and early '60s singles, instead of subjecting us to "My Ding-a-Ling" (#1 Oct.)?

But overall it still is one of my favorite years and it probably didn't hurt that I was having a blast with my new- found freedom as a freshman at Brown.

1973
"We're An American Band"

1973 was a memorable year for rock music and for me personally. During the summer of 1973, I spent two months in Switzerland in the Experiment in International Living residing with a family (the Blasis) in Biel and traveling and hiking in the Alps with other college students in our EIL group of 12. It was an exciting and memorable summer, one of the best in my life. Strangely enough, it was one of the few summers of my life that I was completely out of touch with pop/rock music in the U.S.

Rockin' in the U.S.A.

1973 was a year when rock music in the U.S. remained ascendant. (However, this was soon to change in 1974 when disco music began to sweep the airwaves.) By far and away the most important artist of 1973 was **Stevie Wonder**, who had two extraordinary albums that for the first time in his career were all self-written and self-arranged material. His first release, which was officially in late 1972, *Talking Book,* featured the rock/soul fusion classic "Superstition" (#1 Jan.) and the beautiful and soulful ballad "You Are the Sunshine of My Life" (#1 May). He topped the success of this first album with *Innervisions*, which is one of the best albums ever and featured the hit singles "Higher Ground" (#4 Oct.), "Living for the City" (#8 Jan. '74), and "Don't You Worry 'Bout a Thing" (#16 May '74), though every track was good. Beginning with *Talking Book*, Stevie Wonder had discovered the Hohner clavinet keyboard that he used most distinctively in "Superstition" and later in "Higher Ground".

Preceding "Superstition" at the top of the charts in January 1973 was one of my favorite songs of the year, "You're So Vain" (#1 Jan.) by **Carly Simon**. It was also the only time I ever heard the word "gavotte" in a song as in the everyday phrase: *"You had one eye in the mirror as you watched yourself gavotte"*. However, the top female vocalist song in 1973 was unquestionably **Roberta Flack**'s "Killing Me Softly" (#1 Mar.) *("Singing my life with his words")*. This is one of my favorite slow songs ever and Roberta's silky smooth voice makes it truly beautiful.

American rock music was led symbolically by **Grand Funk Railroad**'s "We're An American Band" (#1 Sep.) with its infectious drumming and bass line and the almost stereotypical rock-band lyrics as they *"proceeded to tear that hotel down"*. From California, the **Doobie Brothers** emerged as a dominant, new, popular rock group as two singles, "Listen to the Music" (#11 Oct. '72) and "Jesus Is Just Alright" (#35 Feb.), from their first album *Toulouse Street* received ample airplay in late 1972 and early 1973. However, the Doobies' strong first album was eclipsed by the even better album *The Captain and Me* in 1973. This album featured six superb songs: "Long Train Runnin'" (#8 June) *("Without love where would you be now?")*, "Without You", "China Grove" (#15 Oct.) *("They're just people looking to the East")*, "South City Midnight Lady", "A Natural Thing" *("We all got to be loved")*, and "Clear as the Driven Snow". It is unquestionably among the best rock albums of all time. I was lucky enough to see the Doobie Brothers as the opening act before **Rod Stewart** in a concert in May 1973 in which they played all of these songs.

Steely Dan's debut album, *Can't Buy a Thrill*, released in late 1972, began to receive significant airplay in 1973 as the first single from the album "Do It Again" (#6 Feb.) moved up the charts. Steely Dan's unique rock-jazz fusion sound became a staple of the '70s thereafter. However, it was the outstanding second single from this album, "Reelin' in the Years" (#11 May) *("Are you gathering up the tears? Have you had enough of mine?")*, that really got my attention. I can remember in June 1973 driving to the Catskills with my friend Neil, constantly switching the radio stations on his car radio in order to hear the song, no matter how much static, just one more time! Steely Dan followed up with their second album later in 1973, the similarly innovative and interesting *Countdown to Ecstasy*. The album featured the great musicianship of the up-tempo and sonorous "Bodhisattva" and "My Old School" (#63 Nov.) and Steely Dan's always interesting lyrics such as *"...California tumbles into the sea, that'll be the day I go back to Annandale"*.

Southern rock emerged as a force in 1973 as the **Allman Brothers** released their *Brothers and Sisters* album, which included their biggest hit "Ramblin' Man" (#2 Oct.). The song actually was in the soundtrack of the movie *The Exorcist* featured in the background in a bar scene. In addition, the album included the FM rock jam instrumental extraordinaire "Jessica" (#65 Feb. '74). A new Southern group, **Lynyrd Skynyrd,** released their debut album featuring several songs that were to later become FM rock classics: "Tuesday's Gone" *("with the wind"),* "Gimme Three Steps", and the guitar jam classic "Free Bird". It's interesting that I barely heard these songs in 1973, as they were only to get significant airplay a couple of years later.

Paul Simon released his second solo album, *There Goes Rhymin' Simon,* which still stands today as one of his two best ever (the other being 1986's *Graceland*). The album featured the hit singles "Kodachrome" (#2 July) *("When I think of all the crap I learned in high school, it's a wonder I can think at all")* and "Loves Me Like a Rock" (#2 Sep.) and incorporated the New Orleans jazz sound into Paul's folk melodies. Other favorite songs from the album included "American Tune", "Learn How to Fall" *("Before you learn to fly, learn how to fall")*, "Something So Right", "St. Judy's Comet", and the faux-philosophical "One Man's Ceiling Is Another Man's Floor".

Another folk artist, **Jim Croce**, whom I had first seen in concert in early 1973 as an opening act for **Loggins and Messina**, hit it big with the up-tempo and fun "Bad, Bad Leroy Brown" (#1 July) *("Badder than old King Kong, meaner than a junkyard dog")*. Then, suddenly on September 20, he was gone, killed in a plane crash. His popularity only grew with the subsequent release of two beautiful ballads: "I Got a Name" (#10 Nov.) and the eerily prescient "Time in A Bottle" (#1 Dec.) *("But there never seems to be enough time to do things you want, once you find them")*.

British Rock

Meanwhile over in the U.K., **Elton John** emerged as a superstar with his hit rocker "Crocodile Rock" (#1 Feb.) and then later in the year, with his outstanding double album *Goodbye Yellow Brick Road*. This album remains Elton's best effort and is consistently good throughout. Side 1 was the highlight with three excellent songs "Funeral for a Friend/Love Lies Bleeding", "Candle in the Wind" *("Goodbye Norma Jean")*, and

"Bennie and the Jets" (#1 Apr. '74). But the rest of the album features other excellent songs as well, most notably the rollicking "Saturday's Alright for Fighting" (#12 Sep.) and "All the Girls Love Alice", and the excellent John/Taupin ballads "Goodbye Yellow Brick Road" (#2 Dec.) *("Where the dogs of society howl, you can't let me in your penthouse I'm going back to my plow")*,"Grey Seal" and "Harmony" *("Hello, baby, hello, haven't seen your face for awhile")*.

Most Popular Hits in 1973
  1. **Tie a Yellow Ribbon – Dawn**
  2. **My Love – Paul McCartney**
  3. **Crocodile Rock – Elton John**
  4. **You're So Vain – Carly Simon**
  5. **Let's Get It On – Marvin Gaye**
  6. **Half Breed – Cher**
  7. **Love Train – O'Jays**
  8. **Killing Me Softly With His Song – Roberta Flack**
  9. **Superstition – Stevie Wonder**
  10. **Delta Dawn – Helen Reddy**

Though not as good as *Led Zeppelin IV*, **Led Zeppelin** did have an excellent follow-up with *Houses of the Holy*, which featured four great Zeppelin classics: "Dancing Days", "Over the Hills and Far Away", "D'yer Mak'er" (#20 Dec.), and "The Song Remains the Same", among other good songs. Strangely, the title track did not appear on this album but was on a later Zeppelin album. I confess to barely listening to this album at the time, as it never caught my attention like their previous album. Only several years later did I begin to appreciate how good it was.

The Who had their first album in more than two years when they released *Quadrophenia*, which was a masterpiece in both composition and instrumentation. (Townshend insists it is the best album that The Who ever made.) Not as "catchy" as their previous two albums, upon multiple listening sessions, the music grows on you and is one of my favorite albums to this day. Amazingly, it is a double album without a weak track. All of the songs are very good to excellent.

In his book, Townshend notes, "Recording *Quadrophenia* with The Who was a joyful experience", describing the complexity of recording: "The studio was filled with exotic instruments we rarely played: marimbas, glockenspiels, xylophones..." and John Entwistle playing "twenty or thirty magnificent trumpets, horns and valve trombones...working thru the recording til his lips started to go numb". However, Townshend also relates the problems of doing the *Quadrophenia* tour: "we confronted the most complex difficulties".[24] I got a chance to see it performed live by The Who a few years ago on the album's 40th anniversary, which was a pretty extraordinary concert given the high degree of difficulty in playing, singing and instrumentation.

Pink Floyd released the unique and "ahead of its time" album *Dark Side of the Moon* in 1973. The album is unique in that the songs all blend together and features longer compositions that have become classic rock staples – "Money" (#13 July), "Us and Them", and "Time". The entire album was an instant success on FM radio and in my dorm room at college. In fact, it was one of the few records that I bought a second copy of, as the first copy was so worn out and warped from being overplayed (and being left on the radiator one night). The first copy thereafter became dorm room art, hung from our ceiling by a string.

Another British group, Jeff Lynne's **Electric Light Orchestra,** emerged as a new and distinctive sound with its extraordinary, seven-minute cover version of "Roll Over Beethoven" (#42 July) on *ELO 2,* which featured unusual rock orchestration and great guitar playing. No doubt this version would really get Beethoven to "roll over".

The former **Beatles** generally had a less auspicious 1973. **John Lennon**'s album *Mind Games* was only so-so with the title track "Mind Games" (#18 Dec.) the only really good song. **George Harrison**'s second album, *Living in the Material World,* was not nearly as good as his first album with only "Give Me Love" (#1 June) *("Give me peace on earth")* being particularly memorable. **Paul McCartney**'s *Red Rose Speedway* was a new low for him and even the popular "My Love" (#1 June) was just too schmaltzy for me. Only "Live and Let Die" (#2 Aug.) *("You used to say live and let live"),* a single he released during the summer written for the James Bond movie of the same name, represented a good McCartney effort. (The *Band on the Run* album, released in December, was excellent but I will defer discussion of that until the next chapter when I review 1974, which is when the album and its songs were getting airplay.) Surprisingly, it was **Ringo Starr** who had the best year with his *Ringo* album, featuring three songs written by Paul, John and George as well as the excellent hits "Photograph" (#1 Nov.) *("Everytime I see your face it reminds me of the places we used to go")*, "You're Sixteen" (#1 Jan. '74), and "Oh My My" (#5 Apr. '74).

My Favorite Songs in 1973
 1. Funeral for a Friend – Elton John
 2. Reeling in the Years – Steely Dan
 3. Superstition – Stevie Wonder
 4. Feelin' Stronger Every Day – Chicago
 5. China Grove – Doobie Brothers
 6. Could It Be I'm Falling in Love – Spinners
 7. We're an American Band – Grand Funk Railroad
 8. Frankenstein – Edgar Winter
 9. Killing Me Softly With His Song – Roberta Flack
10. Stuck in the Middle with You – Stealers Wheel

1973 also had a number of other very good songs/singles. "Feelin' Stronger Every Day" (#10 Aug.) *("Knowing that you wanted it this way, I do believe I'm feeling stronger every day")* by **Chicago** was one of my favorites. This upbeat song about breaking up in the fall of 1973 was just what I needed to hear as I was trying to get over my recent Switzerland summer romance. Several hard rock singles were excellent, including "Smoke on the Water" (#4 July) by **Deep Purple** and two by **The Edgar Winter Group** – "Free Ride" (#14 Oct.) *("The mountain is high the valley is low and you're confused about which way to go")*, and the rock instrumental classic "Frankenstein" (#1 May), featuring the former **McCoys** guitarist **Rick Derringer**. Another one of my rock favorites was **Stealers Wheel**'s "Stuck in the Middle with You" (#6 May) *("Clowns to the left of me, jokers to the right, here I am")*, which featured some interesting twangy guitar work (and yes, even some "cowbell"). Lastly, there was a real throwback to the 1940s by **Bette Midler**, "Boogie Woogie Bugle Boy" (#8 July). This latter song reminded me that there were some really good songs from my parents' generation too.

In addition to "Frankenstein", there were three excellent instrumental singles. "Also Sprach Zarathustra" (#2 Mar.) by **Deodato** fused jazz and rock music while covering the classical theme of the movie *2001: A Space Odyssey*. "Hocus Pocus" (#9 May) by **Focus** from Holland featured a repetitive guitar riff chorus that never seemed to grow tiresome, while the multiple verses of the song included whistling, yodeling, scat singing, accordion and organ playing and even **Jethro Tull**-style flute playing. I also liked the instrumental "Dueling Banjos" (#2 Mar.) by **Eric Weisberg**, though I admit that was only when it didn't remind me of the difficult to watch film *Deliverance*.

On the soul and R&B side, **Gladys Knight and the Pips** had their best single, "Midnight Train to Georgia" (#1 Oct.), as did the **O'Jays** with the infectious melody of "Love Train" (#1 Mar.). **The Isley Brothers** featured a new synthesizer funk rock sound with an excellent comeback record, "That Lady" (#6 Oct.). **The Spinners** had two R&B classics with "One of A Kind (Love Affair)" (#11 June), and a song guaranteed to make everyone feel happy, "Could It Be I'm Falling in Love" (#4 Mar.). **War** had several hit songs, the best being "The World Is a Ghetto" (#7 Jan.). Of course, my favorite "soul" song of the year was "Brother Louie" (#1 Aug.) *("She was black as the night. Louie was whiter than white.")* by **The Stories**, which was actually a cover of the original by **Hot Chocolate**. However, I was shocked to discover when seeing them on *The Midnight Special* on TV in late 1973 that they were, in fact, an all-white group.

1973 definitely had its disappointments and bad songs. Two of my favorite groups, **The Moody Blues** and **Yes**, didn't release any new albums or new songs in 1973 (though Yes had an excellent live album, *Yes Songs*). The **Temptations** had their last top 10 single with "Masterpiece" (#7 Apr.), then never again had a top 20 song. **The Rolling Stones** released the album *Goats Head Soup* late in 1973, which had two very good songs, "Angie" (#1 Oct.) *("When will those clouds all disappear?")* and "Doo-Doo-Doo-Doo-Doo (Heartbreaker)" (#15 Feb. 74) *("The police in New York City, they chased a boy right thru the park.*

In a place of mistaken identity, they put a bullet thru his heart"). But the rest of the album was mediocre at best, a huge letdown after the Stones' last three outstanding studio albums (i.e., *Let It Bleed, Sticky Fingers* and *Exile on Main Street*).

Tony Orlando and Dawn drove me crazy with "Tie a Yellow Ribbon" (#1 Apr.), which was played incessantly on the radio. **Cher**'s "Half-Breed" and **Dr. Hook**'s "The Cover of Rolling Stone" were annoying. But perhaps the worst song of the year goes to **Clint Holmes** for "Playground in My Mind" (featuring the prepubescent vocal *"my name is Michael, I got a nickel..."*).

*****

But all in all, 1973 was a pretty darn good year musically and for me personally. However, disco had just begun to hit the pop charts and that was an ominous sign for 1974.

1974
"You Ain't Seen Nothing Yet"

1974 witnessed a big change for rock and popular music generally. Beginning with the instrumental groups **Love Unlimited Orchestra** (directed by **Barry White**) doing "Love's Theme" (#1 Feb.) and **MFSB** (officially, mother, father, sister, brother... unofficially, Mother F#*#ing Son of a B#%ch) doing "TSOP (The Sound of Philadelphia)" (#1 Apr.), disco exploded onto the pop charts during 1974. Disco music was to boast several other of the biggest hits of the year including "Rock the Boat" (#1 July) by the **Hues Corporation**, "Rock Your Baby" (#1 July) by **George McRae** and two vocal hits by **Barry White:** "Can't Get Enough of Your Love Babe" (#1 Sep.) and "You're The First, My Last, My Everything" (#2 Dec.). In fact, disco was to dominate the charts for much of the next five years, a trend that I didn't much enjoy as I generally disliked the music, nor could I disco dance.

The Bad

Meanwhile, rock music was in retreat generally and even three of the former **Beatles** had an off year. After his excellent solo album in 1973, **Ringo** produced little new music in 1974, though two of his best songs from his 1973 album went to the top or near the top of the charts: "You're Sixteen" (#1 Jan.) and "Oh My My" (#5 Apr.). Meanwhile, **John** and **George** produced little new material as well, with only Lennon's "Whatever Gets You Through the Night" (#1 Nov.), including backing vocals from **Elton John**, being a good 1974 rock-'n'-roll song.

In addition to the three Beatles solo acts, many other rock and folk acts had little of note in 1974. Beginning in 1974, **The Moody Blues** disappeared from the airwaves and rock scene producing no new material for almost five years. **The Who** released an album of remnants called *Odds and Sods*, which paled in comparison to the prior year's *Quadrophenia*. **Yes** had only the meandering and loosely constructed *Tales of Topographic Oceans*, a double album which though it had some excellent musicianship and good musical themes was simply too long – over 80 minutes. (This album was a particular sore point for me as a big Yes fan, because at my first and only Yes concert they played ALL four sides of the album, ignoring all of the outstanding material on *The Yes Album* and *Fragile*, except for their "Roundabout" encore.)

Led Zeppelin had no new material, taking a year off from touring and recording. After 1973's superb album, *The Captain and Me*, the **Doobie Brothers** released *What Were Once Vices Are Now Habits,* an album that featured only one outstanding song, "Black Water" (#1 Mar. '75) *("Mississippi moon, won't you keep on shinin' on me?")*, which was released as a single at the end of 1974. Likewise, **Paul Simon**, after two excellent albums in 1972 and 1973 to start his solo career, had nothing new in 1974.

Perhaps the biggest sign of rock's 1974 slump was that some of the most popular rock hits of the year were covers of older songs from the '60s, ranging from the annoying **Blue Swede** rendition *("Ooh-Ga Chucka")* of "Hooked on a Feeling" (#1 Apr.) to **Grand Funk**'s good rendition of "The Locomotion" (#1 May) and the **James Taylor-Carly Simon** duet of "Mockingbird" (#5 Mar.). **Ringo**'s version of "You're Sixteen" (#1 Jan.) was good, but his version of the **Platters**' "Only You" (#6 Dec.) was not so good. The cover of "Another Saturday Night" by **Cat Stevens** (#6 Oct.) was more inspired, though it still paled in comparison to the **Sam Cooke** original.

Another bad sign for 1974 was that two #1 songs and one top 10 hit from the year were bad "novelty" songs headlined by **Ray Stevens**' "The Streak" (#1 May), which wasn't remotely funny, the tiresome though catchy "Kung Fu Fighting" by **Carl Douglas** (#1 Dec.), and **The Guess Who**'s "Clap for the Wolfman" (#6 Sep.), which represented an all-time low for the group (though not surprising given that the group only included one of its original members and disbanded shortly thereafter).

Most Popular Hits in 1974
1. I Honestly Love You – Olivia Newton-John
2. Show and Tell – Al Wilson
3. The Streak – Ray Stevens
4. Seasons in the Sun – Terry Jacks
5. The Way We Were – Barbra Streisand
6. TSOP – MFSB
7. Having My Baby – Paul Anka
8. The Joker – Steve Miller
9. Annie's Song – John Denver
10. Kung Fu Fighting – Carl Douglas

But the worst aspect of 1974 was that several of the top-selling hits of the year rank among my worst singles of all time. This included the awful "Seasons in the Sun" (#1 Mar.) *("We had joy, we had fun, we had seasons in the sun")*, a **Rod McKuen** written song made somehow even worse by **Terry Jacks** and the tinny organ accompaniment; the awful, anti-abortion "(You're) Having My Baby" by **Paul Anka** (#1 Aug.); the extremely annoying "The Night Chicago Died" (#1 Aug.) by **Paper Lace;** and the musically and lyrically inane "Billy Don't be a Hero" (#1 June) by **Bo Donaldson and the Heywoods**. Believe it or not, as bad as these songs were, all four of them made it to #1 on the pop charts.

The Good

Fortunately, there were some bright spots in the rock and pop-rock scene during the year. My favorite album of 1974 (though technically a December 1973 release) was **Paul McCartney and Wings'** *Band on the Run*, which featured three excellent singles: "Helen Wheels" (#10 Jan.), "Jet" (#7 Mar.), and "Band on the Run" (#1 June) *("Stuck inside these four walls")*, which was the best song on the album. In addition, the album was loaded with other great songs, notably "Let Me Roll It", "Picasso's Last Words (Drink to Me)", and my favorite, "1985" *("No one ever left alive in 1985 will ever do")*, which highlights some great piano playing by Paul. Paul wasn't done for 1974 either, releasing at the end of the year the rollicking single "Junior's Farm" (#3 Dec.) *("Take me down to Junior's farm"!)*.

Other British artists excelled. **David Bowie** came out with the excellent rocker "Rebel, Rebel" *("Hot tramp I love you so")*. **Eric Clapton** released the *461 Ocean Boulevard* album featuring the Bob Marley song "I Shot the Sheriff" (#1 Sep.) *("But I did not shoot the deputy")*, which became the first #1 reggae hit in the U.S. The album did include a couple of original Clapton compositions, most notably "Let It Grow" *("Plant your love and let it grow")* and local musician George Terry's excellent song "Mainline Florida". But the main feature of the album was Clapton's excellent renditions of the traditional rhythm and blues tunes "Motherless Children" *("have a harder time, mother is dead, boy")*, "Willie and the Hand Jive", "Steady Rollin' Man", and "I Can't Hold Out".[25]

Though **Elton John**'s *Caribou* album was a disappointment, particularly after his previous three critically acclaimed albums, it did have two excellent singles from the album, first with "Don't Let the Sun Go Down on Me" (#2 July), which had the rare distinction of going to #1 some 17 years later as a live version. But my favorite song from the album was "The Bitch Is Back" (#4 Oct.) *("Stone cold sober as a matter of fact")* featuring backing vocals by **Dusty Springfield**. Finally, Elton was not to miss the trend towards covering '60s songs with his outstanding cover of "Lucy in the Sky with Diamonds" (#1 Jan. '75) at the end of the year.

Steely Dan released its *Pretzel Logic* album that had several excellent songs, most notably the wonderful "Rikki Don't Lose That Number" (#4 July) *("You don't want to call nobody else")*. In addition, "Pretzel Logic" (#57 Oct.) *("I have never met Napolean, but I plan to find the time")*, "Night by Night", and "Any Major Dude Will Tell You" are Steely Dan classics. The album demonstrated the group's further movement to a unique rock-jazz fusion sound begun with the prior year's *Countdown to Ecstasy* album.

Notable new groups for the year included the Canadian group **Bachman Turner Overdrive** (BTO), featuring **Randy Bachman** (the founder of the **Guess Who**). BTO emerged in 1974 with three excellent singles: the lively "Let It Ride" (#23 Apr.), the classic "Takin' Care of Business" (#12 Aug.) *("And working overtime")*, and lastly my personal favorite "You Ain't Seen Nothing Yet" (#1 Nov.) *("Here's something you're* *never going to forget. You know, you know. You ain't seen nothing yet").* In the latter song, Randy famously mimicked his younger brother's stuttering problem. (Imagine trying to do that today in a popular song!)

Another new group, **Bad Company**, had the spirited rock hit "Can't Get Enough" (#5 Oct.). A group that had been around for several years, **Lynyrd Skynyrd**, had their first commercial success with the classic "Sweet Home Alabama" (#8 Oct.), a direct response to Neil Young's "Southern Man" *("I hope Neil Young will remember. Southern man don't need him around anyhow").* And though not a new group by any means, the **Steve Miller Band** had their first big hit with the very mellow and carefree "The Joker" (#1 Jan.) with the immortal line, *"I really love your peaches. Wanna shake your tree".*

My Favorite Songs in 1974
 1. Band on the Run – Paul McCartney
 2. You Ain't Seen Nothing Yet – BTO
 3. Sweet Home Alabama – Lynyrd Skynyrd
 4. You Haven't Done Nothing – Stevie Wonder
 5. Already Gone – The Eagles
 6. I Shot the Sheriff – Eric Clapton
 7. The Bitch is Back – Elton John
 8. Rikki Don't Lose that Number – Steely Dan
 9. Beach Baby – First Class
10. 1985 – Paul McCartney

On the soul and R&B side, **Stevie Wonder** released his third original solo album *Fulfillingness' First Finale*, which though not as good as his first two original albums, did have several excellent songs, most notably "You Haven't Done Nothin'" (#1 Oct.) *("If you really want to hear our views")* and "Boogie on Reggae Woman" (#3 Jan. '75). **Kool and the Gang** got us in the groove with their first top 10 funk song "Jungle Boogie" (#4 Mar. '74) while **Billy Preston** had his best vocal single "Nothing from Nothing" (#1 Oct.) and the **Jackson 5** had one of their best R&B songs with the more mature sounding "Dancing Machine" (#2 May), the last top ten song for the group. Former **Temptations** lead singer **Eddie Kendricks** outshone his former group with his second and last noteworthy R&B hit "Boogie Down" (#2 Mar.). Meanwhile, **Aretha Franklin** had the beautiful and soulful "Until You Come Back to Me

(That's What I'm Gonna Do)" (#3 Feb.). And **Dionne Warwick** and the **Spinners** merged their great singing talents together with the upbeat "Then Came You" (#1 Oct.).

1974 also featured several excellent softer folk-rock hits such as the haunting "Can't Get It Out of My Head" *("Midnight on the water, I saw the ocean's daughter")* by **ELO** (#9 Mar. '75), **Carly Simon**'s uplifting "Haven't Got Time for the Pain" (#14 June) (one of the best songs of her career), **Harry Chapin**'s musical and lyrical masterpiece "Cat's in the Cradle" (#1 Dec.) *("When you coming home dad. I don't know when. We'll get together then")*. **Gordon Lightfoot**'s beautiful "Sundown" (#1 June), **Joni Mitchell**'s "Help Me" (#7 June), **Carole King**'s "Jazzman" (#2 Nov.) and **America**'s "Tin Man" (#4 Nov.) *("Oz didn't give nothing to the Tin Man that he didn't already have")* rounded out the list of folk-rock classics.

The Eagles released their first hit single, "Already Gone", from their 1974 album *On The Border*, which was one of my favorite songs by the Eagles. "Already Gone" (#32 June) *("Cause I'm already gone, and I'm feeling strong, I will sing this victory song")* was a panacea for the bad breakup, impossible not to sing along with. Lastly, the year featured a surf sound throwback with the very catchy and totally enjoyable "Beach Baby" by **First Class** (#4 Sep.), a group from a very "unbeachlike" England of all places.

1974 was in many respects a disappointing year for rock-pop music and it paled in comparison to 1973 and 1972. And perhaps that was fitting for me in the midst of my "sophomore/junior slump" in college. However, there were still many songs worth remembering and it held out the hope that when it would come to 1975, "You Ain't Seen Nothing Yet"!

1975
"Thank God My Music's Still Alive"

1975 was a year that started with a new president in office, Gerald Ford, who had taken over after Richard Nixon's resignation in late 1974. He was the only "unelected" president in American history (as he was appointed vice president after Spiro Agnew resigned due to his own scandal two years earlier). America was in the doldrums, after Vietnam, Watergate and the economic recession of 1974-75.

Personally, 1975 also began at the nadir of my junior year of Brown. I was still looking for love and already worried what I would do after graduation. Fortunately, by later in the year, I was in love with my first long-term girlfriend and enjoying the fall of my senior year and at least temporarily not worried about my future.

The British Are Coming?

In 1975, rock music, which had been led by the success of the British Invasion since the mid-1960s, was also in a holding pattern, while disco music ruled the pop charts. Notably, stalwarts like **The Rolling Stones** or the former **Beatles** produced little of note in 1975. **John Lennon** was relegated to doing covers of old rock-'n'-roll songs on his *Rock 'N' Roll* album. (However, he did have one good song, "#9 Dream" (#9 Feb.), in early 1975 from his 1974 *Walls and Bridges* album.) **George Harrison** had no new album and had grown increasingly musically irrelevant since his outstanding first album *All Things Must Pass* in late 1970. Only his song "Dark Horse" (#15 Dec. 1974) was of note in 1975.

After a dominant early 1970s, **Yes** had no new material. **The Moody Blues** were in the midst of an almost six-year period of no new albums. **Eric Clapton** had nothing of note in 1975, after his excellent *461 Ocean Boulevard* album in 1974. **Led Zeppelin** released the interminably long, double album *Physical Graffiti* with arguably only three strong tracks (the excellent "Kashmir", as well as "Houses of the Holy" and "Trampled Under Foot"). Even Zeppelin fans found the record wanting after their previous two, much more cohesive, single albums (*Houses of the Holy* and *Untitled - Led Zeppelin IV*). Nonetheless, Britain continued to play an important role in the rock music scene with **Pink Floyd, The Who, Fleetwood Mac,** and **McCartney** all with very good to excellent albums in 1975, and **Elton John** with several excellent pop singles which made him the best-selling artist of 1975 even amidst the disco boom.

After late 1973's extraordinary *Dark Side of the Moon,* **Pink Floyd**'s next effort was bound to suffer in comparison. Still, the *Wish You Were Here* album boasted the same outstanding musicianship, excellent musical themes and a new unconventional structure that was the hallmark of *Dark Side*.... The album begins with the 13-minute+ composition "Shine on You Crazy Diamond (Parts I-V)" and ends with the 12-minute+ "Shine on You Crazy Diamond (Parts VI-IX)". The song paid homage to founding member **Syd Barrett** who had to leave the group due to a mental breakdown seven years earlier. As group leader Roger Waters noted in 2012, "It's my homage to Syd and my heartfelt expression of ... my admiration for the talent and my sadness for the loss of the friend. There are no generalities really in that song. It's not about all the crazy diamonds. It's about Syd."[26]

Roger Waters, who was the lead composer and lyricist for the group, developed a simple yet vibrant central vocal and lyrical theme for "Shine On". But it was **David Gilmour** and his brilliant guitar playing and excellent keyboards along with Waters' bass and back-up guitars and seamless use of synthesizer that drove "Shine On..." as the centerpiece of the album. But the other three tracks on the album were excellent musically, too, with the biting satire about the music industry of "Welcome to the Machine" and "Have a Cigar" and the beautiful, emotional longing expressed succinctly in "Wish You Were Here". Of course, the album played second fiddle to *Dark Side*, but what a great second fiddle it was.

During the late 1960s and early 1970s, the British group **Fleetwood Mac** had constant personnel turnover. But with the departure of lead guitarist and songwriter **Bob Welch**, the remaining three group stalwarts – drummer **Mick Fleetwood**, singer and keyboardist **Christine McVie** and bassist **John McVie** – looked to California for reinforcement and brought in guitarist/vocalist **Lindsey Buckingham** and singer **Stevie**

Nicks. (They originally just wanted Lindsey, but they wisely were convinced by Buckingham to take his girlfriend Nicks as well.)[27]

The formula instantly worked and the 1975 *Fleetwood Mac* album was by far their biggest commercial and critical success to date. The soft but upbeat rock sound and beautiful and catchy tunes and vocals were the hallmark of the album. I absolutely loved Christine McVie's soothing voice (and songwriting) with "Over My Head" (#20 Jan. 1976) *("You can take me to paradise and then again you can be as cold as ice")*, "Warm Ways", "Say You Love Me" (#11 Sep. 1976), and "Sugar Daddy", all outstanding tracks on the album. But Stevie Nicks' "Rhiannon" (#11 June 1976) and "Landslide" were excellent too, as well as Lindsey Buckingham's rousing "Monday Morning", "Blue Letter", and "I'm So Afraid" (with some excellent guitar work as well). All in all, a tour de force for a group that was in tatters just a few months earlier.

In 1975, **The Who** released *Who By Numbers*. It was their first new studio album after the extraordinary trifecta of albums produced by The Who in the early 1970s – *Tommy*, *Who's Next* and *Quadrophenia* – and thus, couldn't help but be disappointing by comparison. Further, The Who recorded the album amidst **Keith Moon**'s spiraling drug and alcohol problems, as well as **Daltrey** and **Townshend**'s barbs at each other in the British press.[28]

Nonetheless, *Who By Numbers* was a very good album – emotionally darker than anything The Who had done before and achingly personal for Pete Townshend. The album opens with perhaps its best track "Slip Kid", a song about the responsibility of growing up *("there's no easy way to be free")*. "However Much I Booze" was written the day Townshend quit alcohol and provides the answer, *"there ain't no way out"*. Other excellent tracks include "They're All in Love", a bitter song about loneliness and anger, "Dreaming from the Waist", a song of sexual frustration, and atypically for the album, a beautiful and heartfelt love song "Blue, Red and Gray".

Most Popular Hits in 1975
1. Jive Talkin' – Bee Gees
2. Rhinestone Cowboy – Glen Campbell
3. That's the Way I Like It – KC & the Sunshine Band
4. Philadelphia Freedom – Elton John
5. Fly Robin Fly – Silver Convention
6. Have You Never Been Mellow – Olivia Newton-John
7. Island Girl – Elton John
8. Lovin' You – Minnie Riperton
9. Lady Marmalade – LaBelle
10. Bad Blood – Neil Sedaka

Meanwhile, bassist **John Entwistle**'s excellent contribution "Success Story" captured The Who's mood at the time perfectly: *"Back in the studio, to make our latest number 1. Take 276, you know this used to be fun"*. Ironically, the only single from the album, the catchy "Squeeze Box" (#16 Feb. '76) *("Mama's got a squeeze box, daddy never sleeps at night")* was Townshend's sole humorous track on the album and clearly doesn't fit the deeply personal theme of Townshend's fear of growing up and being old and lonely. Musically and vocally, the album is superb with Daltrey's vocals, Townshend's guitar playing, Entwistle's bass playing and Moon's drumming being particularly noteworthy. Overall, the album was a back-to-basics effort by The Who (no rock opera or glitzy use of synthesizer) but a very strong one at that.

After the critical and popular success of *Band on the Run*, **Paul McCartney and Wings** produced a solid next album, *Venus and Mars*. The highlights of the album included the excellent opening track, "Venus and Mars/Rock Show" (#12 Dec.) *("Rock and roll at the Hollywood Bowl")*, which was pure rock-'n'-roll fun and reminded one of McCartney's vocals as an early Beatle in songs like "I'm Down" and "Dizzie Miss Lizzie". Two other songs, "Letting Go" (#39 Oct.) *("Ah she tastes like wine")* and "Call Me Back Again", also were excellent rockers driven again by superb but very different McCartney vocal styles. "Love in Song" revealed a rare side of McCartney, a more emotionally bare Paul than was typical in his love songs. "Listen to What the Man Said" (#1 July) was a catchy pop tune (complete with clarinet), albeit one with McCartney's familiar schmaltz. A new member of

Wings, guitarist **Jimmy McCulloch**, in addition to providing solid lead guitar work on the album, penned and sang lead on "Medicine Jar", another strong track. There were some misses on the album, most notably the somewhat inane "Spirits of Ancient Egypt" (with **Denny Laine** singing lead vocal) and "Magneto and Titanium Man". Overall, *Venus and Mars* was a solid, albeit under-appreciated, follow-up to *Band on the Run*.

Elton John was prolific in 1975 with the release of two new albums: *Captain Fantastic and the Brown Dirt Cowboy* and *Rock of the Westies*, as well as a re-release of his first album, *Empty Sky*. I didn't buy either new album and know little of the music from these two other than the singles. "Captain Fantastic" was autobiographical about Taupin and John's early years as songwriters. The single from the album, "Someone Saved My Life" (#4 Aug.) *("You nearly had me roped and tied, all about hypnotized")*, was one of John's best songs both musically and lyrically. The song focused on Elton's marriage engagement and conflict with his musical career, his contemplated suicide in 1969 and his (very wise) decision to ultimately break off the engagement. This was clearly a deeply emotional song for Elton and you can feel it in his piano playing and his singing.

Rock of the Westies had much less going for it. Its two singles, "Island Girl" (#1 Nov.) and "Grow Some Funk of Your Own" (#14 Feb. '76), were decent songs but grew very tiresome when heard on the radio constantly in 1975 and early 1976. Elton did succeed with another upbeat single earlier in the year, "Philadelphia Freedom" (#1 Apr.) *("I live and breathe this Philadelphia freedom")*, which he and Taupin wrote to honor Billie Jean King and her newly founded professional tennis team, the Philadelphia Freedoms. The song was vintage Elton John pop/rock and was the #3 song of the year. For some reason, I never tired of hearing it, no doubt because of its infectious chorus. Later in the year, Elton even teamed up with **Neil Sedaka** and scored with the catchy "Bad Blood" (#1 Oct.).

My Favorite Songs in 1975
1. Born to Run – Bruce Springsteen
2. Someone Saved My Life Tonight – Elton John
3. Free Bird – Lynyrd Skynyrd
4. Magic – Pilot
5. Over My Head – Fleetwood Mac
6. Thunder Road – Bruce Springsteen
7. Hey You – BTO
8. Killer Queen – Queen
9. Doctor Wu – Steely Dan
10. Fire on High – ELO

In addition to Fleetwood Mac, McCartney and Elton John's singles successes, other U.K. artists also had a strong year:

David Bowie had his most successful year in 1975 with his first #1 single in the U.S., the excellent rock song "Fame" (#1 Sep.). The song was co-written by **John Lennon**, who also sang backup. "Young Americans" (#28 May) *("All night, she was a young American")* did not chart as well (reaching #28 in the U.S.) but also was a very good song. Both songs came from Bowie's *Young Americans* album, released in early 1975, which saw a shift in Bowie's music genre from glitter/space rock to blue-eyed rock-'n'-soul.

Electric Light Orchestra's had their first top 40 hit with the release of the beautiful "Can't Get It Out of My Head" (#9 Mar.) from its 1974 *Eldorado* album. But it was the *Face the Music* album from 1975 that spawned two successful singles for the group, "Evil Woman" (#10 Feb. '76) released in late 1975 and "Strange Magic" (#14 May '76) in early 1976. Both were up-tempo, catchy songs that continued the unique ELO rock/orchestration sound as well as featuring Jeff Lynne's excellent vocals. However, the highlight of the album was the brilliant "Fire on High", an instrumental masterpiece which featured interesting orchestration with vocal snippets of the "Hallelujah Chorus", excellent guitar and drumming as well as the ELO drummer speaking backwards, apparently saying (if you played the record backwards), *"The music is reversible, but time is not. Turn back, turn back."*

Queen had their first successful U.S. single, "Killer Queen" (#12 May) *("She keeps Moet Chandon in her pretty cabinet, 'Let them eat cake', she says just like Marie Antoinette")*. The song was like nothing I had ever heard before, either lyrically or musically, and I enjoyed it immensely.

A new Scottish group, **Pilot**, had the very catchy rock song "Magic" (#5 July) *("Oh, oh, oh, it's magic, you know, never believe it's not so")*, which became one of my favorites of the summer of 1975. I can remember driving back from an unsuccessful date that summer, blaring the song from the car's speakers at full blast.

Another Scottish group, **Average White Band**, had two instrumental funk hits in 1975 with "Pick Up the Pieces" (#1 Feb.) and "Cut the Cake" (#10 June). I particularly enjoyed the excellent saxophone playing and tune of "Pick Up the Pieces".

God Bless America

In America, rock music had increasingly moved to a softer rock-jazz fusion sound but there were a few notable exceptions. One such exception came from comparative newcomer **Bruce Springsteen** who, with the release of his third album *Born to Run*, became one of the best "new" artists of 1975 (even featured on the cover of *Time*). Of course, his first and particularly his second album were quite good. But it was *Born to Run* that was to become his most popular effort to date and created an entire new legion of Springsteen fans.

Born to Run featured the heartfelt musical drama of "She's the One", "Backstreets", "Thunder Road" *("The screen door slammed")*, "Tenth Avenue Freeze Out" (#83 Feb. '76), "Jungleland" *("The Rangers had a homecoming in Harlem late last night")* and the title track "Born To Run" (#23 Nov.) *("Highways jammed with broken heroes on a last chance power drive")*. Lyrically and musically, the album was outstanding with not a single weak track. Some compared Springsteen to an electric **Dylan** (à la "Like a Rolling Stone") but Springsteen took the music further with more complex arrangements and orchestration than Dylan ever contemplated (some critics likened it to the **Phil Spector** "wall of sound"). And he had a great band featuring **Clarence Clemons** on sax. *Born to Run*, in my opinion, is Springsteen's best album and the title track his best single of his long and illustrious career.

Paul Simon released the album *Still Crazy After All These Years* in October 1975, winning the Grammy for Best Album in 1976. (In his tongue-in-cheek acceptance speech, Simon thanked **Stevie Wonder** for not releasing an album in 1975!) The album includes four outstanding compositions: "Still Crazy After All These Years" (#40 May '76), *("I met my old lover on the street last night")*,"Fifty Ways to Leave Your Lover" (#1 Feb. '76) *("Drop off the key, Lee and get yourself free")*, "Gone at Last" (with **Phoebe Snow**) (#23 Sep.), and "My Little Town" (with **Art Garfunkel**) (#9 Dec.). (Simon immortalized his hit song "Still Crazy…" a year later by appearing on *Saturday Night Live* in a turkey costume in the first scene of the pre-Thanksgiving show in 1976. When he began to sing "Still Crazy…" the audience went into hysterics.) Simon's album has an interesting and unique jazz/rock/folk fusion feel to it. At about the same time, Art Garfunkel released a reasonably good new album, *Breakaway,* with two relatively good songs: the original song "Breakaway" (#39 Jan. '76) and the cover of **Stevie Wonder**'s "I Believe". However, the highlight was his superb rendition of "I Only Have Eyes for You" (#18 Nov.), which even surpassed **The Flamingos'** original version from the late 1950s.

The Eagles released their most successful album to date, *One of These Nights*. The title track "One of These Nights" (#1 July) *("Swear I'm gonna find you one of these nights")* was an outstanding example of the folk-rock sound that the **Byrds** and **Dylan** had begun in 1965, and was one of the best songs of 1975. My other favorite song from the album was "Take It to the Limit" (#4 Mar. '76) *("If it all fell to pieces tomorrow, would you still be mine"),* which wasn't released as a single until the end of the year. The other hit song from the album, "Lyin' Eyes" (#2 Nov.), is a decent song but one that I tired of quickly (perhaps its six-minute length and its constant airplay and the ever-repeating chorus had something to do with that). Early 1975 also featured the chart-topping "Best of My Love" (#1 Feb.). The song was okay, but also grew tiresome with extensive airplay.

Steely Dan released their *Katy Lied* album, which was a solid effort but not quite as good as the previous year's *Pretzel Logic*. However, it did boast four very good tracks, including "Black Friday" (#37 June), "Bad Sneakers", "Any World", and one of Steely Dan's best songs ever, "Doctor Wu" *("You walked in, and my life began again")*. The album marked the end of touring for the group (in mid-1974) and the departure of several original members, in particular, guitarist extraordinaire **Jeff "Skunk" Baxter** who joined the **Doobie Brothers**. However, Steely Dan's signature sound, a unique blend of rock and jazz, remained ever-present as group founders Fagan and Becker continued to dominate vocals and songwriting, and increasingly used session musicians to record albums.

Other notable North American artists during 1975 included:

The Canadian group **Bachman-Turner Overdrive** had two more rollicking rock hits: "Hey You" (#21 June) *("you say you wanna change the world")* and "Roll On Down the Highway" (#14 Feb.). While their music had become pretty formulaic, it was a hard rock formula that I really enjoyed.

Lynyrd Skynyrd had no new material of note, but they did release their classic rock jam song "Free Bird" as a four-minute single (#19 Jan.) as well as a second top 40 hit single, "Saturday Night Special" (#27 July). "Free Bird", particularly in its more familiar ten-minute rock jam version, was to become one of the top classic rock songs of all time. (Like many, I never bought the single, but instead eventually taped the long version from one of my friends.)

A new group **Styx** had a good effort with "Lady" (#6 Mar.). The song was recorded originally in 1973, but it took two years for it to crack the top 10 in early 1975.

Chicago released a pretty ordinary *Chicago VIII* album, but it did boast one of Chicago's best songs and one of my personal favorites of the year: the upbeat rock-'n'-roll song "Old Days" (#5 June) *("good times I remember")*.

Linda Ronstadt had her first three solo hits (after her original hit "Different Drum" with the **Stone Poneys** in 1968). The best of the three, "You're No Good" (#1 Feb.), was a more conventional rock song, featuring Ronstadt's great voice. Almost as good was "When Will I Be Loved" (#2 June) *("I've been cheated, been mistreated")*, a great country-rock cover of a hallmark Everly Brothers song. She also did an excellent rock version of Martha and the Vandellas' "Heat Wave" (#5 Nov.).

America scored big with two hits during the year. "Sister Golden Hair" (#1 June) *("Well, I keep on thinkin' 'bout you, sister golden hair surprise")* was one of the best songs of the summer with a great folk-rock sound. I also liked "Lonely People" (#5 Mar.), perhaps because it fit my "I wish I had a girlfriend" mood in 1975 with the lyrics, *"Thinking that love had passed them by, don't give up til you drink from the silver cup, you never know until you try."*

James Taylor continued his popular success with his folk-rock sound and two hits: "How Sweet It Is" (#5 Aug.), a cover of the **Marvin Gaye** hit, and the original "Mexico" (#49 Nov.). I liked the latter song, but "How Sweet It Is" suffered in comparison to the Marvin Gaye original.

Another soft rock-pop hit was **Orleans**' "Dance with Me" (#6 Oct.) *("I want to be your partner")* which was a wonderful romantic song, but without the oozing schmaltz of so many other songs in 1975.

I also liked "Laughter in the Rain" (#1 Jan.) by **Neil Sedaka** even though it was clearly overly sentimental, but I suppose even then I was sucker for a comeback hit from an early 1960s artist who last had a top 40 hit in 1963.

Janis Ian scored with the excellent "At Seventeen" (#3 Sep.), her first big hit since 1967's "Society's Child" (a song she originally wrote three years earlier at age 14!).

A relatively new group, the **Ozark Mountain Daredevils**, had the catchy and soothing, country-rock song "Jackie Blue" (#3 May) *("You like your life in a free form style. You'll take an inch but you'd love a mile")*, which surprisingly turned out to be their only major success on the pop charts. (Interestingly, at the time, I thought the singer was a woman, but I learned later, in fact, it was the high voice of drummer Larry Lee.)

The Doobie Brothers had a new, but fairly ordinary, album *Stampede* in 1975. However, it did boast a pretty good rendition of the Motown song "Take Me in Your Arms" (#11 June). Meanwhile, "Black Water" (#1 Mar.) *("Mississippi moon, won't you keep on shinin' on me?")*, the highlight of the weak 1974 album *What Were Once Vices Are Now Habits*, topped the charts early in the year.

Grand Funk Railroad had the excellent tune "Bad Time" (#4 June) *("But I must have picked a bad time to be in love")*, one of my favorites of the spring of 1975.

Soul, Funk and Disco: The Good

For the most part, I found only a limited number of songs/artists that I liked in 1975 in the soul, funk and disco genres. On the soul and funk side, this included:

Chicago-based **Earth Wind & Fire** was one of my favorite groups of the year. They had their first popular success with "Shining Star" (#1 May) and at the end of the year with "Sing a Song" (#5 Feb. '76). Both were prime examples of EW&F's great formula – wonderful, lively brass arrangements, excellent vocals and harmonies, great tunes and a unique funk/soul fusion sound.

The Ohio Players had the huge hit "Fire" (#1 Feb.) and another top 10 single "Love Rollercoaster" (#1 Jan. '76) released in November, which were probably the best popular examples of the funk genre in 1975. I'll confess to liking the Ohio Players much more in retrospect. At the time, I disliked the song "Fire" intensely (probably because I can remember being kept awake at 3AM at Brown during the winter of 1975 by the bass line of the song which I could hear booming across the quad).

The Spinners had the excellent, tuneful and upbeat soul hit "Games People Play" (#5 Oct.), which features their great mix of soprano, tenor, alto and bass voices including most notably bass singer **Pervis Jackson**

hitting his exceptionally low notes on his verse – *"12:45 heading for the subway line..."*

LaBelle scored with the rousing and overtly sexual "Lady Marmalade" (#1 Mar.) *("Voulez-vous coucher avec moi se soir?")*, which, though overplayed, was still an excellent song. The leader, **Patti LaBelle**, had been lead singer for the 1960s girl doo-wop group **Patti LaBelle and the Bluebelles**. The song was co-written by Bob Crewe (best known as the Four Seasons songwriter and producer) and Kenny Nolan (sang/wrote "I Like Dreamin'").

The Latin funk sound of the group **War** featured a very appealing sound on its two chart hits, "Why Can't We Be Friends" (#6 Aug.) and "Low Rider" (#7 Nov.).

There were only a few pure disco songs that I liked:

The Bee Gees had perhaps the best disco song of the year with their first entry in the genre, "Jive Talkin'" (#1 Aug.).

A reformulated **Four Seasons** managed to convert their great '60s sound to '70s disco with the lively "Who Loves You" (#3 Nov.). I particularly enjoyed the instrumental section of the long version of this song and of course **Frankie Valli**'s vocal.

The Bad and the Ugly

Unfortunately, there were a lot of bad and even ugly songs in 1975.

I know **Minnie Riperton** had a great voice, but the abysmal "Lovin' You" (#1 Mar.), complete with a sing-song melody, Minnie's very high-pitch "la-las" and outright screeches and a song opening with birds chirping, literally made it impossible to listen to (and made it one of the worst songs of the year). This song had one redeeming feature, however. If it came on in the morning on my clock-radio alarm, it was sure to get me up for class.

Barry Manilow knows how to write a good tune and I'll admit the first time or two I hear one of his songs, I'll find myself humming it. However, the saccharine sweetness of the musical arrangements and lyrics eventually overpower me and I feel like I do when I eat too much – sick to my stomach. In early 1975, I could tolerate "Mandy" (#1 Jan.) and even liked it a bit, but by the time he reached "Could It Be Magic" (#6 Sep.) and "I Write the Songs" (#1 Jan. '76) later in the year, I was having severe gastrointestinal distress. I know what he means when he says *"and I wrote the very first song…I am Music and I write the songs"* BUT does he realize how obnoxious and pompous this sounds!

Olivia Newton-John had two big hits: "Have You Never Been Mellow" (#1 Mar.) and "Please Mr. Please" (#3 Aug.), both cloying and featuring Olivia's very average voice. Like many in my generation, however, I did like Olivia's looks. This fact was not lost on a 'girl' friend of mine several years later who bought me Olivia's greatest hits album for my birthday solely because of its album cover featuring Olivia's beautiful face.

Jefferson Starship had an okay album, *Red Octopus*, but the main single "Miracles" (#3 Oct.) was incessantly played and extremely repetitive. (I have never counted but I think the chorus *"If only you believe, like I believe…"* is sung way too many times.)

As noted, I found many disco songs just mediocre at best, but **KC and the Sunshine Band** probably had the worst of the lot with "Get Down Tonight" (#1 Aug.) *("Do a little dance, make a little love, get down tonight")* and "That's the Way I Like It" *("uh huh uh huh")* (#1 Nov.).

*****

Overall, 1975 wasn't a bad year. It was the coming out of Bruce Springsteen and Queen, and a happy time for me by the fall of 1975. And America's bicentennial and graduation were right around the corner.

1976
"Don't Go Breaking My Heart"

Forty-one years ago in 1976, America celebrated its bicentennial with tall ships in New York Harbor on the Fourth of July. It was also the year that the U.S. started to emerge from the deep 1974-75 stock market crash and recession. But for me, when it came to 1976, Charles Dickens may have described it best: "It was the best of times, it was the worst of times". I had fallen in love in my senior year with Molly, a sophomore at Brown, who I subsequently dated for two years. I had a single in Miller Hall with my good friend John just down the hall. And I already had enough credits to graduate so I only took the minimum of three classes per semester. In many ways, senior year was my best year at Brown. And the end of the year was the best – graduation weekend and the campus dance at Brown, my first trip to Chicago were part of a whirlwind end of May, early June that I still remember fondly to this day.

But I had also learned at the end of 1975 that my father had lymphoma and it had not been caught early. He had surgery removing lymph nodes in his neck but the cancer had spread requiring more major surgery in late January 1976. They removed his spleen and a significant portion of his stomach but they couldn't get all the cancer and the prognosis was not good. He was sent home in February and then my brother and I came home to be with my mother and sister to wait out the inevitable. He died on March 25. He was only 58.

The reality of life quickly followed his death. I started work at a Newark bank in June and experienced "the first job after college" syndrome that so many do. Moving from a great college social community to a more isolated life in New York City and reverse commuting for two hours a day to a job I didn't really like at all was depressing to say the least. When coupled with a distance relationship with my girlfriend and still grieving the loss of my father, life in New York seemed almost unbearable.

Music in 1976 followed an eerily similar pattern. While there were some excellent albums, most notably the best ever from the **Eagles**, **Boston**, **ELO** and the **Steve Miller Band** and a few other excellent rock songs (e.g., **Blue Öyster Cult**'s "Don't Fear the Reaper", the **Four Seasons'** "December 1963", and **Kansas'** "Carry on Wayward Son"), a lot of music in 1976 was downright dreary or simply bad.

Most Popular Hits in 1976
1. Afternoon Delight – Starland Vocal Band
2. Silly Love Songs – Wings
3. Tonight's the Night (Gonna Be Alright) – Rod Stewart
4. I Write the Songs – Barry Manilow
5. Kiss and Say Goodbye – Manhattans
6. Disco Duck (Part 1) – Rick Dees
7. A Fifth of Beethoven – Walter Murphy
8. Convoy – C.W. McCall
9. Welcome Back – John Sebastian
10. Muskrat Love – Captain and Tennille

Was Rock Music Dead?

In 1976, British rock music was particularly disappointing. There was no new material from **The Who, Yes** or **The Moody Blues** (i.e., three of my favorite groups). **Fleetwood Mac**'s self-titled and excellent late-1975 album was all over the radio in 1976, including three top 20 hits with "Over My Head", "Rhiannon" and "Say You Love Me", but it wasn't until 1977 when the superb *Rumours* album came out that they would have any new material. **Led Zeppelin** had a sub-par album, *Presence*, though I did like the hard rocker "Nobody's Fault but Mine". The **Rolling Stones** had a decent album, *Black and Blue,* but only the song "Fool to Cry" (#10 June) was particularly memorable. **Elton John** had his two sub-par albums, *Blue Moves* and *Here and There* and only his duet with Kiki Dee, "Don't Go Breaking My Heart" (#1 Aug.) *("I couldn't if I tried")*, made me smile. In the U.S., **Bruce Springsteen,** after his successful and excellent *Born to Run* album in 1975, was prevented for almost three years by a court injunction from recording new material owing to a bitter legal dispute over royalties with manager Mike Appel.[29]

Meanwhile, the former Beatles' solo careers had fallen to a new low. **Lennon** began a five-year period without any new recordings (apparently a lot of it spent partying) before his excellent comeback album with Yoko, *Double Fantasy* in 1980. **Harrison**'s *Thirty Three and 1/3* was better than his most recent disastrous efforts (e.g., the *Dark Horse* album) and did contain two decent songs, "Crackerbox Palace" (#19 Mar. 1977) and "This Song" (#25 Dec.) (George's comment about the "My Sweet Lord" plagiarizing "He's So Fine" lawsuit), but the rest of the album was not memorable. **Ringo Starr** sank further with his *Ringo's Rotogravure* album and **Paul McCartney and Wings**' *Wings At The Speed of Sound* was another step down for the group from 1975's *Venus and Mars* though at least it boasted two good songs, "Silly Love Songs" (#1 June) and "Let 'Em In" (#3 Aug.). The former became a favorite of mine in April possibly because it was an upbeat love song, in contrast to many others in 1976.

British rock was clearly suffering, while disco ruled the American charts and the rise of punk and new wave was still a year or two away. However, rock music did have some excellent music in 1976 albeit mostly during the second half of the year and with American groups in the lead.

In December 1976, the **Eagles** released by far and away their best album, *Hotel California*. Joe Walsh, formerly of the James Gang and best known for his solo rocker "Rocky Mountain Way" (#23 Sep.'73), joined the group in 1976 and *Hotel California* benefits mightily from his addition. The album is a fusion of folk-rock and more mainstream rock and works very nicely. It features more traditional-style Eagles songs such as "New Kid in Town" (#1 Feb. 1977), an excellent folk-rock tune that was the first single from the album, as well as "Wasted Time" and "Try and Love Again", two excellent album cuts that could have easily come from any of the Eagles earlier albums. But it is the Joe Walsh-influenced electric guitar songs "Life in the Fast Lane" (#11 June 1977) (which Walsh co-wrote) and "Victim of Love" (B-side of "New Kid in Town") along with the title track "Hotel California" (#1 Apr. 1977) that really make the album soar. The former two songs are great rockers, but "Hotel California" was a very special song. Building slowly with acoustic guitars, then a slow rhythm track and great infectious tune and vocals from Don Henley, the song finishes with an extraordinary guitar duet from Don Felder and Joe Walsh. This melding of folk-rock and hard rock works perfectly and makes "Hotel California" one of the best rock songs ever and my favorite in 1976 or for that matter in 1977 when it received most of its airplay.

Boston released their self-titled debut album in August, which was every bit the equal of *Hotel California* by the Eagles in terms of overall quality. Led by writer/producer and lead guitarist Tom Scholz and vocalist Brad Delp, Boston had a unique rock sound that made their music irresistible. Highlighted by the soaring single "More Than A Feeling" (#5 Dec.) *("I closed my eyes and I slipped away")*, the *Boston* album features nine tracks which all could have been hit singles. "Foreplay/Long Time" was another favorite, particularly the link between the instrumental "Foreplay" and "Long Time" (#22 Feb. 1977) *("It's been such a long time, I think I should be going")*. "Peace of Mind" (#38 June 1977) as well as the album cuts "Hitch a Ride" *("Gonna hitch a ride. Head for the other side")* and "Something About You" were not far behind. Great guitar hooks, nice vocals and strong melodies make *Boston* one of my favorite rock albums of all time.

Heart had their U.S. release of their first album *Dreamboat Annie* in February. The album's success was primarily due to two superb songs: "Magic Man" (#9 Oct.) and "Crazy on You" (#35 June). After Nancy Wilson's excellent acoustic guitar intro, "Crazy on You" morphs into a hard rock ballad featuring an unforgettable guitar riff and Ann Wilson's soaring vocals. The rest of the album doesn't offer anything comparable, but it isn't bad either. "Dreamboat Annie" (#42 Jan. 1977) is a nice folk-rock song that was also a successful single and is reprised to good effect at the end of the album. Another folk-rock song "How Deep It Goes" and the rocker "White Lightning" are also good.

The **Steve Miller Band** and their album *Fly Like an Eagle,* released in May, soared to #3 on the album charts. The album is the best single album the group ever did, highlighted by three very catchy hit singles – "Take the Money and Run" (#11 July) *("This is the story about Billy Joe and Bobby Sue")*, "Rock N Me" (#1 Oct.), and "Fly Like an Eagle" (#2

Mar. 1977). But the album featured much more, most notably two very good songs, "Serenade" and "Dance, Dance, Dance" (which both also appeared on the group's *Greatest Hits* album in 1978) and the interesting rock-blues song "Mercury Blues".

Takin' It to the Streets, the **Doobie Brothers**' fifth album, was their best since the excellent *The Captain and Me*. In late 1975, Michael McDonald joined the group, effectively replacing lead singer Tom Johnston who was having serious health issues. McDonald's keyboards, vocals and blue-eyed soul sound permeate the album. And the best two songs on the album were McDonald compositions with his distinctive vocal style – "It Keeps You Running" (#37 Jan. 1977), a great soul ballad, and the up-tempo "Takin' It to the Streets" (#13 June) *("You don't know me but I'm your brother")*, one of my favorite songs by the Doobie Brothers.

Steely Dan had another strong album, *The Royal Scam*. I'll admit I didn't listen to it much in 1976, but grew to love four songs in particular from the album (after I listened to them repeatedly on a "Best of" collection in 1978) – "The Fez" (#59 Oct.), "Don't Take Me Alive", "Haitian Divorce", and "Kid Charlemagne" (#82 July) *("Every A-Frame had your number on the wall, you must have had it all")*. All four were catchy with Steely Dan's very distinctive rock-jazz fusion sound and their usual interesting lyrics.

English rockers the **Electric Light Orchestra (ELO)** released their best album in September, *A New World Record*. Consistently good throughout and featuring Jeff Lynne's distinctive, orchestrated rock sound, the album was also ELO's most popular to date. It features three singles: "Livin' Thing" (#13 Dec.) *("It's a terrible thing to lose")*, "Do Ya" (#24 Mar. 1977), and "Telephone Line" (#7 Sep. 1977) as well as several other good rock-'n'-roll songs, notably "Rockaria" and "So Fine". My two favorites from the album were "Livin' Thing" *("I'm taking a dive")*, a nice lively upbeat song, and "Do Ya" *("Do ya, do ya, want my love")*, an excellent rock-'n'-roll song. I bought this album in 1977 and played it constantly.

Peter Frampton released the highly successful live double album *Frampton Comes Alive* in early 1976. The album spent 10 weeks at #1 and spawned three top-20 hits in 1976, "Show Me the Way" (#6 May), "Baby, I Love Your Way" (#12 Aug.), and "Do You Feel Like We Do" (#10 Nov.). The album was one of the first live albums I can remember where the music quality was actually quite good. Nonetheless, while I enjoyed the three hit songs from the album, particularly the long version of "Do You Feel Like We Do" as well as another album cut "Shine On", the rest of the double album was underwhelming for me and didn't live up to its popular hype.

My Favorite Songs in 1976
  1. Hotel California – Eagles
  2. Bohemian Rhapsody – **Queen**
  3. Crazy on You – Heart
  4. Carry on Wayward Son – Kansas
  5. More Than a Feeling – Boston
  6. Don't Fear the Reaper – Blue Öyster Cult
  7. Rock'n Me – Steve Miller Band
  8. Foreplay/Long Time – Boston
  9. Dream On – Aerosmith
  10. Magic Man – Heart

Other rock songs that I enjoyed included:

Queen's "Bohemian Rhapsody" (#9 Apr.) *("So you think you can stone me and spit in my eye? So you think you can love me and leave me to die?")* was one of the best songs of the year – a rock-opera hit featuring great guitar and contrapuntal vocals that was great fun even after multiple listenings. The song has the rare distinction of actually charting 16 years later and reaching #2 on the charts after it was featured in the movie *Wayne's World*. Queen also had the very good song "Somebody to Love" (#13 Jan. 1977) *("can anybody find me somebody to love?")*, which featured some great singing by Freddie Mercury and the rest of Queen as well as the excellent single "You're My Best Friend" (#16 July).

Blue Öyster Cult had their first hit and best song with "Don't Fear The Reaper" (#12 Oct.), which is one of my favorites of 1976. It was the source material for a great *SNL* skit in the 1990s featuring Christopher Walken as the music producer who demands "more cowbell" from band member Will Ferrell.

Boston-based **Aerosmith** had its first two top 10 hits with its re-release of the 1973 song "Dream On" (#6 Apr.) *("Dream until your dream comes true")* in 1976 and the release of "Walk This Way" in November (#10 Jan. 1977), two of the best songs the group has ever done. "Sweet Emotion", which barely made the top 40 in 1975, was another excellent Aerosmith song that received more airplay in 1976, because of the group's newfound popularity. While having their own distinctive style, both musically and vocally, Aerosmith's early hits reminded me of an American version of Led Zeppelin.

Gordon Lightfoot had the lengthy epic song "Wreck of the Edmund Fitzgerald" (#2 Nov.), one of those rare recordings that tells a riveting story through an excellent song.

"Carry on Wayward Son" (#11 Feb. 1977) *("Don't you cry no more")* by **Kansas** was a great rock song. Taken from the 1976 *Leftoverture* album, the single was released in December 1976 and became the trademark hit for the group and is among my favorites.

Gary Wright had two very catchy pop-rock singles – the synthesizer heavy "Dream Weaver" (#2 Mar.), and "Love Alive" (#2 July) *("My heart is on fire, my soul's like a wheel that's turning")*.

"Love Is a Drug" (#30 Mar.) by **Roxy Music** from England was an interesting art-rock song that presaged the beginning of new wave in 1977.

English rockers **Foghat** had their best song "Slow Ride" (#20 Mar.) *("Slow ride, take it easy")* with a unique pacing and rhythm for a hard rock song. Later, they had the catchy "Fool for the City" (#45 July).

Thin Lizzy from Dublin had their first and only major U.S. hit "The Boys Are Back in Town" (#12 July).

Manfred Mann had a huge comeback hit in late 1976 when they successfully covered Bruce Springsteen's "Blinded by the Light" (#1 Feb. 77). This was the group's first top 40 hit since "Mighty Quinn" in 1968.

And speaking of comebacks, "Rock and Roll Music" (#5 Aug.) by The Beach Boys was an excellent remake of the Chuck Berry classic and was The Beach Boys' first top 40 song in nine years. Technically, The Beatles also had a comeback hit except it was just a re-release of an album cut from the 1966 album *Revolver,* "Got to Get You into My Life" (#7 July). That the song was a re-release of a 10-year-old song as a single and still made the top 10 is a good indication of the dearth of strong rock songs in 1976.

The longtime British artist **Cliff Richard** had fourteen #1 hits in the U.K. but had never had a top 20 hit in the U.S. However, with "Devil Woman" (#6 Sep.) *("She's just a devil woman, with evil on her mind")*, Richard finally had an American hit single and a pretty good one at that.

"All By Myself"

Music in 1976 raises an interesting "chicken or the egg" question. Did so many songs seem depressing to me because I was feeling down in the dumps during much of 1976 or was I depressed because there were so many dreary songs? While logic says that it was the former, some of the songs didn't help matters much. Songs about breakups, relationships on the rocks or loneliness were particularly difficult for me to listen to even though I will admit that a few of them were good songs. Consider some egregious examples from 1976:

"If You Leave Me Now" (#1 Oct.), **Chicago** – *"If you leave me now, you'll take away the greatest part of me, ooh no, please don't go...you'll take away the very heart of me."*

"Here Comes Those Tears Again" (#23 Mar. 1977), **Jackson Browne** – *"Here comes those tears again, just when I was getting over you, just when I was going to make it thru another night without missing you."*

"You'll Never Find Another Love Like Mine" (#2 Sep.), **Lou Rawls** – *"Late in the midnight hour, baby (you're gonna miss my lovin'). When it's cold outside (you're gonna miss my loving'), you're gonna miss, you're gonna miss my lo-o-ove."*

"The Pretender" (#58 June 1977), **Jackson Browne** – *"And when the evening rolls around, I'll go home and lay my body down, and when the morning sun comes streaming in I'll get up and do it again, Amen... Caught between the longing for love and the struggle for the legal tender... Out into the cool of the evening strolls the pretender."*

"Kiss and Say Goodbye" (#1 July), **The Manhattans** – *"This has to be the saddest day of my life... I'm gonna miss you, I can't lie (I'm gonna miss you)*, *Understand me, won't you try (I'm gonna miss you) It's gonna hurt me, I can't lie (I'm gonna miss you)...Let's just kiss and say goodbye."*

"Sorry Seems to Be the Hardest Word" (#6 Dec.), **Elton John** – *"What I've got to do to make you love me, what I've got to do to make you care...it's sad, so sad, it's a sad sad situation."* (To make matters worse, this song featured a VERY dreary vocal style and music.)

"It's Over" (#38 May), **Boz Scaggs** – *"Why can't you get it thru your head, it's over, it's over now. Yes, you heard me clearly now I said, it's over, it's over now."*

"She's Gone" (#7 Oct.), **Hall and Oates** – *"Everybody's high on consolation. Everybody's trying to tell me what is right for me, yeah, I need a drink and a quick decision. Now it's up to me. Ooooh, what will be. She's gone, oh why, oh why, I better learn how to face it, she's gone, she's gone, oh why, oh why, I'd pay the devil to replace her, she's gone, she's gone oh why, what went wrong?"*

This last song caused me to trash one clock radio when I woke up to this song a few mornings after Molly and I broke up in November 1977. (At least, I was angry instead of depressed!).

But the king of depressing songs in 1976 was the **Eric Carmen** hit "All By Myself" (#2 Mar.):

When I was young
I never needed anyone
and making love was just for fun.
Those days are gone.

Living alone
I think of all the friends I've known,
but when I dial the telephone
Nobody's home.

All by myself
Don't want to be all by myself anymore
All by myself
Don't want to live all by myself anymore

This song should come with a warning: "Do not listen to when all alone in your apartment!" Fittingly, Carmen had the follow-up hit "Never Gonna Fall in Love Again" (#11 July), to which my response was, "Well yeah, particularly if you depress everybody."

Disco, Funk and Soul

While most disco songs were pretty bad, there were a few exceptions. My favorite disco songs were by artists that were not disco acts per se. The best was "December 1963 (Oh What a Night)" (#1 Mar.) by the **Four Seasons**, a catchy comeback song for Frankie Valli on the heels of "Who Loves You" (the Four Seasons' first disco hit) in late 1975. My other favorite disco hit was "Love Hangover" (#1 May) *("I don't want to get over")* by **Diana Ross** probably indicating my general preferences for '60s artists.

But the rest of disco was pretty dismal. Among the most popular, but still bad, a faux classic "A Fifth of Beethoven" by **Walter Murphy** (#1 Oct.), the instrumental disco song that certainly had Beethoven "rolling over" in his grave, yet another **KC and the Sunshine Band** disco hit "(Shake, Shake, Shake) Shake Your Booty" (#1 Sep.), and "Love to Love You Baby" (#2 Feb.), the orgasmic first hit by the "Queen of Disco" **Donna Summer.**

Fortunately, funk and soul music was quite a bit better. **War** had their best song with the mellow and picturesque "Summer" (#7 Sep.) *("Riding round town with the all the windows down...Yes it's summer, my time of year")*. **Earth, Wind and Fire** had yet another excellent funk and soul hit "Getaway" (#12 Oct.) featuring their unique harmonies. **Brothers Johnson** had the soulful "I'll Be Good to You" (#3 July). And my favorite funk song of the year was "Play That Funky Music" (#1 Sep.) by **Wild Cherry** that would get even the most reclusive types on the dance floor.

The Bad

Unfortunately, there were a number of bad songs, even beyond disco. **Captain and Tennille** did such a saccharine version of "Muskrat Love" (#4 Nov.), I found myself pining for the original by America, even though it was never a favorite of mine. **The Carpenters** destroyed a nice **Herman's Hermits** hit "There's a Kind of a Hush" (#12 Apr.). **Barry Manilow** sang "Tryin' to Get the Feeling Again" (#10 May) and I sorely wished he wouldn't try! Then, there was the #1 song of the year "Afternoon Delight" (#1 July) which took saccharine to new heights both musically and lyrically – *"Gonna find my baby, gonna hold her tight...skyrockets in sight, afternoon delight."* But perhaps the worst song of the year (if you can call it a song) was **C.W. McCall**'s "Convoy" (#1 Feb.), which combined trucker C.B. slang with a silly tune. I can still remember one of my friends putting that on the jukebox at our favorite pizza joint at Brown and having some woman scream out, "What asshole put that song on?!"

*****

Despite the bad and dreary songs, 1976 was a decent year for music. For the Eagles, Steve Miller, Boston and Heart, their 1976 records ultimately represented the best of their careers. And there was promise that 1977-1978 would be even better with a new album, *Rumours,* on the way from Fleetwood Mac, and several new wave groups, The Police, the Talking Heads and the Cars, beginning to gain in popularity. In 1977, rock would be taking a new turn and in December 1977, I learned I would be heading west to Stanford Business School and a new chapter in my life.

Section II
The Lists

Part 1
Favorite Song Lists

Best Summer Songs
"There Is Danger
in the Summer Moon Above"

As I write this chapter, summer is nearly over. The kids in our neighborhood are back in school and the unofficial end of summer (Labor Day Weekend) is nearly upon us. (I realize that the "official" end of summer comes with the autumnal equinox, but I have never felt that September was anything but a fall month.) So in honor of the summer before it departs (sigh), I thought I would present my list of 20 favorite summer songs.

But first, here are a few ground rules as to what I define as a "summer song". I don't count songs that happened to be recorded or charted during the summer months. Instead, the song must have "summer" or "summertime" or a summer month (i.e., "June", "July" or "August") in the title OR in the lyrics to qualify. Also, to keep this manageable, I have restricted it to songs recorded in the 1960s and 1970s. I am sure that there are some great, earlier and later era songs that I am missing, but so be it. So here they are in approximate order though not much separates #1 from #20:

1. "Summer in the City" – Lovin' Spoonful (1966)
Mark Sebastian co-wrote this song for his older brother's group. Since he was in the same class as my sister in high school at Friends Seminary in New York, I can't help but feel very connected to this song. I love this song for its poignant lyrics that are all about New York City and remind me of my summers growing up: *"...back of my neck, getting dirt and gritty...All around, people looking half dead. Walking on the sidewalk, hotter than a match head."* The song is also an uncharacteristic rocker given the normal folk-rock sound of John Sebastian and the Spoonful and includes great keyboards and electric guitar. In other words, it has it all.

2. "See You in September" – The Happenings (1966)
"There is danger in the summer moon above." Though not the original version (the Regents recorded the original back in 1959), this '60s

rendition features the Happenings' great voices and is a bit faster than the original. It is irresistibly catchy, both lyrically and musically. Though certainly not a rock song, it was one of my early favorites (and among my first 45 purchases) when I starting listening to WABC constantly in the summer of 1966.

3. "Sunny Afternoon" – The Kinks (1966)
"Lazing on a sunny afternoon in the summertime." This song oozes summer laziness which all of us have experienced at one time or another. It doesn't hurt that it is also, in my opinion, one of the Kinks' best songs with an infectious guitar, bass line and tune.

4. "Hot Fun in the Summertime" – Sly and the Family Stone (1969)
"End of the spring and here she comes back, high, high, high, yeah, those summer days." This is by far the best soul song about summer. And it is a hard one not to love since it makes you feel really good about the summer (though strangely sad when you hear it post-September).

5. "Summertime Blues" – Eddie Cochran (1958)/The Who (1970)
"Sometimes I wonder what I'm gonna do, cause there ain't no cure for the summertime blues." Okay, I cheated a bit on this one. I love Eddie Cochran's original version with its late '50s guitar rhythms, so I made an exception for the list. But I also like The Who's hard rock version (particularly their "Live at Leeds" recording) as well. So I put them both on the list tied at #5.

6. "Summer Rain" – Johnny Rivers (1968)
I have always been a huge Johnny Rivers fan. I love his voice. This is a particularly good ballad, an original hit song with lyrics that had us all remembering the summer of 1967. *"All summer long, we were dancing in the sand. Everybody just kept on playing Sgt. Pepper's Lonely Hearts Club Band."* (At least, I remember experiencing the second part of that line from the summer of 1967.)

7. "Saturday in the Park" – Chicago (1972)
"I think it was the 4th of July." This song captures the spirit of Grant Park in Chicago on a summer Saturday. But it just as easily could have been New York or any other major city in the 1970s with *"a man selling*

ice cream, and singing Italian songs". It's a great tune featuring Chicago's interesting brass arrangement.

8. "Surfin' U.S.A." – Beach Boys (1963)
"We'll all be gone for the summer. We're on safari to stay. Tell the teacher we're surfin' surfin' U.S.A.". This is one of several great Beach Boys songs about beaches and surfing. However, it is one of just two that mention summer. (The other is the song "All Summer Long".)

9. "A Summer Song" – Chad and Jeremy (1964)
This is the best folk ballad about summer. It's hard not to listen to it imagining that it's summer again. *"Trees swaying in the summer breeze; showing off their silver leaves."*

10. "Beach Baby" – First Class (1974)
"Beach, baby beach, baby; there on the sand from July to the end of September." I really love this tune and how it waxes nostalgic about summer on the beach. It was a big hit in 1974, well after the peak of popularity of The Beach Boys, though it sounds as if it comes from that era.

11. "Brother Love's Travelin' Salvation Show" – Neil Diamond (1969)
"Hot August night and the leaves hangin' down. And the grass on the ground smellin' sweet." I love the way this song builds lyrically and musically from a sultry night scene to wild evangelism. This is possibly Neil's best song.

12. "Everybody's Talkin'" – Nilsson (1969)
"Sailin' on a summer breeze." This is just a really good song, reminding me of the movie *Midnight Cowboy* and walking through NYC in the summer.

13. "4th of July, Asbury Park (Sandy)" – Bruce Springsteen (1973)
"Sandy, the fireworks are hailin' over little Eden tonight...Sandy, the aurora is rising behind us." A great Fourth of July scene at Asbury Park is painted by Springsteen's interesting lyrics and lazy summer vocals and music.

14. "Summer Breeze" – Seals and Crofts (1972)
"Sweet days of summer, the jasmine's in bloom." A great duet about summer, though "Hummingbird" is still my favorite by them.

15. "Bus Stop" – Hollies (1966)
"Please share my umbrella...All that summer we enjoyed it. That umbrella, we employed it. By August, she was mine." This great Hollies song features the great vocal harmonies of Graham Nash.

16. "Rain on the Roof" – Lovin' Spoonful (1966)
"Caught up in a summer shower, maybe it will last for hours."

17. "Green Grass" – Gary Lewis & the Playboys (1966)
"We will love the summer long."

18. "Summer" – War (1976)
"Yes, it's summer, my time of year." War's best song really makes you feel like it is summer both musically and lyrically.

19. "Turn Down Day" – The Cyrkle (1966)
"Soft summer breeze and the surf rolls in."

20. "Summertime" – Billy Stewart (1966)
The best rock era version of the famous Gershwin tune from *Porgy and Bess* that Billie Holiday recorded in 1936. I like the original version better but the Billy Stewart arrangement is very interesting.

Near Misses/Honorable Mentions:
"Hot Summer Day" – It's A Beautiful Day

"Theme from a Summer Place" – Percy Faith and His Orchestra

"Hot August Night" – Meat Loaf

Best Rain Songs
"Listen to the Rhythm of the Falling Rain"

As I write this chapter, it is January in Columbus and is raining/cloudy for what seems like the twentieth consecutive day. (I think I saw the sun this morning but I may have forgotten what it looks like.) So naturally it got me thinking about my favorite rain or stormy weather songs. To qualify, the song must mention rain or stormy weather in the title. Also, I chose only one song per artist. So here is my list of my 30 favorites of the 1960s and 1970s in chronological order by first chart date. A *** indicates songs that include the sounds of rain or a rainstorm:

1. "Raindrops"* – Dee Clark (May '61)**
"It must be raindrops, so many raindrops, it feels like raindrops falling from my eyes."

2. "Crying in the Rain" – Everly Brothers (Jan. '62)
"I'll do my crying in the rain."

3. "Rhythm of the Rain"* – Cascades (Jan. '63)**
"Listen to the rhythm of the falling rain, pitter, patter."

4. "Don't Let the Rain Come Down" – Serendipity Singers (Feb. '64)
"My roof's got a hole in it and I might drown."

5. "Walking in the Rain"* – Ronettes (Oct. '64)**
"And I'll be certain he's my guy, by the things he likes to do...like walking in the rain."

6. "Baby the Rain Must Fall" – Glenn Yarbrough (Mar. '65)
"Wherever my heart must lead me, baby I must go."

7. "Lightin' Strikes" – Lou Christie (Dec. '65)
"When I see lips beggin' to be kissed, I can't stop ...Lightning is striking again." Lou couldn't get enough of rain songs, as his follow-up hit in the spring of 1966 was "Rhapsody in the Rain".

8. "Rainy Day Woman #12 & 35" – Bob Dylan (Apr. '66)
"Everybody must get stoned." This is a "rain" song with neither a mention of rain, nor any part of its title in the lyrics.

9. "Flowers Never Bend with the Rainfall" – Simon and Garfunkel (May '66)
"So I continue to pretend, my life will never end, and flowers never bend with the rainfall."

10. "Rain" – The Beatles (June '66)
"Rain, I don't mind. Shine. The weather's fine."

11. "Rain on the Roof" – Lovin' Spoonful (Oct. '66)
"Me and you and rain on the roof, caught up in a summer shower, maybe it will last for hours, waiting out the sun." This song is on both my rain and summer lists!

12. "Tell It to the Rain"*** – Four Seasons (Dec. '66)
"Tell it to the rain, and the stars that shine above, that it is me you're thinking of, and I'm your love."

13. "Don't Let the Rain Come Down on Me" – The Critters (July '67)
"Don't let it wash away my memories."

14. "Summer Rain"*** – Johnny Rivers (Nov. '67)
"Summer rain taps at my window..." This song also has the honor of being on both my summer and rain lists!

15. "The Rain, the Park & Other Things"*** – The Cowsills (Dec. '67)
"I saw her sitting in the rain. Raindrops falling on her...Flowers in her hair, flowers everywhere, I love the flower girl."

16. "I Wish it Would Rain"*** – Temptations (Jan. '68)
"Sunshine, blue skies please go away...I know to you it might sound strange, but I wish it would rain".

17. "Stormy" – Classics IV (Oct. '68)
"All of a sudden that old rain's falling down, and my world is cloudy and gray. You've gone away. Oh stormy, bring back that sunny day."

18. "Raindrops Keep Fallin' on My Head" – B.J. Thomas (Nov. '69)
"But there is one thing I know, the blues they send to meet me, won't defeat me." I'll admit I tired of this song, because of its excessive

airplay. But any song featured in the movie *Butch Cassidy and the Sundance Kid* has to be on the list!

19. "Rainy Night in Georgia" – Brook Benton (Jan. '70)
"Heavy rain falling. Seems I hear your voice calling 'it's alright'."

20. "Who'll Stop the Rain" – Creedence Clearwater Revival (Jan. '70)
"And I wonder, still I wonder, who'll stop the rain." CCR also had another rain song, which was nearly as good: "Have You Ever Seen the Rain?"

21. "Kentucky Rain" – Elvis Presley (Feb. '70)
"So I'm walking in the rain, on this lonely Kentucky back road...Kentucky rain keeps pouring down."

22. "Fire and Rain" – James Taylor (Sep. '70)
"I've seen fire and I've seen rain. I've seen sunny days I thought would never end...but I always thought I would see you one more time again."

23. "Here Comes That Rainy Day Feeling Again" – The Fortunes (May '71)
"And soon my tears will be falling like rain."

24. "Rainy Days and Mondays" – The Carpenters (May '71)
"Hanging around, nothing to do but frown, rainy days and Mondays always get me down."

25. "Riders on the Storm"*** – The Doors (July '71)
"Riders on the storm...into this world were thrown like a dog without a bone, an actor out alone. ...There's a killer on the road, his brain is squirming like a toad...if you give this man a ride, sweet memory will die..." Ironically, this song first hit the Top 100 on July 3, 1971, the day Jim Morrison died. It was also the Doors' last successful single.

26. "In the Rain"*** – The Dramatics (Feb. '72)
"I'm gonna go outside...in the rain. It may sound crazy."

27. "Let It Rain" – Eric Clapton (Sep. '72)
"Let it rain, let your love rain down on me."

28. "It Never Rains in Southern California" – Albert Hammond (Oct. '72)

"It never rains in California, but girl don't they warn you, it pours, man it pours."

29. "Love Reign O'er Me"*** – The Who (Dec. '73)

"Only love can make it rain, like a sweat of lovebirds laying in the fields. Love reign on me." While this song doesn't have rain or storms in the title, I made an exception because the title is used interchangeably as "love rain over me" in the song. And like several others on the list, the song begins with a rainstorm.

30. "Fool in the Rain" – Led Zeppelin (Dec. '79)

"And the storm that I thought would blow over, clouds the light of the love that I found, found." Led Zeppelin also recorded "The Rain Song".

Best Christmas Songs
"Santa Claus Is Coming to Town"

Every Christmas season brings the onslaught of secular and religious songs and hymns. I have no complaint about Christmas carols and hymns. In fact, some of the best religious music is Christmas music with standouts like "Joy to the World", "Silent Night", "Angels We Have Heard on High" and "O Holy Night" or "Hallelujah Chorus" by Handel, which might be the best single song of the Baroque period. I suspect many of you feel the same way. And there is a good reason for this. During the Baroque and Classical and even Romantic eras, most of the top-flight music was largely religious and produced by the greatest composers of all time such as Handel, Bach, Mozart and Beethoven. Christmas carols were no exception with Mendelssohn's "Hark! The Herald Angels Sing" a prime example. It is not surprising that Christmas hymns and carols were among the most popular songs of their era.

But when it comes to popular, *secular* Christmas songs, the sheer quantity of songs or versions of the same song over and over and over again doesn't translate into quality in most cases. In fact, it seems like every popular music artist has recorded a Christmas album, which can result in the same songs being sung ad nauseum every Christmas. Fortunately, there are a few exceptions to the rule. So here is my Top 10 list of popular, secular Christmas songs:

1. "Sleigh Ride" – The Ronettes
This is an outstanding version of a great Christmas song, a well-sung and happy song that is really hard to resist at Christmastime. (Honorable mentions: "Winter Wonderland" and "Frosty the Snowman" also by Darlene Love and the Ronettes, with the same great Phil Spector production).

2. "The Christmas Song" – Nat King Cole
What a great voice he had! There hasn't been anything close to this song for setting the Christmas mood since it was recorded in 1961.

3a. "Santa Claus Is Coming to Town" – Bruce Springsteen
Only Springsteen could turn this into a live rocker including a Clarence Clemons sax solo and Santa arriving at the end, and somehow pull it off.

3b. "Santa Claus Is Coming to Town" – Jackson 5
Okay, so I cheated and have two versions tied at #3. (However, it's my list and I'll do what I want!) This very spirited and enjoyable version makes it sound like Michael believes Santa is really coming. Given that he was around 12 at the time, he probably did.

4. "Silent Night" – The Temptations
This unique, soulful rendition of "Silent Night" reminds me that I love this hymn whether it is sung by The Vienna Boys Choir or by the Temptations. (This is definitely not a "secular" song, but the Temps are a very popular "secular" group.)

5. "Run Rudolph Run" – Chuck Berry
I always remember the time capsule that the U.S. sent into outer space on the Voyager Missions in the 1970s, which included music from Mozart and Beethoven as well as "Johnny B. Goode", a few other songs and other spoken messages. Supposedly, this was our way of communicating in the event that there really was intelligent life out there. The joke goes that the very first message that came back to earth from alien life was, "Send More Chuck Berry!"

6. "Little Saint Nick" – The Beach Boys
This original Christmas song showcases The Beach Boys' great harmonies. And that's good enough for this Beach Boys fan!

7. "Happy Xmas (The War is Over)" – John Lennon
This is the best of the former Beatles' Christmas songs and the only one that doesn't drive my wife crazy.

8. "Wonderful Christmastime" – Paul McCartney
I had to put a song on the list from one of my favorite singer-songwriters ever. However, I confess that my ulterior motive is that this song drives my wife crazy!

9. "Snoopy's Christmas" – The Royal Guardsmen
This is another light Christmas song that continues the enjoyable Snoopy

song series. (I highly recommend you also listen to "Snoopy vs the Red Baron" and "The Return of the Red Baron".) And how many Christmas songs do you know where a guy with a bad German accent says to a dog, "Merry Christmas, My Friend"?

10. "The Twelve Days of Christmas" – John Denver and the Muppets

I know the Twelve Days of Christmas is your classic, VERY REPETITIVE Christmas song with a chorus that repeats TWELVE times. However, the Muppets version has to make you chuckle and that is enough to vault this song into my Top 10.

*****

Two obvious missing songs from this list: "Jingle Bell Rock" by Bobby Helms and "White Christmas" by Bing Crosby. However, these are songs that I have heard so many times that they have grown old. Maybe in a few years, I'll change my mind.

Finally, I should note that there are several very good instrumental collections of holiday music ranging from Windham Hill "new age" jazz to the Boston Pops. A broader collection called *Charlie Brown's Holiday Hits* by the Vince Guaraldi Trio (which is mostly jazz piano) is also excellent.

So when it comes to Christmas time, enjoy the music, whatever your favorites are.

Best Comedy Singles
"Please Mr. Custer, I Don't Want to Go"

The goal of music should not only be to entertain us or be interesting musically and lyrically, but in a few cases to make us laugh. Surprisingly, there are precious few songs that are truly funny. Great comedians seldom released singles and the rare ones that they did release were usually only okay (e.g., "Little Ole Man" by Bill Cosby, basically a cover of "Uptight" with Cosby's lyrics). For example, two excellent, singing-comedy acts (The Smothers Brothers and Tom Lehrer) issued only one single between them.

Also, the two most successful "comedy" artists/musicians really didn't do anything that was very funny (or at least not to me). This includes Ray Stevens, who is perhaps best known for his #1 hit "The Streak", which wasn't that funny or his two earlier top ten hits, "Gitarzan" and "Ahab the Arab", which were equally unfunny. It also includes Dickie Goodman (and, in earlier singles, his partner Bill Buchanan) who pioneered the "break-in" records that strung together bits of then popular songs along with narration for comic effect. This began with "The Flying Saucer Pts. 1 and 2" back in 1956 and Goodman's last successful single, "Mr. Jaws", in 1975. Unfortunately, aside from the novelty of this approach in 1956, the humor just seems stupid to me.

Fortunately, there are a few exceptions to this rule and several singles succeeded largely because they were clever, or unique and at least elicited a chuckle even now. I expanded the list into the early '80s to account for a couple of these. So in honor of the now more than 75-year-old Dr. Demento, who loved playing weird and bizarre and usually humorous songs on his weekly radio show, here is my Demented Double Dix in chronological order:

1. "Jingle Bells" – The Singing Dogs (1955, 1971, 1972, 1973, 1983, 1984)
Yes, it is easy to get sick of this one around Christmastime, but the concept and execution are still pretty funny.

2. "Beep, Beep" – The Playmates (#4 Dec. '58)
"Hey Buddy how do I get this car out of second gear?" It is hard not to smile when I hear this song. It is a great car song.

3. "Mr. Custer" – Larry Verne (#1 Oct. '61)
"Please Mr. Custer, I don't wanna go." Verne's song is a parody of the slew of war-related songs at the time that talked about the likes of Davy Crockett or the Battle of New Orleans.

4. "Monster Mash" – Bobby "Boris" Pickett and the Crypt Kicker Five (#1 Oct. '62)
"It was a graveyard smash." The song was a great parody concept, no doubt even funnier when first released in the early 1960s during the music dance craze (e.g., "The Twist", "The Locomotion", etc.). It has gotten old over the years because of constant play but still a classic.

5. "Hello Muddah/Hello Faddah – A Letter from Camp" – Allan Sherman (#2 Sep. '63)
"Oh please don't make me stay, I've been here ONE – WHOLE – DAY!" This might be the most wickedly funny song ever. The lyrics are brilliant. *"You remember Jeffrey Hardy, they're about to organize a searching party".*

6. "Martian Hop" – The Ran-dells (#16 Sep. '63)
"We have just discovered an important note from space, the Martians plan to throw a dance for all the human race." If you listen to this song, not only will you smile and chuckle, but you will probably want to dance, too.

7. "Pretoria" – Smothers Brothers (1964)
"We are marching to Pretoria." I cheated on this one. This wasn't a single, but my brother-in-law Peter would have killed me if I didn't include at least one Smothers Brothers song. And this one is very funny!

8. "New Math" – Tom Lehrer (1965)
"So you have 13 tens, so you take away 7 and that leaves five, well six actually." While I am cheating, I included the brilliant singer-comedian Tom Lehrer with one of my favorites, "New Math" from his *That Was the Year That Was* album. Lehrer also had no singles probably because

his albums sold very nicely and included many really funny songs (e.g., "Pollution", "The Elements", "The Vatican Rag", to name just a few).

9. "Leader of the Laundromat" – The Detergents (#19 Jan. '65)
"My folks were always putting her down (down, down), because my laundry always came back brown." The ultimate parody song of the Shangrilas hit "Leader of the Pack", it even sounds like it was recorded in a laundromat!

10. "May the Bird of Paradise Fly Up Your Nose" – Little Jimmy Dickens (#5 Nov. '65)
"One fine day as I was a-walkin' down the street. Spied a beggar man with rags upon his feet. Took a penny from my pocket. In his tin cup I did drop it. I heard him say as I made my retreat 'May the bird of paradise fly up your nose, may an elephant caress you with his toes'..." Perhaps with inspiration from Johnny Carson and Carnac the Magnificent, this country song took insults to a pretty funny level.

11. "Wild Thing" – Senator Bobby (#20 Jan. '67)
"Ah you move me, yes...press ahead Wild Thing". A great Kennedy imitation by comedian Bill Minkin and some clever lines throughout make this a very funny song. The B-side is the same song except by Senator Everett Dirksen.

12. "Here Comes the Judge" – Shorty Long (#8 July '68)
"Can't dance? That'll be 90 days, 30 days for the boogaloo, 30 days to learn how to shing-a-ling, and 30 more for the Afro twist." Using the "here comes the judge" catchline from TV's *Rowan and Martin's Laugh-In*, Shorty Long developed a catchy and amusing song featuring the deep voice of the Spinners' Pervis Jackson as the judge. Sadly, Shorty drowned in a boating accident one year later.

13. "A Boy Named Sue" – Johnny Cash (#2 Aug. '69)
"My name is Sue, how do you do! Now you gonna die." This song is highlighted by Shel Silverstein's clever lyrics and the recording is live in front of a delighted San Quentin prison audience. Silverstein, who is perhaps best known for his popular children's books, also wrote several other excellent songs including "The Unicorn". But when it came to "A Boy Named Sue" only Johnny Cash could do justice singing his brilliant

lyrics such as *"kicking and gouging in the mud and the blood and the beer"*.

14. "Alice's Restaurant Massacree" – Arlo Guthrie (1967, charting later in a much shorter version "Alice's Rock & Roll Restaurant" (#97 Dec. '69))
"You can get everything you want at Alice's Restaurant." Hard to exclude one of the funniest shaggy dog stories/songs ever even though it was never a single. The fact that it was 18 minutes long of course had a lot to do with it, but even so it was played constantly on progressive FM stations during the late '60s/early '70s.

15. "Lola" – The Kinks (#9 Oct. '70)
"Girls will be boys and boys will be girls. It's a mixed up muddled up shook up world". Was it comedy, satire or were the Kinks simply way ahead of their time in 1970? Who can say, but my friends and I loved listening to it. Lola is representative of many excellent Kinks songs that range between biting satire and comedy.

16. "Deteriorata" – National Lampoon (#91 Oct. '72)
"You are a fluke of the universe, you have no right to be here but whether you can hear it or not, the universe is laughing behind your back." This is a very funny parody of Les Crane's "Desiderata" with the opposite message! National Lampoon has a number of funny parodies, but this was the only one to actually chart on *Billboard*. My favorite might be "Magical Misery Tour", a parody of John Lennon, which given that it used f-bombs every several words was not released as a single for an understandable reason (spelled FCC).

17. "Junk Food Junkie" – Larry Groce (#9 Mar. '76)
"In the daytime I'm Mr. Natural, just as healthy as I can be...but at night I'm a junk food junkie, good lord have pity on me." Groce's homage to "closet" junk food eaters (both figuratively AND literally) is superb and hysterical.

18. "King Tut" – Steve Martin (#17 July '78)
"Buried with a donkey, he's my favorite honky." Nothing beats watching Steve Martin performing this song on *SNL* in 1978 dressed as an ancient

Egyptian king, but the single is quite clever and timely as it coincided with the tour of the newly discovered King Tut treasures in the U.S.

19. "Another One Rides the Bus" – Weird Al Yankovich (#104 in '81)
"And another one on and another one off, another one rides the bus." The best of Weird Al's many parody songs was this very clever takeoff of "Another One Bites the Dust" by Queen. It was Yankovich's first song to make the charts (albeit "bubbling under" the top 100 Billboard charts at #104). It has the nice feature of being understated musically as well, with most of the music from Weird Al's accordion.

20. "Take Off" – Doug and Bob McKenzie (#16 Mar. '82)
"Take off to the great white north, take off, it's a beauty way to go." I always enjoy these two Canadians played by two Canadians in real life, Dave Thomas and Rick Moranis, both from *Second City TV* and later in a number of comic movie roles. Geddy Lee (lead vocalist of Rush) does a great job with the melody.

Honorable Mentions:
"Purple People Eater" – Sheb Wooley

"Snoopy vs. The Red Baron" – The Royal Guardsmen

Now "Politically Incorrect", Honorable Mentions:
"Big Bruce" – Steve Greenburg

"Basketball Jones" – Cheech and Chong

My Favorite Rock Instrumentals

While there have been many instrumentals during the rock era, there are only a few that qualify as "rock" or rockers. Many instrumentals are fully orchestrated with no percussion or drum track, let alone electric guitar and are much more sedate, such as "Theme from a Summer Place", "Love Theme from Romeo and Juliet", "Stranger on the Shore", "Love is Blue", etc. These are very nice instrumentals but hardly rockers.

Also, to be considered an instrumental, the song cannot contain any lyrics that are sung conventionally. So here is my list of 25 favorites from the 1960s and 1970s in chronological order:

1. "Walk, Don't Run" – Ventures (1960)
Perhaps the first true "rock" instrumental, it is mostly guitars and drums. It also was one of the first beach-rock songs.

2. "Nut Rocker" – B. Bumble and the Stingers (1962)
Emerson, Lake and Palmer also recorded a live version of "Nut Rocker". Both versions are wonderfully lively instrumentals. Nonetheless, both artists owe apologies to Tchaikovsky.

3. "Telstar" – Tornados (1962)
I love how this song features the fake sound of the Telstar satellite at the beginning and end. Also, it uses an electronic keyboard (either the clavioline or Univox) that gives it a very distinct sound.

4. "Wild Weekend" – Rockin' Rebels (1963)
This great beach rocker is fueled by a nice sax and guitar sound and is only surpassed by "Wipeout".

5. "Wipeout" – Surfaris (1963)
Lively drumming and spirited guitar playing make this the all-time beach rock classic.

6. "Java" – Al Hirt (1964)
Great trumpet playing made this a very lively instrumental. Sure, it's more jazz than rock, but this great song has to be on my list.

7. "The In Crowd" – Ramsey Lewis Trio (1965)
While also more of a jazz song than a rock song, it was upbeat enough with a rock beat to qualify and of course, it is a great song.

8. "A Taste of Honey" – Herb Alpert and the Tijuana Brass (1965)
Since I wasn't a regular listener of the radio yet, I first remember hearing this song before the previews at a movie theater and was instantly hooked.

9. "Soul Finger" – The Bar-Kays (1967)
The great horn section drives this song but it also includes a wonderful rhythm section. Though a bit jazzy, it qualifies as a rock instrumental under my admittedly subjective definition. (Though the kids in the background are yelling "Soul Finger", it still is an instrumental in my book.)

10. "Third Stone from the Sun" – Jimi Hendrix (1967)
This rare "instrumental" by Hendrix is from his first album and one of his better songs. It includes a spoken track that has been intentionally slowed down and describes a visit from an alien ship to Earth (if you speed up the turntable). This song narrowly edged out Hendrix's more well-known instrumental version of "The Star-Spangled Banner".

11. "Classical Gas" – Mason Williams (1968)
This is probably my favorite instrumental of the 1960s. I particularly liked Williams' merging of full orchestration with his acoustic guitar.

12. "Soulful Strut" – Young-Holt Unlimited (1968)
This great soul-jazz fusion song features great trumpet and keyboards and is just lively enough to count as a rockin' instrumental.

13. "Hawaii Five-O" – Ventures (1969)
The opening drumroll ushers in visions of a large wave cresting, followed by a wonderfully light, fast-paced instrumental. It is also the best TV show theme song ever!

14. "Overture from Tommy" – The Who (1969)
This lengthy introduction to the rock opera *Tommy* is perhaps my favorite rock instrumental. It features some brilliant acoustic guitar work by Townshend and French horn played by John Entwistle.

15. "Soul Sacrifice" – Santana (1969)
Played at Woodstock in 1969, this song is Santana's best instrumental. He still plays this very well in concert as I can attest to from seeing him in Las Vegas in 2017.

16. "Time Is Tight" – Booker T. and the MGs (1969)
Several are excellent by Booker T. but this is my favorite. The jazzier "Green Onions" is my next favorite, but not really a rocker.

17. "Glad" – Traffic (from *John Barleycorn Must Die*) (1970)
Traffic's most enduring album was spearheaded by this lively piano and saxophone-led instrumental.

18. "Joy" – Apollo 100 (1972)
This rockin' version of a well-known Bach piece was recorded by this British studio group.

19. "Outa-Space" – Billy Preston (1972)
This great R&B rocker by Billy Preston was his first big hit as a solo artist. Preston had served as a great studio musician, most notably credited on keyboards for several Beatles songs and albums. I actually got to see him in concert as part of the band backing up Eric Clapton about a decade ago and only months before Preston's death.

20. "Rock and Roll Part 2" – Gary Glitter (1972)
A largely unknown song when released, it became famous from its use during timeouts at basketball arenas during the 1980s.

21. "Also Sprach Zarathustra" – Deodato (1973)
This rock/jazzy version of a classical piece is best known as the unofficial theme to the movie *2001: A Space Odyssey*.

22. "Frankenstein" – Edgar Winter Group (1973)
This is a great rock instrumental that includes drum solos, wailing saxophone, Rick Derringer on guitar, and lots of synthesizer. I remember watching this performed on the *Midnight Special* TV show with Derringer playing a great guitar and Winter running around and playing just about everything else.

23. "Hocus Pocus" – Focus (1973)
Strange song from this Norwegian group that had one short electric guitar chorus strung together with verses that included whistling, scat singing and flute playing. Focus sings "bah-dee-yada, bah-dee-yada, bup bah!" before most of the choruses, but this is still an instrumental in my book.

24. "Jessica" – Allman Brothers (1973)
Other than diehard Allman fans, most everyone bought the *Brothers and Sisters* album for the hit song "Ramblin' Man" and this superb guitar-laden instrumental.

25. "Fire on High" – Electric Light Orchestra (from *Face the Music*) (1975)
This is a highly unusual rock instrumental to say the least, that included backwards talking, and a background of "Hallelujah Chorus". For more discussion, see the 1975 chapter in Section I.

Honorable Mentions:
"The Horse"- Cliff Nobles

"I Was Kaiser Bill's Batman" – Whistling Jack Smith
This is a rarity among popular songs, an all-whistling song. Didn't quite make the list, but would be #1 on my all- whistling song list.

"Feels So Good" – Chuck Mangione
This is a good song, but too overplayed in the late 1970s and not quite enough of a rocker to make the list.

Best B-sides (ex. The Beatles)
"Wham Bam Thank You Ma'am!"

When I first starting buying 45 rpm records or "singles", I had a very small record collection – a couple of Beatles albums and only a handful of singles. As a result, I played both the A-sides AND the B-sides despite the fact that these were usually throwaway songs by the group. This included unmemorable B-sides such as "Love Me Like Before" by Sam the Sham and the Pharaohs (A-side "Little Red Riding Hood"); "He Thinks He's a Hero" by The Happenings (A-side "See You in September"). In fact, it was rare, with the exception of The Beatles, that a B-side of a single was a good song. So naturally, I wondered what were my favorite B-sides of the 1960s and 1970s.

However, in order to avoid pure domination by The Beatles, I have created a separate Best Beatles B-sides list (see next list). Also, to avoid several entries by a few other key groups (e.g., The Rolling Stones, CCR and a few other artists on my list), I have limited it to no more than ONE song per artist. Also, in some cases, the original B-side out-charted the original A-side. Here, I use Joel Whitburn's definition where the B-side is the side that is less successful on the charts.

So herewith my 45 favorite (non-Beatles) B-sides of the 1960s and 1970s in order by the date it first charted as a B-side:

1. "Hello Mary Lou" – Ricky Nelson (A-side "Travelin' Man") May 1961
"Hello Mary Lou, goodbye heart." This B-side made the top 10 (reaching #9 in the U.S.) and is one of Ricky Nelson's very best and most recognizable songs. It is also one of the earliest pop songs I can remember hearing as a 6-year-old.

2. "Blue Bayou" – Roy Orbison (A-side "Mean Woman Blues") Sep. 1963
"Savin' nickels, savin' dimes. Workin' till the sun don't shine. Looking forward to happier times on blue bayou." This B-side was part of a double-sided hit by Orbison and in 1977 became a very popular hit song by Linda Ronstadt.

3. "Bad to Me" – Billy J. Kramer (A-side "Little Children") May 1964
"The birds in the sky would be sad and lonely if they knew that I lost my one and only, they'd be sad if you're bad to me." A classic love song penned by Lennon-McCartney, which is also Kramer's best song.

4. "A Change Is Gonna Come" – Sam Cooke (A-side "Shake") Jan. 1965
"It's been a long, a long time coming, but I know a change is gonna come, oh yes it will." Perhaps the most famous B-side ever written, it served as inspiration for the Civil Rights movement in 1965. By the time it had charted, however, Sam Cooke had been shot by a motel owner and died of his wounds on December 11, 1964.

5. "We've Got a Groovy Thing Going Baby" – Simon and Garfunkel (A-side "Sounds of Silence") Nov. 1965
"Bad news, bad news I hear you're packing to leave...oh baby baby, you must be out of your mind, do you know what you're kicking away?" It was hard to choose among the many, very good S&G B-sides. I like this one a lot, because it is an unusually up-tempo S&G song. Other great B-sides include "Flowers Never Bend", "Baby Driver", "59th Street Bridge Song", "The Only Living Boy in New York", "For Emily Whenever I Find Her", "April Come She Will", "Old Friends", and "Keep the Customer Satisfied".

6. "With a Girl Like You" – The Troggs (A-side "Wild Thing") June 1966
"I want to spend my life with a girl like you." I had an email exchange about this B-side with Lou Simon, host of Sirius XM Radio's *'60s Satellite Survey*. There were actually two B-sides for "Wild Thing", this one and another with a pretty mediocre song "From Home". Naturally, I bought the bad version, and Lou bought the good one.

7. "God Only Knows" – Beach Boys (A-side "Wouldn't It Be Nice") Aug. 1966
"God only knows what I'd be without you." This is one of the most beautiful love songs ever, also on the superb album *Pet Sounds*. The Beach Boys had a few other excellent B-sides, most notably "Little Deuce Coupe", "In My Room", and "Let Him Run Wild".

8. "I'm Not Your Steppin' Stone" – Monkees (A-side "I'm a Believer") Dec. 1966
"You're reading all those mod fashion magazines. The clothes you're wearing girl are causing public scenes." This cover of a Paul Revere and the Raiders song in early 1966 is not only the Monkees' best B-side, but is one of their best songs.

9. "Let's Spend the Night Together" – The Rolling Stones (A-side "Ruby Tuesday") Jan. 1967
"Now I need you more than ever." The Stones were forced to sing: "let's spend some *time* together" on the Ed Sullivan show owing to the song's explicit sexual message. How times have changed! The Stones also had a number of good B-sides, most notably "Bitch", "2000 Light Years from Home", "Lady Jane", and "You Can't Always Get What You Want". The last song would have been my first choice but for the much longer album version that is included in my "long song" list.

10. "There's No Stopping Us Now" – Supremes (A-side "Love Is Here and Now You're Gone") Jan. 1967
"There's no stopping us now, now that we found our way." The Supremes had a number of excellent B-sides including "Ask Any Girl", "Standing at the Crossroads of Love", and "Whisper You Love Me Boy". All could have been A-sides.

11. "No Milk Today" – Herman's Hermits (A-side "Kind of a Hush") Feb. 1967
"No milk today, my love is gone away, the bottle stands forlorn, a symbol of the dawn...How could they know just what this message means, the end of all my hopes, the end of all my dreams?" The lyrics refer to a note left out for the milkman not to deliver the usual bottle of milk, because "my love is gone away". An interesting song lyrically as well as musically, this is one of the Hermits' best songs.

12. "Crystal Ship" – Doors (A-side "Light My Fire") June 1967
"The days are bright and filled with pain, enclose me in your gentle rain."

13. "Hey Joe" – Jimi Hendrix (A-side "Foxey Lady") Dec. 1967
"Where you going with that gun in your hand?" A Hendrix classic is also a B-side.

14. "I Say a Little Prayer" – Dionne Warwick (A-side "Theme from the Valley of the Dolls") Jan. 1968
"The moment I wake up, before I put on my makeup..." Dionne's best song ever is only a B-side "technically". It originally was the A-side (and reached #4 on the charts in 1967) but then "Valley of the Dolls" became an even bigger hit in early 1968.

15. "Voices in the Sky" – Moody Blues (A-side "Ride My See Saw") Oct. 1968
"Bluebird, flying high, tell me what you'd say, if you could talk to me, what news would you bring, of voices in the sky." This is a beautiful song from one of my favorite groups, known primarily for their albums. "Candle of Life", "Melancholy Man", and "For My Lady" are very good B-sides as well.

16. "The Time It Is Today" – Association (A-side "Goodbye Columbus") Mar. 1969
"Sunrise, sunset, what you're born with is what you get." The Association waited until 1969 to release this excellent song from their fourth album (from early 1968) as a B-side.

17. "Everybody Is a Star" – Sly and the Family Stone (A-side "Thank You Falettinme Be Mice Elf Agin") Jan. 1970
"I love you for who you are, not the one you feel you need to be." Sly had several excellent B-sides such as "I Want to Take U Higher", "M-Lady", and "Stand", but my favorite is the upbeat and optimistic "Everybody is a Star".

18. "Who'll Stop the Rain" – Creedence Clearwater Revival (A-side "Travelin' Band") Jan. 1970
"And I wonder still I wonder who'll stop the rain?" Starting with "Bad Moon Rising/Lodi" in 1969, CCR had seven double-sided hits (i.e., both sides charted). Of these, "Who'll Stop the Rain" was my favorite B-side, but "Fortunate Son" and "Hey Tonight" were also excellent.

19. "No Sugar Tonight" – Guess Who (A-side "American Woman") Apr. 1970
"No sugar tonight in my coffee, no sugar tonight in my tea." The Guess Who also had another excellent B-side "Undun" (A-side "Laughing").

20. "Carry On" – Crosby, Stills, Nash & Young (A-side "Teach Your Children") June 1970
"Rejoice, rejoice, we have no choice, but to carry on...Carry on, love is coming, love is coming to us all." During its heyday, CSN and CSNY had SIX top 40 singles taken from its first two albums. The B-sides from five of these were from these same two albums and also included "Helplessly Hoping", "Helpless", "Long Time Gone", and "Déjà Vu".

21. "Colour My World" – Chicago (A-side "Make Me Smile" and "Beginnings") July 1970
"Colour my world with hope of loving you." The song is a rarity in that it appeared on two separate singles. In the second version with "Beginnings" as the A-side, the song received a lot of airplay on both FM and AM radio and became one of the more popular Chicago songs.

22. "Isn't It a Pity" – George Harrison (A-side "My Sweet Lord") Nov. 1970
"Isn't it a pity, now isn't it a shame, how we break each other's hearts, and cause each other pain?" It is no surprise that this B-side comes from *All Things Must Pass*, Harrison's first and best solo album.

23. "Take Me to the Pilot" – Elton John (A-side "Your Song") Nov. 1970
"Take me to the pilot for control, take me to the pilot of your soul." This is one of my favorite Elton songs and a great piano rocker. "Harmony" (A-side "Bennie and the Jets") is a close second.

24. "Miles from Nowhere" – Cat Stevens (A-side "Wild World") Feb. 1971
"Miles from nowhere, I guess I'll take my time, oh yeah, to reach there." This is not only Cat Stevens' best B-side, but it is one of his best songs.

25. "Sunny Skies" – James Taylor (A-side "Country Road") Feb. 1971
"You will be pleased to know that sunny skies hasn't a friend."

26. "I Feel the Earth Move" – Carole King (A-side "It's Too Late") June 1971
"I feel my heart start to trembling whenever you're around." This is Carole's best true rock song and a superlative B-side.

27. "Mandolin Wind" – Rod Stewart (A-side "I Know I'm Losing You") Nov. 1971

"Through the coldest winter in almost 14 years, I couldn't believe you kept a smile." One of several excellent songs from Rod Stewart's first solo album, this was my favorite B-side. Another B-side "Reason to Believe" is also good, but the fact that "Mandolin Wind" was a Stewart-penned song, rather than a cover of a Tim Hardin song made the difference.

28. "My Wife" – The Who (A-side "Behind Blue Eyes") Nov. 1971

"I ain't been home since Saturday night and now my wife is coming after me..." This classic song was written and sung by bass player John Entwistle and features outstanding lyrics. *"Give me police protection gotta find someone to look out for No. 1, give me a black-belt judo expert with a machine gun..."* Other very good Who B-sides include "Overture from Tommy" (which is on my best instrumental list) and "We're Not Gonna Take It", both from the album *Tommy*.

29. "Long Distance Runaround" – Yes (A-side "Roundabout") Feb. 1972

"I still remember the dream there, I still remember the time you said goodbye, did we really tell lies, letting in the sunshine, did we really count to one hundred."

30. "The Needle and the Damage Done" – Neil Young (A-side "Old Man") Apr. 1972

"I caught you knocking at my cellar door. I love you baby can I have some more? Ooh the damage done." This is an excellent anti-drug ballad. Interesting fact about Neil Young B-sides: three of his first four singles had the same B-side, "Sugar Mountain".

31. "Suffragette City" – David Bowie (A-side "Starman") July 1972

"Ohhh...wham bam thank you ma'am!" How is it even possible that this great Bowie song, my favorite by him, was only the B-side of "Starman"?

32. "Rockin' Down the Highway" – Doobie Brothers (A-side "Jesus is Just Alright") Dec. 1972

"I can't stop, gotta keep moving or I'll lose my mind, oh rockin' down the highway." The Doobies had several good B-sides, including "Black

Water" which was later put on a different single as an A-side and became their first #1 in early 1975.

33. "Dancing Days" - Led Zeppelin (A-side "Over the Hills and Far Away") June 1973
"You'll be only, my one and only, is that the way it should start?" Other excellent B-sides include "Living Loving Maid", "Misty Mountain Hop", "Hey, Hey What Can I Do?" and "Communication Breakdown", although almost all fans were buying Led Zeppelin albums and not Led Zeppelin singles at the time.

34. "Learn How to Fall" – Paul Simon (A-side "Loves Me Like a Rock") Aug. 1973
"You got to learn how to fall before you learn to fly."

35. "Too High" – Stevie Wonder (A-side "You Are the Sunshine of My Life") Aug. 1973
"I'm too high, but I ain't touched the sky." This was a tough choice for me since "Visions", "Big Brother", and "He's Misstra Know It All" are also very good B-sides.

36. "Nineteen Hundred and Eighty Five" – Paul McCartney (A-side "Band on the Run") Apr. 1974
"No one ever left alive in 1985 will ever do." This song is carried by McCartney's great piano playing and his stellar voice. McCartney usually saved his better compositions for his albums rather than B-sides. How else can one explain such B-sides as "C-Moon" and "Cook of the House"?

37. "Kow Kow Calqulator" – Steve Miller Band (A-side "Living in the U.S.A.") May 1974
"Turn on your love light, let it shine." Before the Steve Miller Band became quite popular in late 1973 with "The Joker", they produced five interesting blues-psychedelic rock fusion albums during 1968-1972. "Kow Kow Calqulator" is one of those gems from these early albums that found its way onto the second single release of "Living in the U.S.A.".

38. "10538 Overture" – Electric Light Orchestra (A-side "Evil Woman") Nov. 1975
"Did you see your friend crying from his eyes today?" This is the first song by ELO to receive much airplay from their first album in early 1972 and showcases the multiple layers of orchestration that would become their trademark. However, the song wasn't a B-side until "Evil Woman" was released as a single.

39. "She's the One" – Bruce Springsteen (A-side "Tenth Avenue Freeze Out") Jan. 1976
"And if there is somebody calling me on, she's the one." The best of Springsteen's '70s B-sides, but Bruce had only four singles in the '70s so hardly a big song list.

40. "Shine On" – Peter Frampton (A-side "Show Me the Way") Feb. 1976
"Shine on, shine on me, shine on you." Peter Frampton's triple album *Frampton Comes Alive* represented the pinnacle of his brief popularity during 1976-78. This B-side might well be the best song from the whole album.

41. "Monday Morning" – Fleetwood Mac (A-side "Say You Love Me") July 1976
"I've got nothing but love for you, tell me what you really want to do."

42. "Victim of Love" – Eagles (A-side "New Kid in Town") Dec. 1976
"What kind of love have you got? You should be home but you're not." I was surprised when I learned that "Victim of Love" wasn't a single on its own as it is better than its A-side.

43. "We Will Rock You" – Queen (A-side "We Are the Champions") Oct. 1977
"You got mud on your face, you big disgrace, kicking your can all over the place." This was a true double-sided hit in that the album has the two songs segued together and radio stations always played them together.

44. "Black Cow" – Steely Dan (A-side "Josie") Aug. 1978
"I can't cry anymore while you run around. Break away. Just when it seems so clear that it's over now, drink your big black cow and get out of

here." "Black Cow" is a great upbeat "breakup" song and the clear-cut best of several good Steely Dan B-sides.

45. "All Mixed Up" – Cars (A-side "Good Times Roll") Mar. 1979
"She tricks me into thinking, I can't believe my eyes. I wait for her forever, but she never does arrive... She's always making pictures. She's always making scenes. She's always out the window when it comes to making dreams. It's all mixed up... She says to leave it to me, everything will be alright." From the Cars' first and best album, this is a song about a failing relationship written by Ric Ocasek. It features a great vocal from bass player, Benjamin Orr.

Best Beatles B-Sides
"Don't You Know It's Gonna Be Alright"

The Beatles had so many great songs that it is no surprise that they alone have an excellent list of B-sides. As I listened to them, 20 B-sides emerged as my favorites. However, since I found them almost impossible to rank, I used the excellent book by Spignesi and Lewis, *100 Best Beatles Songs: An Informed Fans Guide,* to do so. So, here are my 20 favorite Beatles B-sides with the first 14 ordered by their rank in Spignesi and Lewis:

1. **"Strawberry Fields Forever"** (A-side "Penny Lane") (#2 in *100 Best*)

2. **"Revolution"** (A-side "Hey Jude") (#9 in *100 Best*)

3. **"I Am the Walrus"** (A-side "Hello Goodbye") (#11 in *100 Best*)

4. **"Eleanor Rigby"** (A-side "Yellow Submarine") (#27 in *100 Best*)

5. **"Something"** (A-side "Come Together") (#28 in *100 Best*)

6. **"Day Tripper"** (A-side "We Can Work It Out") (#32 in *100 Best*)

7. **"This Boy"** (A-side "All My Loving") (#43 in *100 Best*)

8. **"If I Fell"** (A-side "And I Love Her") (#46 in *100 Best*)

9. **"I Should Have Known Better"** (A-side "A Hard Day's Night") (#55 in *100 Best*)

10. **"Baby, You're a Rich Man"** (A-side "All You Need is Love") (#61 in *100 Best*)

11. **"Don't Let Me Down"** (A-side "Get Back") (#83 in *100 Best*)

12. **"I Saw Her Standing There"** (A-side "I Want to Hold Your Hand") (#84 in *100 Best*)

13. "I'm Happy Just to Dance With You" (A-side "I'll Cry Instead") (#87 in *100 Best*)

14. "Rain" (A-side "Paperback Writer") (#93 in *100 Best*)

15. "She's a Woman" (A-side "I Feel Fine")

16. "I'm Down" (A-side "Help!")

17. "P.S. I Love You" (A-side "Love Me Do")

18. "You Can't Do That" (A-side "Can't Buy Me Love")

19. "From Me to You" (A-side "Please Please Me")

20. "Act Naturally" (A-side "Yesterday")

Best Long Songs
"Take a Sad Song and Make It Better"

Perhaps the most famous songs in the history of rock are the so-called rock anthems, songs that define rock groups and artists. Not surprisingly many of these songs are long, in some cases eight minutes or more. So it got me thinking about my favorite "long" rock songs. First, I had to define what a "long" song is. I looked at my iTunes library of rock and popular songs (about 10,000+) and determined a good cutoff was six minutes. Less than that and there were too many songs; much more than that and some excellent, lengthy songs would be excluded. Second, I placed a limit of only one song per artist. This was to avoid having the list being dominated by a few groups (e.g., Yes, Led Zeppelin, The Who, Rolling Stones, etc.). Also, rock instrumentals are NOT included (see "Best Instrumentals" chapter).

So what are the best long songs? Here is my list of my 20 favorites from the 1960s (and late 1950s) and my 30 favorites from the 1970s in approximate order.

1960s

1. "Light My Fire" – Doors (1967) – 7:07. *"The time to hesitate is thru, no time to wallow in the mire, try now we could only lose and our love become a funeral pyre."* Close behind by the Doors: "Riders on the Storm" and "L.A. Woman" from 1971.

2. "Hey Jude" – Beatles (1968) – 7:10. *"Take a sad song and make it better."* Hands down the best by The Beatles, who did only a few "long" songs. "I Want You (She's So Heavy)" gets honorable mention.

3. "You Can't Always Get What You Want" – Rolling Stones (1969) – 7:16. *"But if you try some time, you just might find you get what you need."* This is my clear-cut favorite by the Stones, though there are several other great ones including "Midnight Rambler" and "Sympathy for the Devil".

4. **"Legend of a Mind" – Moody Blues (1968)** – 6:37. *"He'll fly his astral plane, take you trips around the bay."* "Nights in White Satin" is a very close second!

5. **"Like a Rolling Stone" – Bob Dylan (1965)** – 6:10. *"How does it feel to be on your own, with no direction shown, like a complete unknown, like a rolling stone."* The master of many long rock songs with plentiful lyrics, this song is ultimately his most famous and his best.

6. **"Down by the River" – Neil Young (1969)** – 9:00. *"Down by the river, I shot my lady, down by the river, dead, ooh, shot her dead."* "Cowgirl in the Sand" is also quite good, but this is my favorite song by Neil, featuring a very lengthy guitar jam that never gets boring.

7. **"What'd I Say" – Ray Charles (1959)** – 6:28. *"Tell your mom, tell your pop, I'm gonna send you back to Arkansas."* This classic from 1959 is my favorite long song by a soul/R&B artist. It neatly links an instrumental first half featuring some great keyboards and a vocal second half.

8. **"Sky Pilot" – Animals (1968)** – 7:30. *"How high can you fly, you'll never, never reach the sky."*

9. **"Alice's Restaurant" – Arlo Guthrie (1967)** – 18:37. *"Officer, I cannot tell a lie, I put that envelope under that garbage."*

10. **"Beginnings" – Chicago (1969)** – 6:27. *"Only the beginning, only just the start."* I love the percussion ending to this song.

11. **"You Keep Me Hangin' On" – Vanilla Fudge (1968)** – 7:20. *"Let me get over you the way you gotten over me."* This great rock version of the Supremes song nicely changes the pacing and the instrumentation of the original.

12. **"Court of the Crimson King" – King Crimson (1969)** – 9:26. *"The rusted chains of prison moons are shattered by the sun."* "Epitaph" and "21st Century Schizoid Man" are also excellent long songs. Too bad Greg Lake then left King Crimson.

13. "Had to Cry Today" – Blind Faith (1969) – 8:48. If you like Eric Clapton and Steve Winwood on dueling guitars, you will love this song.

14. "Time Has Come Today" – Chambers Brothers (1968) – 11:07. *"Now the time has come, no chance to realize."* The song is great and admittedly this long version feels a bit endless, but it made such an excellent background to the climactic scene in the Jane Fonda movie *Coming Home* that it had to be on my list.

15. "I Heard It Through the Grapevine" (album version) – Creedence Clearwater Revival (1969) – 8:37. Near tie: "Suzie Q" (album version).

16. "I'm So Glad" (live) – Cream (1969) – 9:13. Arguably, Cream was the first group (along with the Doors) to make long jam songs popular. This is their best example, though "Toad" and "Spoonful" from their *Wheels of Fire* album are also very good.

17. "Fingertips Pts. 1 and 2" – Stevie Wonder (1963) – 6:53. *"Everybody say Yeh!"* The short version (Fingertips Pt. 2) is much better known and very good, but I love hearing even more harmonica from the 12-year-old genius in this lengthier version.

18. "Season of the Witch" – Al Kooper/Stephen Stills/Mike Bloomfield (1968) – 11:04. The highlight of the *Super Session* album was this lengthy version of the Donovan song. I used to play this album/song a lot while learning to touch-type to reduce the boredom. Really!

19. "Voodoo Chile" – Jimi Hendrix (1968) – 14:59. This nearly 15-minute Hendrix jam is his best long song. Though not one of my favorites by him, this jam session certainly showcases his talents and that of several backup musicians including Steve Winwood.

20. (Tie) "MacArthur Park" – Richard Harris (1968) – 7:26. *"And I'll never have the recipe again, Oh no!"* This song is saved by wonderful orchestration, but Harris' vocals and the song lyrics can become a bit much and even comical if you are in the right mood. Nonetheless, I still enjoyed it.

20. (Tie) "In-A-Gadda-Da-Vida" – Iron Butterfly (1968) – 17:03. Certainly one of the first "famous" long songs, this unmistakable guitar riff is played almost continuously (and often interminably) for the entire 17-minute length. I bought the album but other than the title track barely listened to it. I'll admit this is only on my list because it is either a famous or infamous part of rock history.

1970s

1. "Stairway to Heaven" – Led Zeppelin (1971) – 8:00. *"There's a lady that knows all that glitters is gold."* What can be said about this song that hasn't already been said.

2. "Layla" – Derek and the Dominoes (1970) – 7:04. *"You got me on my knees!"* This two-part song is one of the all-time best with Part 1 including Clapton's great vocal and Part 2 including Clapton's guitar jam along with a great, stately organ solo.

3. "Funeral for a Friend/Love Lies Bleeding" (1973) – Elton John – 11:08. ("Tiny Dancer" and "Someone Saved My Life Tonight" are almost as good.) This is possibly the best piece of music that Elton ever recorded.

4. "Roundabout" – Yes (1971) – 8:32. *"In and around the lake, mountains come out of the sky, they stand there."* This is my favorite by the group with many others, e.g., "America", "And You and I", "Heart of the Sunrise", "Yours Is No Disgrace", "I've Seen All Good People", and "Starship Trooper" not far behind.

5. "Won't Get Fooled Again" – The Who (1971) – 8:31. *"Meet the new boss same as the old boss."* This is the best by The Who and a rock classic. However, "Who Are You" is a close second.

6. "Hotel California" – Eagles (1976) – 6:28. *"On a dark desert highway, cool wind in my hair."* Many consider this rock's greatest song. I wouldn't go quite that far, but it is certainly close.

7. "I'm Your Captain" – Grand Funk Railroad (1970) – 10:04. *"I'm getting closer to my home."* Hands down, the best song the group ever did.

8. "American Pie" – Don McLean (1971) – 8:37. *"Now for ten years we've been on our own, but moss grows fast on a rolling stone."* There has never been a longer rock allegory than "American Pie".

9. "Aqualung" – Jethro Tull (1971) – 6:33. *"Sitting on a park bench, eyeing little girls with bad intent."* The master of long songs/jams, including full 20-minute sides of the album *Thick as a Brick*, "Aqualung" is still his best.

10. "Trilogy (Lovin' Me, To Make a Woman Feel Wanted, Peace of Mind)" – Loggins and Messina (1972) – 11:14. *"You don't need change in your pocket, you don't need soles on your shoes, to make a woman feel wanted."* "Angry Eyes" is also great.

11. "Free Bird" – Lynyrd Skynyrd (1973) – 9:10. *"And this bird you cannot change."* This is perhaps the most famous guitar jam song ever.

12. "Foreplay/Long Time" – Boston (1976) – 7:49. *"It's been such a long time, I think I will be going."*

13. "Papa Was a Rolling Stone" – Temptations (1972) – 6:58. *"It was the third of September, a day I'll always remember."* The instrumental 2-minute lead-in to this song is BRILLIANT, but the song itself is also great.

14. "Jungleland" – Bruce Springsteen (1975) – 9:34. *"The hungry and the hunted, explode into rock n' roll bands."* "Rosalita" a near miss.

15. "Roll Over Beethoven" – Electric Light Orchestra (1973) – 8:09. What a fabulous cover of the Chuck Berry song! ELO pulls out all the stops on this one.

16. "Low Spark of High Heeled Boys" – Traffic (1971) – 11:44. This is the quintessential jazz-jam song, loosely constructed around the recurring *"low spark of high-heeled boys"* vocal. What can I say? I love Steve Winwood!

17. "Green Grass and High Tides" – Outlaws (1975) – 9:52. *"Green grass and high tides forever."* This country-rock jam song is very catchy and has some excellent guitar playing.

18. "Paradise by the Dashboard Light" – Meat Loaf (1977) – 8:29. *"Stop right there I gotta know right now! Before you go any further do you love me?..."* The duet singing of Meat Loaf and Ellen Foley is the highlight of this song. And any song that manages to include baseball-style 'play-by-play' commentary of sexual activity by Phil Rizzuto has to be on my list.

19. "Life's Been Good" – Joe Walsh (1978) – 8:56. *"I lost my license, now I don't drive."* Walsh's excellent song about being a rock star is probably more autobiographical than he would care to admit.

20. "Wreck of the Edmund Fitzgerald" – Gordon Lightfoot (1976) – 6:29. *"At 7 PM, the main hatchway gave in, he said 'fellas it's been good to know you'."* This is the best long song that tells a historical story. In this case, it is the story of the wreck of a ship carrying iron ore on its way to Cleveland during a hellacious, early winter storm. The ship sank in Lake Superior near Whitefish Point, Michigan on November 10, 1975.

21. "Us and Them" – Pink Floyd (1973) – 7:49. It's hard to choose among Pink Floyd's great long songs. I could easily have picked "Time", "Comfortably Numb", "Money", or "Shine on You Crazy Diamond", depending on my mood.

22. "Scenes from an Italian Restaurant" – Billy Joel (1977) – 7:33. *"Bottle of white, bottle of red, perhaps a bottle of rose instead."* Love the way this song starts slowly as the two former lovers meet in the restaurant, then speeds up as they reminisce, becomes frenetic when they talk about Brenda and Eddie, and then finally winds down as they finish their meal. It's a mini rock opera in one song.

23. "Taxi" – Harry Chapin (1972) – 6:43. *"Me I'm driving in my taxi, taking tips and getting stoned."* "Taxi" is one of the most famous long lyrical songs. It's sad (the story of two former lovers meeting by chance), yet I never seem to tire hearing it.

24. "Aja" – Steely Dan (1977) – 8:00. *"Aja, when all my dime dancing is thru, I run to you."* I particularly love the instrumental Far Eastern sound that permeates this song.

25. "Running Hard" – Renaissance (1974) – 9:37. *"Towards what used to be. Losing ground in changes sliding endlessly."* Great opening piano solo and Annie Haslam's beautiful vocals makes this my favorite song by Renaissance. It also opened their concert that I attended in the Felt Forum in NYC in 1977.

26. "White Bird" – It's a Beautiful Day (1972) – 6:12. *"White bird in a golden cage on winter's day in the rain."* The group's unique sound was powered by excellent violin playing by David LaFlamme, his wife Linda on keyboards, and lead vocalist Patti Santos.

27. "Green Eyed Lady" – Sugarloaf (1970) – 6:51 *"Green eyed lady, ocean lady, soothing every wave that comes."* I love this song even in its lengthier album version.

28. "Celluloid Heroes" – Kinks (1972) – 6:22. *"You can see all the stars as you walk down Hollywood Boulevard..."*

29. "Do You Feel Like We Do" – Peter Frampton (1976) – 14:18.

30. "Highway Song" – Aztec Two-Step (1972) – 6:38. This is a classic, folk-rock song that always makes me a bit sad.

Honorable Mentions:
"Trilogy" – Emerson, Lake & Palmer – 8:52.

"Highway Star" – Deep Purple – 6:08.

"Give It to Me" – J. Geils Band – 6:30.

Best Rockin' Love Songs
"And You Know You Should Be Glad"

While most people talk about their favorite love songs, they think of slow, romantic songs from the likes of Streisand and Sinatra. However, I decided to compile my favorite love songs in an unconventional manner. I wondered what the best songs were with "love", "loving", etc. in the title AND which were up-tempo rock songs. In other words, there are no slow songs on this list (apologies to those who were hoping to find "Love is Blue", "To Sir With Love", "My Love", "And I Love Her", "Love (Can Make You Happy)", etc.).

To keep this list manageable, I have limited it to only one song per artist. Also, there are no soul and R&B songs on the list, so apologies to the Supremes (e.g., "Love Child", "Love Is Here and Now You're Gone", "Baby Love", "You Can't Hurry Love"), Four Tops ("Standing in the Shadows of Love"), Stevie Wonder ("I Was Made to Love Her"), The Jackson 5 ("The Love You Save") or The O'Jays ("Love Train"). So here are my favorite rockin' love songs from the '60s and '70s in chronological order:

1. "Do You Love Me" – Contours (1962)
"Do you love me, now that I can dance?" One of the earliest Motown R&B songs is on the list because it is one of the earliest rock songs as well. Featured in the movie *Dirty Dancing*, this is one of my all-time favorites.

2. "Baby, I Love You" – Ronettes (1963)
"Have I ever told you how good it feels to hold you?" I'll admit this is a stretch as a "rock" song, but it is the Ronettes and I had to have one girl group hit on my list. (Andy Kim's version is more of a rocker for those who are purists).

3. "She Loves You" – Beatles (1964)
"She loves you and you know you should be glad." The Beatles had several excellent rockin' love songs which also included "Can't Buy Me Love", "All My Loving", and "All You Need is Love". But the fast-paced "She Loves You" is one of my favorites by them so it gets the nod.

4. "For Your Love" – Yardbirds (1965)
"I'll bring you diamond rings and things right to your door." This is the best Yardbirds song and a great rock song.

5. "Good Lovin'" – Young Rascals (1966)
"Doctor, Mr. MD, can you tell me what's ailing me." The Rascals' harder rock arrangement of this Olympics song from 1965 might be their best song ever.

6. "Gimme Some Lovin'" – Spencer Davis Group (1967)
"So glad you made it, so glad you made it, you got to gimme some lovin'." This is one of my favorite Winwood songs and rock songs in general and the first of many excellent songs by him over his career.

7. "Somebody to Love" – Jefferson Airplane (1967)
"You better find somebody to love." Jefferson Airplane's first hit was probably what I had in mind when I created this rockin' love song list.

8. "Sunshine of Your Love" – Cream (1967)
"I'll soon be with you my love, give you my dawn surprise." Cream's most popular song is a great rockin' love song.

9. "I Love You" – People (1968)
"Yes I do, but the words won't come." While this is a fairly simple, pop-rock song, for some reason I like it a lot. Maybe it's because of the psychedelic sounding intro with a building guitar riff. More likely I was prescient, because the group was from San Jose only 20 miles from where I would meet my future wife.

10. "Will You Love Me Tomorrow" – Four Seasons (1968)
"So tell me now so I won't ask again." This cover of the Shirelles hit is excellent because it turned a pop girl group song into more of a rock-'n'-roll song.

11. "Whole Lotta Love" – Led Zeppelin (1969)
"Way down inside, honey you and me, I'm gonna give you my love." This quintessential hard rock song began Zeppelin's popular career. "All My Love" is also a good Zeppelin hard rocker.

12. "Love the One You're With" – Stephen Stills (1970)
"If you're down and confused and you don't remember who you're talking to." This is the best and arguably the only really good song in Stills' solo career.

13. "I'd Love to Change the World" – Ten Years After (1971)
"Everywhere theres freaks and hairies." I love the guitar line in this hard rocker.

14. "Looking for a Love" – J. Geils Band (1971)
"Looking everywhere. Looking for a love to call my own". This is the first single and noteworthy song from this Boston group. Sadly, the excellent "Love Stinks" released in 1980 is a few months too late to qualify for this list.

15. "Love Her Madly" – Doors (1971)
"Don't you love her as she's walking out the door, like she did one thousand times before." This is my favorite of the Doors' love songs that also includes "Hello, I Love You" and "Love Me Two Times".

16. "When You Dance I Can Really Love" – Neil Young (1971)
"When you dance, do your senses tingle and take a chance." From Neil's second solo album *After the Gold Rush*, it is definitely his most rockin' love song and a favorite of mine.

17. "Love Reign O'er Me" – The Who (1973)
"Like the sweat of lovebirds laying in the field."

18. "Radar Love" – Golden Earring (1974)
"We got a thing that's called radar love." This hard rock group hailed from The Hague, Netherlands.

19. "Love Is the Drug" – Roxy Music (1975)
"And I need to score." This art-rock British group perhaps heralded in the new wave of the late 1970s with this hit.

20. "When Will I Be Loved" – Linda Ronstadt (1975)
"I've been cheated, been mistreated." This is a great country-rock cover of the Everly Brothers hit and is one of my favorites by Ronstadt.

21. "Say You Love Me" – Fleetwood Mac (1976)
"Guess I'm not as strong as I used to be, and if you use me again it'll be the end of me."

22. "Victim of Love" – Eagles (1976)
"What kind of love have you got? You should be home but you're not." This song was one of the first hard rock songs by the group featuring new arrival Joe Walsh.

23. "Jungle Love" – Steve Miller Band (1977)
"It's driving me mad, it's making me crazy." One of Steve Miller's best up-tempo rockers is also one of my favorites.

24. "Bye Bye Love" – Cars (1978)
"It's an orangy sky. Always it's some other guy. It's just a broken lullaby." This is a great new wave rocker!

25. "I Need a Lover" – John Cougar Mellencamp (1979)
"Who won't drive me crazy." Mellencamp's hardest rock song was his first and only single from the 1970s.

Best Numeric or Alphanumeric Songs
"1-2-3"

I have always liked numbers, enjoyed math and statistics. As a kid, I gravitated to the city of Digitopolis in *The Phantom Tollbooth*. So it is probably no surprise that I wondered what are the best songs with numbers in their titles, either numeric or alphanumeric. For this list, I expanded my timeframe from 1955 to 1989 and occasionally later decades. I excluded "Part 1" and "Part 2" as numbered songs. So herewith are my favorites in "numeric" order with special attention in making sure to fill in at least one song from #1 through #30 (though I failed to find a #29 song):

1. TIE: "You're the One" – The Vogues (1965); "One" – Three Dog Night (1969) *"One is the loneliest number that you'll ever do"*; **"Revolution #1" – The Beatles (1968)**
There are numerous songs that mention "One". Accordingly, I have a three-way tie for my favorite. Several other good ones include "I'm One" by The Who, "One Way Out" by the Allman Brothers, "One Way or Another" by Blondie, "One of These Nights" by the Eagles, and "One Fine Day" by the Chiffons.

2. "Love Me Two Times" – The Doors (1968)
"Love me twice today...One for tomorrow and one just for today."
Honorable Mentions: "Two of Us" by The Beatles; "Two Divided By Love" by The Grassroots; "Two Faces Have I" by Lou Christie.

3. "1-2-3" – Len Barry (1965)
Honorable Mention: "Quarter to Three" by Gary U.S. Bonds; Dishonorable Mentions: "Knock Three Times" by Dawn; "1, 2, 3 Red Light" by 1910 Fruitgum Co.

4. "Positively 4th Street" – Bob Dylan (1965)
"You've got a lot of nerve to say you are my friend, when I was down you just stood there grinning". My second favorite song by Dylan is also the best "four" song, but nary a mention of the "4th" or the title in the lyrics.

5. "Five O'Clock World" – The Vogues (1965)
"It's a five o'clock world when the whistle blows, no one owns a piece of my time." Honorable Mentions: "5D (Fifth Dimension)" by The Byrds; "Five to One" by The Doors.

6. "Six O'Clock" – Lovin' Spoonful (1967)
"There's something special about six o'clock, in the morning when it's too early to knock." Honorable Mention: "Six Man Band" by the Association.

7. "Seven Rooms of Gloom" – The Four Tops (1967)
Honorable Mention: "Seven Bridges Road" by the Eagles.

8. TIE: "Eight Days a Week" – The Beatles (1965) *"Is not enough to show I care"*; **"Eight Miles High" – The Byrds (1965)** *"And when you touch down, you'll find it is stranger than known."*

9. TIE: "Cloud Nine" – Temptations (1968) *"I'm doing fine on cloud nine"*; **"Love Potion #9" – The Searchers (1964)**
Honorable Mentions include "Karn Evil 9" by Emerson, Lake and Palmer; "#9 Dream" by John Lennon, though neither song ever mentions "9" in the lyrics.

10. "3/5 of a Mile in 10 Seconds" – Jefferson Airplane (1967) *"Know I love you baby yes I do."* This song is my favorite non-single by the Jefferson Airplane, a great rocker.

Honorable Mention: "Ten Commandments of Love" by Harvey and the Moonglows**.** I had to go back to 1958 to find this song, the ONLY top 40 "ten" song I could find.

The Beach Boys also had a rendition of "Ten Little Indians" which made #49 in late 1962, but is sufficiently bad that it doesn't warrant inclusion.

11. "11 O'Clock Tick Tock" – U2 (1980)
"Hear the children crying, I know it's time to go." A nice album cut from U2's 1980 debut album was all I could find for "11". And it never mentions "11".

12. "Twelve-Thirty" – Mamas and Papas (1967)
"Outside my window was a steeple, with a clock that always said 12:30."

13. "13 Question Method" – Chuck Berry (1961)
"Is the one to use when you want to go have some fun" This is an interesting Chuck Berry song from 1961, but not a charting single so not very well known.

14. "14" – Paula Cole (2007)
"But I was 14 with my passion and 15 with my best and 16 with ego and zero with the rest." I "discovered" Paula Cole while researching this list and enjoy this 2007 song. And I sure couldn't find anything else.

15. TIE: "5:15" – The Who (1973) *"Inside, outside, Where have I been? Out of my brain on the 5:15"*; **"15" – Taylor Swift (2008)**
The first is a gem from *Quadrophenia* and one of the best songs The Who ever recorded. The second is a purer "fifteen" song from 2008. I put this one on the list to make my daughters happy (and show that their Dad is up with more current music).

16. "16 Candles" – The Crests (1959)
"You're only sixteen, but you're my teenage queen." This 1959 song is a doo-wop classic! Honorable Mentions: "Sixteen Tons" by Tennessee Ernie Ford; "Happy Birthday, Sweet Sixteen" by Neil Sedaka.

17. TIE: "Edge of Seventeen" – Stevie Nicks (1982) *"just like the white winged dove"*; **"Opus 17 (Don't You Worry 'Bout Me)" – Four Seasons (1966)** *"I can see there ain't no room for me."*

The former is Nicks' best solo effort. The latter song is one of my favorites by the Four Seasons, but like several others on this list doesn't ever mention the title. Honorable Mention: "At Seventeen" by Janis Ian.

18. "Eighteen" – Alice Cooper (1971)
"I'm in the middle without any plans, I'm a boy and I'm a man." This is Alice Cooper's best song, released when I was still 17.

19. TIE: "19th Nervous Breakdown" – Rolling Stones (1966); "Hey Nineteen" – Steely Dan (1980)

20. "Twentieth Century Boy" – T. Rex (1973)
"Well it's plain to see you were meant for me, I'm your boy, your twentieth century toy." Honorable Mention: "20th Century Fox" by The Doors. These are both excellent album cuts.

21. "21st Century Schizoid Man" – King Crimson (1969)
"Cat's foot iron claw. Neuro-surgeons scream for more. At paranoia's poison door. Twenty first century schizoid man..." I rest my case.

22. "22" – Taylor Swift (2013)
"I don't know about you, but I'm feeling 22." See discussion for #15. It's hard not to enjoy Taylor Swift's music. Maybe if I wait a few decades Taylor will fill in all my missing numbers.

23. "Strawberry Letter #23" – Brothers Johnson (1977)
"A present from you, Strawberry Letter 22. The music plays, I sit in for a few." What a great song! I love the harmonies and the backing instrumental tracks. Twenty-three is not mentioned because the song itself is "Strawberry Letter #23".

24. "4 + 20" – Crosby, Stills, Nash & Young (1970)
This is just one of the many great tracks from the *Déjà Vu* album. Do the math!

25. TIE: "25 or 6 to 4" – Chicago (1970); "Twenty-Five Miles" – Edwin Starr (1969)
Chicago's best song and Edwin Starr's other big hit.

26. "26 Miles (Santa Catalina)" – The Four Preps (1958)
This #2 song is a nice folk tune, albeit not particularly well known except among folk song enthusiasts.

27. "27" – Fall Out Boy (2003)
I like this 2003 hit, a nice upbeat 21st century rock song. I can just see them saying, "Dad is so cool!"

28. "Twenty-Eight" – The Weeknd (2011)
I just discovered this Canadian alternative R&B song researching this list of numbered songs. It's pretty good.

30. "Thirty Days"- Chuck Berry (1955)
"I'm gonna give you thirty days to get back home." Send more Chuck Berry!

31. "Thirty-One Flavors" – Shirelles (1963)
Only big Shirelles fans (such as yours truly) know this song, let alone own it. (It only made #97 on the charts in 1963). This song was featured in the movie *It's a Mad, Mad, Mad, Mad World* but since I saw it when I was 9, I don't remember that, or much else about the movie. *"Peach, banana, coconut too..."*

35. "Rainy Day Women #12 and 35" – Bob Dylan (1966)
Also on the "rain" song list, this song doesn't mention its title in the lyrics.

40. "Forty Miles of Bad Road" – Duanne Eddy (1959)
This country and western/rock-'n'-roll guitarist has a great twangy sound and produced many excellent instrumentals during the late 1950s/early 1960s. He is considered early rock-'n'-roll's #1 instrumentalist. This was one of his three top tens, along with "Rebel Rouser" and "Because They're Young".

41. "Forty-One Days" – Boozoo Chavis (1991)
While this 1991 single never charted, this zydeco musician (Creole music from southwestern Louisiana) played the accordion and sang songs that became zydeco standards. My god, look what I have learned by undertaking this list!

42. "Forty Two" – The Afters (2008)

49. "Funk #49" – James Gang (1970)
This song featured Joe Walsh's familiar guitar sound and is a classic rock staple, but no mention of #49 in the song.

50. "Fifty Ways to Leave Your Lover" – Paul Simon (1976)
"Hop on the bus, Gus."

55. "I Can't Drive 55" – Sammy Hagar (1984)
Was Hagar responsible for getting speed limits changed back to 65? Interestingly, less than three years after this song the federal maximum speed limit was raised to 65 for most limited access highways.

59. "59th Street Bridge Song (Feelin' Groovy)" – Harpers Bizarre (1967)/Simon and Garfunkel (1966)
"Slow down you move too fast, you've got to make the morning last". This is one of those cases where I like the cover as much as the original Simon and Garfunkel song.

60. "Sixty Years On" – Elton John (1970)
"Who'll walk me down to church when I'm sixty years of age..." This is an excellent song from Elton's breakthrough album, but 60 must have seemed really old then!

64. "When I'm Sixty-Four" – The Beatles (1967)
"Will you still need me, will you still feed me, when I'm sixty-four." I sure hope so! Sixty-four is only about a year away for me.

65. "'65 Love Affair" – Paul Davis (1982)
"You sang do wop diddy wop diddy wop doo" I think Paul Davis has a very different recollection of music in 1965 than I do.

66. "Route 66 Theme" – Nelson Riddle (1962)
I confess I don't really remember this theme song or TV show from 1962. It was past my bedtime then.

67&68. "Questions 67 & 68" – Chicago (1969)
"Can this feeling that we have together suddenly exist between?" This two-fer is from Chicago's first album from 1969.

69. "Summer of '69" – Bryan Adams (1985)
"Those were the best days of my life."

75. "20-75" – Willie Mitchell (1964)
This R&B keyboardist from Memphis led the house band in a number of instrumentals and later became President of Hi Records. His best-known song is "Soul Serenade" (#23 in 1968), but this one isn't bad and also made the top 40. The title is the label number.

90. "30-60-90"- Willie Mitchell (1969)

96. "96 Tears" – ? & The Mysterians (1966)
"Too many teardrops for one heart to carry on."

98.6. "98.6" – Keith (1967)
"It's good to have you back again."

99. "99 Luftballons" – Nena (1984)

100. "A Hundred Pounds of Clay" – Gene McDaniels (1961)
The biggest and first hit by this Omaha R&B singer.

409. "409" – The Beach Boys (1962)
"She's real fine, my 409."

500. "I'm Gonna Be (500 Miles)" – The Proclaimers (1993)

909. "One After 909" – The Beatles (1970)

1000. TIE: "Land of 1000 Dances" – Cannibal and the Headhunters (1965); "Thousand Miles" – Vanessa Carlton (2002)
"Land of 1000 Dances" was also sung by Wilson Pickett, but I prefer the original. Vanessa Carlton was a staple around my household during our girls' early teen years.

1921. "1921" – The Who (1969)
"Have a feeling 21 is gonna be a good year, especially if you and me see it in together...What about the boy, he saw it all...you didn't hear it, you didn't see it..." Excellent opening song of *Tommy* that leads to Tommy becoming deaf, dumb and blind.

1941. "New York Mining Disaster, 1941" – Bee Gees (1967)
"In the event of something happening to me."

1963. "December 1963" – Four Seasons (1976)
"Oh, what a night!"

1985. TIE: "Nineteen Hundred Eighty-Five" – Paul McCartney and Wings (1973); "1985" – Bowling for Soup (2004)
Two excellent songs with two very opposite views of 1985: McCartney's apocalyptic *"No one left alive in 1985..."* and Bowling for Soup's fond

memories: *"...Springsteen, Madonna, waiting for Nirvana, there was U2 and Blondie and music still on MTV. Her two kids in high school tell her that's she's uncool cause she's still preoccupied with 19, 19, 1985."*

1999. "1999" – Prince (1982)
"And tonight we're gonna party like it's 1999." No more needs to be said.

2000. TIE: "2000 Light Years from Home" – Rolling Stones (1968); "2000 Miles" – The Pretenders (1984)

2001. "Also Sprach Zarathustra (2001)" – Deodato (1973)

2112. "2112 Overture/The Temples of Syrinx" – Rush (1976)
This Rush tune has grown on me over time.

2525. "In the Year 2525" – Zager and Evans (1969)
"If man is still alive, if woman can survive...they may find..."

10538. "10538 Overture" – Electric Light Orchestra (1972)

22000. "22,000 Miles" – The Moody Blues (1981)

45789. "Beechwood 4-5789" – The Marvelettes (1962)
This is the first of the phone number songs and a decent one at that.

1000000. "A Million to One" – Jimmy Charles (1960)

6345789. "634-5789 (Soulsville, U.S.A.) – Wilson Pickett (1966)

8675309. "867-5309/Jenny" – Tommy Tutone (1982)

Best Originals/Cover Pairs
"It Takes Two, Baby, Me and You"

"Covers" of original songs have always fascinated me. A good cover does not simply take the original or previous hit version and sing/play it just like the original but often changes the tempo, the singing style, the instrumentation and sometimes even the musical notes in places. But ultimately a good cover requires a good original song to be successful. So here are my favorite song pairs in approximate order (usually the original hit with a good cover version) and a few cases song trios (where there were two covers that I liked). To qualify, the original or near-original version must have been recorded during the rock era (i.e., 1955 or later) and the cover must have been recorded during the 1960s or 1970s.

As I developed this list, I noticed several interesting trends. Not surprisingly, The Beatles are the most popular group on this list with six original songs and two cover versions. Motown artists appear on seven of the songs (either as cover acts, originals or both) and Chuck Berry has three original hits on the list. So herewith my top 40 in "very" approximate order:

1. "I Heard It Thru The Grapevine" – Gladys Knight and the Pips (1967); Marvin Gaye (1968)
"Bet you're wondering how I knew." Gladys Knight's original version includes an almost angry vocal in this up-tempo R&B song. Marvin Gaye's version is a beautiful, mournful, soul song. Gaye's version is the best song he ever did, but Gladys Knight's version is quite good too.

2. "Proud Mary" – Creedence Clearwater Revival (1969); Ike and Tina Turner (1971)
"Rollin' on a river." One of Creedence's best country rock songs was turned into a tour de force by Ike and Tina, a combination slow soul song featuring Ike's bass voice and then a wild, up-tempo R&B/rock-'n'-roll vocal by Tina.

3. "We Can Work It Out" – The Beatles (1966); Stevie Wonder (1971)

"Try to see things my way." This soft rock song is one of The Beatles' finest hits. However, I love how it was completely transformed by Stevie Wonder into a brilliant up-tempo R&B rocker. This is the best cover of ANY Beatles song and given that it was one of my favorites by the group, that is no small feat.

4. "Lucy in the Sky with Diamonds" – The Beatles (1967); Elton John (1974)

This great John Lennon song from the *Sgt. Pepper* album is nicely covered by Elton John as only he can. It certainly helps that the single credits "the Reggae guitars of Dr. Winston O'Boogie" (a.k.a. John Lennon).

5. "Good Golly Miss Molly" – Little Richard (1958); "Devil With the Blue Dress On/ Good Golly Miss Molly" – Mitch Ryder and the Detroit Wheels (1966)

"From the early early morning to the early early night." "Good Golly Miss Molly" ranks as Little Richard's most famous song and was his last of four top 10s (including "Long Tall Sally", "Jenny, Jenny" and "Keep a Knockin'") and served as inspiration for the rock-'n'-roll sound imitated by The Beatles. Mitch Ryder changed the sound to more '60s rock and combined it with "Devil With the Blue Dress On" (Shorty Long's original 1964 version only made #125 on the charts) to make a great single and the best medley ever.

6. "Ain't No Mountain High Enough" – Marvin Gaye/Tammi Terrell (1967); Diana Ross (1970)

Though I prefer the original, which was Gaye/Terrell's first and best hit together (though surprisingly only reached #20 on the charts), it is hard to complain about Ross' version which reached #1 on the charts and featured Diana's unique vocal style.

7. "With a Little Help from My Friends" – The Beatles (1967); Joe Cocker (1968)

This excellent song from *Sgt. Pepper* was redone brilliantly by Joe Cocker. Cocker performed the song at Woodstock and it arguably catapulted his popular career. Joe Cocker became the king of cover versions with excellent renditions of #17 below, "She Came in Thru the Bathroom Window" (Beatles), "Feelin Alright" (Dave Mason) and "Cry Me a River" (Julie London).

8. "Roll Over Beethoven" – Chuck Berry (1956); The Beatles (1964); Electric Light Orchestra (1973)

The Beatles do a great job covering one of Chuck Berry's finest hits. However, ELO's version is fabulous, including great orchestration and a bit of Beethoven's *Fifth Symphony* to start the record.

9. "America" – Simon and Garfunkel (1968); Yes (1972)

"I said 'Be careful his bowtie is really a camera.'" One of my favorite Simon and Garfunkel songs is turned into an excellent hard-rock jam song by Yes.

10. "Twist and Shout" – Isley Brothers (1962); The Beatles (1964)

"Shake it up baby now." As much as I love the Isleys' R&B version, it's hard to resist John Lennon screaming vocals in The Beatles' rock-'n'-roll version. Even the Isleys' version was not the original single, which was recorded first by the Top Notes in 1961 but failed to chart.

11. "Pinball Wizard" – The Who (1969); Elton John (1975)

"That deaf, dumb, blind kid sure plays a mean pinball." The Who's original version is one of classic rock's finest featuring a great acoustic guitar throughout. Elton John's version was one of the few bright moments of the movie *Tommy* and highlights Elton's rock voice and excellent keyboard playing.

12. "Here Comes the Sun" – The Beatles (1969); Richie Havens (1971)

"Little darling it's been a long long lonely winter." This George Harrison composition is my favorite by him either as a Beatle or after. Havens, a great folk guitarist, had his best song and only hit single with a lively acoustic rendition of the song.

13. "Get Ready" – Temptations (1966); Rare Earth (1970)

"So fee, fi, fo, fum, look out baby, cause here I come." This excellent early R&B hit by the Temptations surprisingly only reached #29 on the charts. Detroit-based Rare Earth, one of the first white groups to be signed by Motown, turned it into an excellent hard-rock song that

reached #4 on Billboard in its two-and-a-half-minute version. The album version is over 20 minutes long and was often played on the phonograph prior to our physics class. (In retrospect, our often late-arriving physics teacher Ed North must have had a pretty good sense of humor.)

14. "I've Got You Under My Skin" – Frank Sinatra (1956); Four Seasons (1966)
"I've got you deep in the heart of me." While this Cole Porter tune originally was sung in the 1930s, it became one of Sinatra's trademark songs and ultimately was released on an album in 1956. However, the Four Seasons recorded my favorite rendition ten years later, featuring a great intro and a great false ending.

15. "Can't Take My Eyes Off You" – Frankie Valli (1967); "Can't Take My Eyes Off You/Going Out of My Head" – The Lettermen (1968)
"You're just too good to be true." Valli's best solo hit is combined with Little Anthony's great song to produce an excellent medley by the Lettermen. Only Mitch Ryder's "Devil with the Blue Dress..." medley is better.

16. "Baby I Need Your Loving" – Four Tops (1964); Johnny Rivers (1967)
"And other days and other nights I long to hold you tight... because I'm so lonely." A very good song by the Four Tops is turned into an even better song by Johnny Rivers courtesy of his silky smooth voice and a slowdown in the tempo of the song.

17. "(I Know) I'm Losing You" – Temptations (1966); Rod Stewart (1971)
"I fooled myself as long as I can, I can feel the presence of another man." This very good Temptations song was transformed into a great rock song by Rod Stewart. Rare Earth also covered this song, but Stewart's version is much better.

18. "Will You Love Me Tomorrow" – Shirelles (1961); Four Seasons (1968)
"Tonight you're mine completely." This is my favorite Shirelles song, probably because it was written by Carole King and Gerry Goffin. The Four Seasons version is a great rock-'n'-roll rendition.

19. "The Letter" – Box Tops (1967); Joe Cocker (1970)
"Gimme a ticket for an aeroplane, ain't got time to take a fast train." Despite being under two minutes in length, the Box Tops' original is a classic popular-rock song that was #1 for four weeks. Cocker's version is more than twice as long and is very unique. Rich with horns, other orchestration, and background singers, Cocker's rough rock voice and a slower tempo, it was to become Cocker's first and only top ten hit until 1975's "You Are So Beautiful".

20. "Dedicated to the One I Love" – Shirelles (1961); Mamas and Papas (1967)
"While I'm far away from you my baby..." While I enjoyed the Shirelles' original, the Mamas and Papas turned this song into one of the most beautiful rock love songs ever. Michelle Phillips gets a rare lead vocal in the intro of this song and though her voice is not nearly as strong or as good as Mama Cass, it works setting the stage for some great contrapuntal singing throughout. This was the Mamas and Papas' second most popular song after "Monday, Monday".

21. "When Will I Be Loved" – Everly Brothers (1960); Linda Ronstadt (1975)
"I've been cheated, been mistreated." The original Everly Brothers version is a good song, but Linda Ronstadt's version is outstanding. The song is more up-tempo, contains nice country rock instrumentation and benefits from Ronstadt's great voice and singing in a higher key. Not surprisingly, the song became Ronstadt's second biggest hit in the 1970s reaching #2 on the charts.

22. "Mr. Tambourine Man" – Bob Dylan (1965); Byrds (1965)
Dylan's famous folk-rock version was turned electric by the Byrds and became their first #1 hit. It featured their great harmonies as well as great electric guitar.

23. "Light My Fire" – Doors (1967); Jose Feliciano (1968)
"Try to set the night on fire." While it's hard to top one of the best rock songs of the 1960s, Feliciano manages to do a good job covering the hit by turning it into an acoustic folk-rock song. While I used to make fun of the song at the time *("Light my fire, light my fire, light my fire, light my*

fire, oh yeah"), with time, my opinion and my ear have mellowed and now enjoy his version too.

24. "If I Had A Hammer" – Peter, Paul and Mary (1962); Trini Lopez (1963)
"It's the hammer of justice, it's the bell of freedom." While Peter, Paul and Mary sing beautifully on this Pete Seeger folk classic, Lopez's lively, Latin-infused version will always be my favorite.

25. "I Only Have Eyes for You" – Flamingos (1959); Art Garfunkel (1975)
"Are the stars out tonight? I don't know if it's cloudy or bright." The Flamingos' doo-wop version is excellent, but Art Garfunkel's great voice transforms it into a beautiful, ethereal-sounding, slow-rock love song.

26. "You Keep Me Hangin' On" – Supremes (1966); Vanilla Fudge (1968)
"You don't care a thing about me, you're just using me." The Supremes' original is a classic fast-paced, Motown hit. The Vanilla Fudge do a great job turning the song into a slower tempo, hard rocker, which became their one and only hit record.

27. "Ain't Too Proud to Beg" – Temptations (1966); Rolling Stones (1974)
"Please don't leave me, don't you go." Who better than the Rolling Stones to turn one of my favorite Temptation soul hits, into a rock-'n'-roll cover?

28. "Rock 'n Roll Music" – Chuck Berry (1957); Beach Boys (1976)
A Chuck Berry path-breaking song is covered to great effect by the Beach Boys nearly two decades later. I love the Beach Boys harmonies, which make their version unique. The Beatles also covered the song in 1964 but not as well as the Beach Boys.

29. "Do You Wanna Dance" – Bobby Freeman (1957); Beach Boys (1965); Bette Midler (1972)
Freeman's original is a rock-'n'-roll classic. The Beach Boys version is similar but adds nice harmonies. Bette Midler's version is a unique, slow, love song, but full of sexual energy in a manner that only she can pull off.

30. "Baby It's You" – Shirelles (1962); Smith (1969)
Yet another Shirelles song (love that group!) is covered very effectively by the pop-rock group Smith (singer Gayle McCormick) turning a sha-la-la classic into a nice rocker. The Beatles also covered this song but not as well as Smith. Unlike the Beatles, however, this was Smith's only top 40 hit.

31. "Baby, I Love You" – Ronettes (1964); Andy Kim (1969)
"Have I ever told you, how good it feels to hold you." The Ronettes have always been a favorite, and this was their second hit record. Andy Kim's version is decidedly more pop-rock, even bubble gum music, but I can't shake the fact that I like it.

32. "The Fool on the Hill" – The Beatles (1967); Sergio Mendes and Brasil '66 (1968)
This Beatles song, another excellent McCartney composition, could have easily been another hit single if The Beatles had chosen to release it. At the time, the Sergio Mendes version seemed very old-fashioned, more suitable for my parents. But with time, I grew to appreciate the female soprano vocals (in contrast to McCartney's tenor voice) as well as pretty good orchestration in the cover version.

33. "Bye Bye Love" – Everly Brothers (1957); Simon and Garfunkel (1970)
The Everlys' first hit has always been a favorite of mine as it established their reputation as country/rock-'n'-roll artists with a unique sound. Simon and Garfunkel's live version on their last album has even greater energy and a very different vocal sound.

34. "You're Sixteen" – Johnny Burnette (1960); Ringo Starr (1974)
This is one of those cases where I like the remake much more than the original. Burnette's original showcases a nice tune and lots of orchestration. It could have easily been a late '40s Sinatra song. Ringo's version turns it into a rock-'n'-roll song that is pure fun. It also helps that there are backing vocals from Harry Nilsson and kazoo playing by Paul McCartney.

35. "Got to Get You Into My Life" – The Beatles (1966); Earth, Wind and Fire (1978)
"Ooh, did I tell you I need you, every single day of my life." This excellent McCartney song, which was an "ode to pot", is turned into a jazzy R&B song by EWF. The song was one of the few bright moments in the disastrous movie *Sgt. Pepper's Lonely Hearts Club Band*.

36. "Memphis" – Chuck Berry (1959); Johnny Rivers (1964)
"Long distance information, give me Memphis Tennessee." It's still hard to believe that Berry's original was only a B-side of "Back in the U.S.A." that only reached #37 on the charts. Rivers' version is very good largely because of his great voice.

37. "I'm a Man" – Spencer Davis Group (1967); Chicago (1969)
"Yes, I am and I can't help but love you so." This early single by Spencer Davis (aka Steve Winwood) is an excellent rock hit. Chicago jazzes it up considerably in its more than 7-minute version, featuring an extended percussion session as well as Chicago's usual panoply of instruments.

38. "Spanish Harlem"- Ben E. King (1961); Aretha Franklin (1971)
"There is a rose in Spanish Harlem." Ben E. King's classic is a soft R&B song. Aretha transforms it into a lively soul song as only she can.

39. "Mercy Mercy Mercy" – Cannonball Adderley (1967); Buckinghams (1967)
The instrumental version by saxophonist Adderley is excellent and was written by Adderley's pianist Joe Zawinul, for those of you who can't hear the attribution by Adderley at the beginning of the song. (I admit I didn't understand it either.) The Buckinghams added lyrics and a full-brass band and had a top ten hit, and a pretty good song as well.

40. "Just One Look" – Doris Troy (1963); Hollies (1964)
Troy's original showcases her soulful voice. She became a famous rock back-up singer for Pink Floyd and the Rolling Stones, among others. The Hollies' version features their great harmonies and was their first charting single in the U.S., though just barely, reaching #98 on the charts.

Honorable Mentions:
"How Sweet It Is"; "Land of 1000 Dances"; "The Locomotion"; "Blue Bayou"; "Blowin' in the Wind"; "59th Street Bridge Song"; "Another Saturday Night".

Part 2

Favorite Artists and Album Lists

My Favorite Concerts
"Get Back to Where You Once Belonged"

I have been to a lot of rock/pop concerts (more than 50) over the past 45 years, beginning with my freshman year at Brown. However, I have begun to realize that I was starting to forget those important moments of my life and now would be a good time to refresh my memories by adding a chapter about my concert experiences. So with a little assistance from friends and Google, I present to you my top concert experiences of all time.

First, a few ground rules. My list is not a ranking of my favorite artists per se, and for a variety of reasons a few of my favorite groups are not even on my list. Also, I have seen several groups multiple times (most notably, The Moody Blues and The Who three times each and Chicago four times), but only included one concert for each of these groups. I based my ranking on several factors, which included: (1) overall performance of the artist(s) at the particular concert; (2) songs played at the concert; (3) concert venue and where I was sitting; (4) opening act (if any) songs and performance; and (5) personal reasons such as who I was going with to the concert. And if you are wondering why The Rolling Stones, Paul Simon (with or without) Garfunkel, Steely Dan, Stevie Wonder, Neil Young or Bob Dylan are not on the list, well unfortunately I have managed to miss them, most recently The Rolling Stones in May 2015 in Columbus.

In the end, I came up with 12 favorites but must admit that I had a lot of favorites that could easily be on the list as well. (See my "honorable mentions" list at the end of the chapter.)

So without further ado, here are my dynamic dozen concerts:

1. "It's Getting Better All the Time" – Paul McCartney, Oct. 10, 2002, Value City Arena at the Schottenstein Center in Columbus, Ohio with my dear wife Anne

Maybe this goes without saying that seeing the last surviving Beatle (other than Ringo) would make the top of my list. But this particular concert and its timing made it even better than my high expectations. For one, after years of touring as Wings or McCartney and playing mostly Wings material, by the late 1990s after Linda's death, McCartney had shifted to doing far more old Beatles songs (particularly HIS Beatles compositions). I hadn't realized that this shift was occurring and was completely blown away by McCartney's performance and his playlist. McCartney's voice was still very strong and melodic (he was 59 at the time, a youngster!). McCartney's playing, particularly keyboards, was excellent and he had a great backup band and singers. The concert began with "Hello Goodbye" and also included such great Beatles songs as "All My Loving", "Getting Better", "We Can Work It Out", "Mother Nature's Son", "You Never Give Me Your Money/Carry That Weight", "Fool on the Hill", "Something" (ukulele version as homage to George), "Eleanor Rigby", "Here, There and Everywhere", "Get Back", "Hey Jude", "Back in the U.S.S.R.", "Blackbird", "Let It Be", "Can't Buy Me Love", "I Saw Her Standing There", "The Long and Winding Road" (minus the Spector overproduction on the *Let It Be* album), "Yesterday", and finishing fittingly with "Sgt. Pepper's (reprise)/The End". And his Wings/McCartney songs included: "Maybe I'm Amazed", "Band on the Run", "Jet", "Live and Let Die", and "Every Night", which are among his best solo compositions. I rest my case!

2. "And I Think It's Gonna Be a Long, Long Time" – Elton John/Billy Joel, Feb. 18, 2001, MGM Grand Hotel in Las Vegas, Nevada with Anne

There are several reasons this concert is #2. First and foremost, after nearly three years of suffering with chronically bad back pain that ultimately required me to take a three-month leave of absence from work during 2000, I was finally traveling again. In fact, the Vegas trip was the first trip Anne and I took alone in more than five years and this concert was the first I had seen in more than a decade. Second, we had great seats in about the tenth row on the side of the stage. Third, I love Elton John and much of Billy Joel's music and they played for more than three hours! The sound quality and piano playing with the two occasionally "dueling" with each other was great and the vocals sounded the same as they did in the '70s.

The set list was extraordinary from start to finish, beginning with "Your Song" and "Just the Way You Are" by both Elton and Billy and then moving to an all-Elton John set which included many of my favorites: "Don't Let the Sun Go Down on Me", "Funeral for a Friend", "Someone Saved My Life", "Philadelphia Freedom", "All the Girls Love Alice", "Rocket Man", "Levon", Tiny Dancer" and "Goodbye Yellow Brick Road". Elton then sang one of his favorite Billy Joel songs, "Uptown Girl", an excellent rendition. Elton then finished his solo set with "Sad Songs", the rollicking "I'm Still Standing", "Crocodile Rock" and "Saturday Night's Alright".

Billy Joel's set was almost as impressive: "I Go to Extremes", "Movin' Out", "Prelude/Angry Young Man", "New York State of Mind", "Scenes from an Italian Restaurant" and finishing with "We Didn't Start the Fire", "It's Still Rock N Roll" and "Only the Good Die Young". Interspersed amidst the hits was Billy's excellent cover of Elton's "Take Me to the Pilot" as well as good covers of "Mack the Knife" and The Beatles' "Oh Darling".

For the encore, John and Joel together did "My Life", "The Bitch is Back", "You May Be Right" (my favorite Billy Joel song), "Bennie and the Jets", "Candle in the Wind" and "Piano Man", as well as excellent versions of Little Richard's "Good Golly Miss Molly" and The Beatles' "Come Together" and "A Hard Day's Night". All in all, it was an unbelievably good concert.

3. "Help Me Now I Just Got to Get Back to the House at Pooh Corner" – Loggins and Messina/Jim Croce, Mar. 7, 1973 at the University of Rhode Island's Keaney Gym with several Brown University friends

This was my first rock, folk or pop concert ever, and as such, I hold a special appreciation for the experience. Further, this was a great concert in almost every respect: (1) Loggins and Messina were at their peak in terms of material, having just released their second album (a good effort) after an outstanding first album, *Sittin' In*; (2) Jim Croce, although comparatively less known at the time, had just released two albums during 1972 and one in early 1973 from which was going to come much of his touring material and most of his hit records ("You Don't Mess Around with Jim", "Time in a Bottle", "Operator", and "Bad, Bad Leroy Brown"); and (3) We were in a relatively small venue and fairly close to the music.

Jim Croce started things off as the opening act. (In retrospect, that he was "only" the opening act was pretty amazing.) Not only was his singing and acoustic guitar playing great, his songs were all interesting and fun. Further, he told stories as lead-ins to some of his songs such as "Bad, Bad Leroy Brown", "Roller Derby Queen", and "You Don't Mess Around with Jim". In fact, he almost stole the whole show as just the opening act!

However, Loggins and Messina were even better. The group included numerous backup musicians playing the flute, violin, and horns as well as the more standard rock-'n'-roll instruments. Their songs were great; their singing was wonderful; and the guitar/bass and orchestration were outstanding. They performed several long jam songs such as "Vahevala" (featuring a lengthy flute solo), "Angry Eyes", "Same Old Wine", and "Trilogy". Loggins performed several great solo renditions of "Danny's Song" and my favorite, "House at Pooh Corner". And, of course, they played their other hits as well, such as "Your Mama Don't Dance", "Thinking of You", "Nobody but You", and "Back to Georgia".

4. "Talkin' 'Bout My Generation" – The Who, Dec. 13, 1975 at the Providence Civic Center by myself

The first time I saw The Who came about almost serendipitously. My girlfriend Molly and I had overslept and missed getting in line for tickets for The Who in the late fall of 1975. However, by chance, one of my dorm friends knew someone who had ONE extra ticket that they would be willing to give me. I REALLY wanted to see The Who so I thought what the heck. With open seating, I didn't end up getting the greatest seat (up high in the middle of the Providence Civic Center – not close but not too far away), because I wasn't willing to line up hours or days before the concert "all by myself". However, once the concert began, I soon forgot where I was sitting or that I was alone.

The Who played all their hits, starting with their 1960s hits: "I Can't Explain", "Substitute", "My Generation", "I Can See for Miles", "Pictures of Lily", "Pinball Wizard", "Magic Bus", and my favorite, "Happy Jack", being the most memorable. Then, they continued with several cuts from their then current album, *Who By Numbers*, such as "Slip Kid", "Squeeze Box", "Success Story", and "Dreaming from the Waist". But they saved the best for last finishing with most of the *Who's Next* album, including GREAT renditions of Entwistle's "My Wife", "Baba O'Riley", "The Song Is Over", "Bargain", "Behind Blue Eyes", and "Won't Get Fooled Again". Though I was somewhat disappointed that The Who didn't play more from *Quadrophenia* and *Tommy*, I still loved the concert.

The Who put on a great show with all four original group members. The very high quality of the vocals and the music was evident. I was also fascinated by The Who's involuntary choreography that began with Townshend's guitar playing splits and leaps, Daltry's almost athletic vocals, contrasted with John Entwistle's virtually stationary bass playing. But Keith Moon stole the show with his violent drumming that periodically resulted in a drumstick flying out of his hand and into the crowd. Never fear, he merely grabbed another from below his drum set.

5. "Good Times I Remember" – Chicago, Feb. 2002, Stardust Casino in Las Vegas, Nevada with brother Geoff and John Lum

Seeing Chicago in concert in a very small venue was an experience I will never forget. Also, it turned out that Geoff was getting married that May and the Vegas trip was an extended bachelor's party of sorts. Even with many of its members in their late 50s or early 60s, the playing, particularly of the brass instruments, was beautiful and the vocals were as good as on the albums. Chicago opened with the beautifully flowing 13-minute set "Ballet for a Girl in Buchannon" (most of Side 2 of *Chicago II*), which included "Make Me Smile" and "Colour My World" interspersed with great musical connecting songs. The evening included just about every important Chicago song over the previous 30+ years, including "25 or 6 to 4", "Old Days", "Does Anybody Want to Know What Time It Is", "Hard to Say I'm Sorry/Get Away", "Lowdown",

"Beginnings", "Stronger Every Day", "Just You and Me", and "Searchin' So Long", among many others.

6. "Reflections of My Mind" – Moody Blues/Adam Kilzer Band, July 1988 at Wolf Trap, Virginia with Anne (and Kathleen in utero) (Also saw almost identical concert a year earlier at Wolf Trap with John Lum)

The Moody Blues have always ranked among my most favorite groups and I own almost every album/CD that they have recorded. Our seats were good (in the pavilion not the lawn) and the music was great. They performed all of my favorites for almost three hours, ranging from their earliest efforts to their most recent albums: from 1967's "Tuesday Afternoon" and "Nights in White Satin"; 1968's "Ride My See-Saw", "Voices in the Sky", and "Legend of a Mind"; 1970's "Question"; 1971's "The Story in Your Eyes" and "One More Time to Live"; 1972's "I'm Just a Singer in A Rock and Roll Band", "You and Me", and "Isn't Life Strange"; to songs from the 1980s ("The Voice", "Gemini Dream", "The Other Side of Life", and "Your Wildest Dreams"). Their vocals were great (particularly Justin Hayward) and John Lodge's guitar playing was particularly good along with surprisingly good flute playing from Ray Thomas. Relative newcomer Patrick Moraz (formerly of Yes) sounded great on the keyboards. I was in seventh heaven and I know Anne enjoyed it as well (albeit a tad uncomfortable). And, unofficially, it was Kathleen's first concert!

7. "It's My Life and I'll Do What I Want" – Eric Burdon and the New Animals, Jan. 2003 in Las Vegas, Nevada with John Lum

While I am a fan of the Animals and own almost all of their music, this concert vaulted to near the top of the list because of the small venue (literally a large side room of a casino) and our seats (second row center only a few feet away from Eric Burdon!). Burdon sang like it was the 1960s again and the song list was an Animals greatest hits list including ALL of my favorites (e.g., "We Gotta Get Out of This Place", "Don't Let Me Be Misunderstood", "Don't Bring Me Down", "It's My Life", "San Franciscan Nights", "When I Was Young", and of course, "House of the Rising Sun"). However, the moment I will never forget is after Burdon did a particularly good rendition of "Sky Pilot" and I was standing and applauding, he came over and high-fived me. Now that was a memory!

8. "And I'll Be There, with a Love That'll Shelter You" – Four Tops, Feb. 1980, Palo Alto Square, Palo Alto, California with Anne

This was my first concert with Anne and one of the most "up-close" experiences with a group that I have ever had. The Palo Alto Square was a restaurant/bar/dance floor, which was comparatively small. When the Four Tops began to play, we were able to get up and dance to the music literally only a few feet away from Levi Stubbs and the other Tops. I felt like we were at a wedding where they had hired the Four Tops to play. They did all their hits, of course, and sounded great. What utter fun!

9. "They're Just People Looking to the East" – Rod Stewart/Doobie Brothers, May 3, 1973 at the Providence Civic Center with several friends from Brown

As part of Brown spring weekend my freshman year, we were able to get floor seats to see the Doobies and Rod Stewart. The Doobie Brothers were the opening act and in my opinion were so outstanding that they stole the show. It didn't hurt that only two months earlier the Doobies had released what was to become one of the greatest rock albums ever, *The Captain and Me*, which included "Long Train Runnin'", "Without You", "South City Midnight Lady", "Clear as the Driven Snow", "Natural Thing", and of course "China Grove". These tracks, when coupled with tracks from their 1972 album *Toulouse Street* with "Jesus is Just Alright" and "Listen to the Music", made for an energetic and wonderful opening act.

Though overshadowed by the Doobies, Rod Stewart gave a great performance as well. This included the excellent guitar work of Ron Wood (later guitarist with the Stones) and the other members of the Faces who performed regularly with Stewart at the time. Rod stuck primarily with material from: (1) his massively successful 1971 album *Every Picture Tells a Story*, including the megahit "Maggie Mae", "I Know I'm Losing You", "Mandolin Wind", "Reason to Believe" and the outstanding title track; and (2) his 1972 album *Never a Dull Moment*, which included his great covers of Hendrix's "Angel" and Sam Cooke's "Twistin' the Night Away" and the 1972 hit "You Wear It Well". And added into the mix was the Faces' "Stay with Me", one of my favorite songs.

10. Heart – Wollman Rink, Central Park, NYC, Summer 1978 with John Lum

The venue was great, outdoors in Central Park, but in a reasonably small grandstand where we sat pretty close. Heart (particularly Nancy Wilson on guitar) and their backup band played great and Ann Wilson's vocals were outstanding. The song list was superb with "Magic Man", "Crazy on You", "Love Alive", "Barracuda", "Heartless", "Straight On", and "Kick It Out" of particular note. And, of course, this was at the peak of popularity for Heart and included other material from their first three albums.

11. Eric Clapton with special guest Steve Winwood – June 2009, Value City Arena, Columbus, Ohio with Anne

Though I had seen Clapton perform individually, seeing him perform with Steve Winwood was a special treat. Winwood's vocals were excellent, his keyboard AND guitar playing were noteworthy, while Clapton's guitar work was per usual outstanding. Of particular note was their playing of four of the six songs from the one and only *Blind Faith* album (a collaboration of Winwood, Clapton, Rich Grech and Ginger Baker in 1969): "Had to Cry Today", "Can't Find My Way Home", "Well Alright" and "Presence of the Lord", where Clapton outdid himself during the guitar solo. In addition, their set list included several Winwood solo or Traffic compositions (e.g., the guitar-infused "Split Decision", "Glad", and "Dear Mr. Fantasy") as well as several Clapton standards from solo/Derek and the Dominoes days (e.g., "Layla", "After Midnight", "Little Wing", "Forever Man", and "Cocaine"). My only complaint, being an even bigger fan of Winwood than Clapton, was that we didn't hear more of Winwood's solo stuff such as "While You See a Chance", "Higher Love", "Back in the High Life", and "The Finer Things", but this was a pretty small complaint in retrospect.

12. Barenaked Ladies/Ingrid Michaelson – May 2010, Palace Theatre, Columbus, Ohio with my daughter Maryanne

My one entry for a post-1980s group is on the list for several reasons. First, it is the only time that I have taken either of my two daughters to a concert and that made it pretty special. Second, we had great seats in about the fifth row of the Palace Theatre in Columbus, Ohio. Third, Ingrid Michaelson was very enjoyable and one of Maryanne's favorites. Fourth, the Barenaked Ladies remain my favorite 1990s-early 2000s group and it was great to hear them live. Their humor, clever lyrics, shotgun-style singing and harmonies and sound musicianship made them unique among the 1990s bands. I loved hearing "One Week", "Pinch Me", "Shoebox", "It's All Been Done" and their other hits as well as their more current songs.

Honorable Mentions:
Springsteen, 2008
Boston/Kansas, 2012
Police/Pretenders, 2008
Fleetwood Mac, 1977
Eagles/Roy Orbison, 1980
John Sebastian, 1977
Monkees/Grass Roots/Herman's Hermits/Gary Puckett, 1986
Santana, 2017

Best Family Groups
"It's a Family Affair"

While the members of most pop and rock groups are unrelated, there are several important exceptions to this rule. Brothers, sisters, husbands and wives, cousins, etc. are part of a number of singing groups. To qualify for this list, groups had to have two or more family members and have significant musical output in the 1960s or 1970s. So herewith my 25 favorite "family" groups of the 1960s and 1970s with a few of my favorite song examples:

1. The Beach Boys – "Good Vibrations", "Sloop John B", "California Girls" – The five-man group included the three Wilson brothers (Brian on keyboards and bass, Carl on guitar, and Dennis on drums) and cousin Mike Love (lead vocals, saxophone).

2. Fleetwood Mac – "Over My Head", "Go Your Own Way", "Don't Stop" – The group included husband and wife John McVie (bass) and Christie McVie (keyboards), though they divorced in 1976 during the height of the group's popularity.

3. Creedence Clearwater Revival – "Proud Mary", "Who'll Stop the Rain", "Fortunate Sun" – The four-member group included two brothers: John Fogerty (guitars, vocals) and Don Fogerty (guitar). However, if you read Fogerty's autobiography, when it came to recording it's pretty clear that John did just about everything.

4. Sly and the Family Stone – "Dance to the Music", "Thank You", "Family Affair" – The seven-person group included Sly Stone (lead singer, keyboards), brother Freddie (guitar), sister Rosie (keyboards), and cousin Larry Graham (bass).

5. Heart – "Crazy on You", "Magic Man", "Straight On" – Four of the original six-person group consisted of sisters Ann Wilson (lead vocals) and Nancy (guitar and keyboards) and brothers Roger and Mike Fisher (guitars). The Fishers left the group in 1979.

6. **The Kinks** – "You Really Got Me", "Lola", "Sunny Afternoon" – The four-man group included brothers Ray Davies (lead vocals, guitar and group leader) and Dave Davies (lead guitar and vocals).

7. **Mamas and Papas** – "Monday, Monday", "California Dreamin'", "I Saw Her Again" – The four-person group included husband and wife John Phillips and Michelle Phillips, who divorced in 1970.

8. **Everly Brothers** – "Cathy's Clown", "Wake Up Little Susie" (1957), "Bye Bye Love" (1957) – This classic brother duo, Phil and Don, had most of their best output in the late 1950s.

9. **Bachman-Turner Overdrive** – "Takin' Care of Business", "You Ain't Seen Nothing Yet", "Roll on Down the Highway" – Quartet included Randy Bachman (vocals and guitar) and brother Robbie (drums).

10. **Allman Brothers** – "Revival (Love Is Everywhere)", "Ramblin' Man", "Jessica". Sextet originally included Duane (lead guitar) and Greg (keyboards). Duane died in 1971.

11. **Earth, Wind and Fire** – "Shining Star", "September", "Boogie Wonderland" – Eight- to ten-person group included Maurice White (drummer, singer, writer, producer) and brother Verdine White (bassist).

12. **Miracles** – "Tracks of My Tears", "Going to a Go-Go", "Tears of a Clown" – Five-member vocal group included Smokey Robinson and Claudette Rogers (married to Smokey, 1958-86).

13. **Jackson 5** – "The Love You Save", " I Want You Back", "Dancing Machine" – The group included the five brothers: Michael, Jermaine, Tito, Marlon and Jackie.

14. **Fifth Dimension** – "Aquarius/Let the Sunshine In", "Up, Up and Away", "Stoned Soul Picnic" – Vocal quintet included Marilyn McCoo and Billy Davis Jr., who married in 1969.

15. **Isley Brothers** – "Twist and Shout", "It's Your Thing", "That Lady" – Vocal trio of brothers O'Kelly, Ronald and Rudolph Isley.

16. Ronettes – "Baby, I Love You", "Be My Baby", "Walkin' in the Rain" – This singing trio included two sisters: Veronica Bennett (who became Ronnie Spector when she married Phil Spector) and Estelle Bennett, as well as cousin Nedra Talley Ross.

17. Bee Gees – "I've Gotta Get a Message to You", "How Can You Mend a Broken Heart", "Jive Talkin'" – Vocal trio of brothers included Barry and twins Maurice and Robin.

18. Gladys Knight and the Pips – "I Heard It Thru the Grapevine", "If I Were Your Woman" – This quintet included Gladys, her brother Merald "Bubba" Knight, sister Brenda, and cousins William and Eleanor Guest.

19. Kool and the Gang "Jungle Boogie", "Hollywood Swinging", "Celebration" (1980) – This R&B-funk sextet included Robert "Kool" Bell (bass) and his brother Ronald (sax).

20. Impressions – "People Get Ready", "It's Alright", "Keep on Pushin'" – Quintet included the brothers Arthur and Richard Brooks. However, both left the group in 1962.

21. Cowsills – "Hair", "The Rain, the Park & Other Things", "Indian Lake" – This vocal septet included brothers Bill, Bob, Paul, Barry and John, sister Susan and mother Barbara.

22. Chambers Brothers – "Time Has Come Today" – Quintet featured four brothers: Willie (guitar), Joe (guitar), Lester (harmonica) and George (bass).

23. Shangri-Las – "Remember (Walkin' in the Sand)", "Leader of the Pack", "I Can Never Go Home Anymore" – Girl group quartet included two pairs of sisters: Mary (lead singer) and Betty Weiss and twin sisters Mary Ann and Marge Ganser.

24. Gerry and the Pacemakers – "Don't Let the Sun Catch You Cryin'", " "How Do You Do It?", "Ferry Cross the Mersey" – Quartet included Gerry Marsden (vocals, guitar) and brother Freddie.

25. McCoys – "Hang on Sloopy", "Fever" – Quartet included brother Rick (vocals, guitar) and Randy Zehringer (drums). Rick later recorded as Rick Derringer.

Honorable Mentions:
The Angels, Archie Bell and the Drells, The Bellamy Brothers, Cannibal and the Headhunters, The Cookies, The Dixie Cups, Exciters, Ike and Tina Turner, The Irish Rovers, The Lettermen, Sister Sledge, Sonny and Cher, The Tokens, Dire Straits (mostly '80s), to mention just a few.

Dishonorable Mentions:
The Carpenters, Captain and Tennille, The Osmonds

Best Rock Albums
"It's Only Teenage Wasteland"

In 2012, *Entertainment Weekly* came out with its top 100 list of albums. As with any subjective list, I had real problems with it. For one, there were many albums from the post-1990 era including hip-hop, rap, etc., which I don't like or follow. Also, I couldn't really figure out what the list was for: the best pop albums? the best rock/soul/R&B albums? the best of all albums? Finally, I don't really like the "critics" picks that predominate the *EW* list. These same critics have kept deserving groups out of the Rock and Roll Hall of Fame (e.g., The Moody Blues) while allowing many lesser groups in, simply because they don't measure up to their subjective views about what constitutes good music.

So naturally this got me thinking about my own list of favorite albums ever. So I created a top 10 list. But with a few ground rules:

No greatest hits albums – These aren't true albums but just compilations of past hits from groups. I love a lot of them (e.g., Four Tops, Supremes, Four Seasons, etc.) but they aren't on this list.

Only albums from the 1960s and 1970s – I only included '60s and '70s albums to be consistent with the theme of this book. However, I did make one exception for one of my favorite artists of the 1960s and 1970s who happened to have his best album in 1986.

No classical music or musicals – I love many classical pieces and musicals but this is about my favorite rock/folk/ soul and pop music.

Finally, I applied one caveat, which is that in my top 10, no artist could have more than one album. I applied the "desert island" rule here, which is if I were shipwrecked on a desert island and had only a phonograph and 10 record albums, I would probably want a lot of variety in those ten albums. (Don't ask why I would happen to have a phonograph on a desert island, when I don't even have a functioning turntable today!).

So with these caveats in mind, here is my top 10, in rough order:

1. *Who's Next* (1971) – The Who

I have many favorite songs and albums by the Who, particularly *Tommy* and *Quadrophenia*. However, *Who's Next* is in my humble opinion the greatest rock album ever recorded. What is amazing is that it came about as an amalgamation of songs from Pete Townshend's *Lifehouse* rock opera project, a project that was abandoned, and other songs that Townshend largely penned separately.[30] But despite this lack of thematic unity, the album has a beautiful musical unity with excellent songs throughout. The playing of Townshend (guitars, keyboards, and synthesizer), John Entwistle on bass and Keith Moon on drums is particularly noteworthy throughout the album.

The album begins with one of the best Who songs, "Baba O'Riley" (*"it's only teenage wasteland"*), which showcases Daltrey's vocal talents, Townshend's use of an infectious synthesizer background and an unforgettable three-chord guitar/piano sequence. "Bargain" follows, another beautiful rock ballad by Townshend that features synthesizer, great guitar work and drumming. "Love Ain't for Keeping" is edgier with Daltrey (and Townshend) reinforcing the title message through their emphatic vocals. "My Wife" follows, both written and sung by Entwistle. It is a great rocker with interesting tongue-in-cheek lyrics, such as, *"I ain't been home since Friday night and now my wife is coming after me...gonna buy a fast car, put on my lead boots and take a long long drive. I may end up spending all my money, but I'll be alive."* (My friend Robbie Carey and I once spent most of an afternoon just trying to figure out all of the lyrics by playing this song over and over.) Side 1 finishes up with the beautiful and haunting "The Song is Over" which always made me happy/sad (particularly if I was going through a relationship breakup) and was one of the songs from the abandoned *Lifehouse*.

Side 2 fittingly starts with "Gettin' in Tune" (another *Lifehouse* song), which is another excellent rock melody, and is followed by Townshend's "Goin' Mobile", a more up-tempo tune which features a very unique use of synthesizer with guitar. "Behind Blue Eyes" follows and is another beautiful rock song which quickly alternates between the slow acoustic guitar of Townshend along with the cherubic voice of Daltrey to the more upbeat and violent electric guitar of Townsend along with the more evil, sinister vocals *("when my wrist clenches, crack it open...")*. Finally, the album concludes with the rock classic, the eight-minute "Won't Get Fooled Again", which may be the best single song that The Who has ever done.

2. *Abbey Road* (1969) – Beatles
In reality, there are five or six Beatles albums that are my favorites depending on my mood. The *White Album* has some of the greatest material The Beatles have ever done. *Sgt. Pepper's* is a landmark achievement with its own unique sound and thematic feel. *Rubber Soul* best exemplifies The Beatles' songwriting talents and vocal harmonies. *A Hard Day's Night* and *Help!* (British versions) evoke memories of the earlier Beatles with great and infectious melodies and the excitement I felt hearing them even as a 10-year-old. But if forced to choose, I have to pick *Abbey Road*, The Beatles' last album that they recorded together. (The *Let It Be* album was actually recorded before *Abbey Road* but lawsuits over recording rights and the change in producer to Phil Spector delayed its release until after *Abbey Road*.)

Side 1 begins with the unique avant-garde "Come Together" *("he got juju eyeballs...hold you in his armchair you can feel his disease")*, which has an infectious guitar/bass line and Lennon's vocal and fascinating lyrics. This is followed by George Harrison's "Something", which is a beautiful love/lust rock ballad. Next are three from McCartney: two tuneful melodies that are upbeat and fun: "Maxwell's Silver Hammer" and "Octopus's Garden" (sung by Ringo), with "Oh! Darling" sandwiched in between. "Oh! Darling" showcases McCartney's rough rock voice and a bluesy ballad at that, which has grown on me over the years. Side 1 climaxes with the emotional and lustful "I Want You (She's So Heavy)" featuring Lennon's heartfelt rock/primal scream vocal and an extraordinary electric guitar/bass ending, which ends abruptly (and appropriately) with no fade out.

Side 2 of *Abbey Road* is The Beatles' best album side, with each song blending seamlessly together. It starts with the upbeat "Here Comes the Sun" (Harrison's greatest composition with The Beatles and the best song on the album). Then, beginning with Lennon's "Because", there is a string of partially completed short songs including "You Never Give Me Your Money", "Sun King", "Mean Mr. Mustard", "Polythene Pam", "She Came in Through the Bathroom Window", "Golden Slumbers", "Carry That Weight" finishing fittingly with the thoroughly enjoyable "The End", which includes a Ringo drum solo and dueling guitars from Paul, George and John. While frenetic at times, Side 2 works beautifully as if it were one song much like a rock opera of sorts. Of course, The Beatles couldn't resist adding in their shortest track ever "Her Majesty" at 23 seconds as the true last track of the album.

It's fair to say that *Abbey Road* was an album that I wore the grooves out. It certainly was one of the best things about the fall of 10th grade in prep school.

3. *Let It Bleed* **(1969) – Rolling Stones**
The Stones have many good albums, but *Let It Bleed* is the best of them all. It features a great fusion of blues and rock music with great guitar playing by Keith Richards, Mick Jagger vocals and three of the best rock songs ever: "Gimme Shelter", "Midnight Rambler", and the finale, "You Can't Always Get What You Want". However, the other six songs are quite good as well and include the rock/bluesy "You Got The Silver" and "Love in Vain", the original country version of "Honky Tonk Women" called "Country Honk" (which I now like almost as much as the more popular rock version), and the rockers "Live With Me", "Let It Bleed", and "Monkey Man". "Monkey Man" is notable for its great piano introduction and guitar work by Richards.

Thematically, *Let It Bleed* conveys the Stones' bad-boy image convincingly. It is clearly about touring and being a world-famous rock band, with drugs and sex the most common themes. In other words, this album is about The Rolling Stones themselves and musically it is their very best.

4. *Back in the High Life* **(1986) – Steve Winwood**
Steve Winwood is one of my favorite artists ever from his earliest days as an 18-year-old with Spencer Davis Group playing keyboards and belting out "Gimme Some Lovin'", to his rock-jazz fusion days with Traffic and, in particular, the albums *John Barleycorn Must Die* and *Low*

Spark of the High-Heeled Boys or his days of collaborating with Eric Clapton on the *Blind Faith* album. However, when he released the *Back in the High Life* album, he reached the pinnacle of his solo career. The album combines Winwood's excellent musicianship (he plays just about everything: keyboards, bass and guitar), songwriting, very soulful and heartfelt singing and a distinctive, upbeat religious theme. The lyrics and music, with the exception of the last track on the album, are happy and upbeat throughout and it is hard to listen to this album without smiling and singing along (or at least it is for me!). The songs are outstanding and there are no mediocre cuts on the album.

The first side starts with "Higher Love", a very catchy tune (and a #1 song), featuring backup singing from Chaka Khan and a distinctive rhythm arrangement, followed by "Take It as It Comes", another excellent song and arrangement. "Freedom Overspill", the third track, was also the second of four singles released from the album and another great arrangement. The first side ends with my favorite song on the album: the slower tempo but optimistic title track "Back in the High Life" (the third single from the album) featuring the backing vocals of James Taylor and a beautiful melody and excellent acoustic guitar. As great as Side 1 is, Side 2 comes close to equaling it starting with the beautiful "The Finer Things" (the fourth hit single from the album) followed by "Wake Me Up on Judgment Day", another soulful song. "Split Decision", a little heavier rock song (not surprisingly co-written by Joe Walsh, who also played guitar on the album), marks a departure from the album's theme and starts with a crescendo of electric guitars. Finally, the album ends with "My Love's Leavin'", the only melancholy and slow song but sung beautifully by Steve Winwood. While I never truly owned the vinyl record (so I can't apply the "did I wear it out" test), I would bet I played the CD (or the taped version that I had in my car) more times than any other CD I owned during the 1980s.

5. *Fragile* (1971) – Yes
Yes recorded three great studio albums in a row: *The Yes Album*, *Fragile* and *Close to the Edge* during 1971 and 1972 that were the pinnacle of the group's music compositions and craftsmanship. *Fragile*, like the others, is built around several long songs like long movements in a rock

symphony. It gets the nod over the other two primarily because the four songs ("Roundabout", "South Side of the Sky", "Long Distance Runaround/The Fish", and "Heart of the Sunrise") are easily among the best songs Yes has ever done. In between, the album provides short solo showcases for each of the five members which are both musically interesting and excellent short pieces. This includes Rick Wakeman's keyboard solo in his arrangement of the classical "Cans and Brahms", John Anderson's vocal "We Have Heaven", Chris Squire's solo bass playing in "The Fish" and Steve Howe's acoustic guitar solo "Mood for a Day".

The album begins with "Roundabout", which is one of my favorite rock songs of all time. In its eight minutes, this song features just about everything musically: Wakeman's complex organ and synthesizer, Squire's intricate and unique rhythmic bass guitar (who I believe was the best bass player in rock history), Howe's acoustic and electric guitar, and Anderson's multi-layered (and multi-tracked) vocals. This song is simply great in every respect. Almost as good as "Roundabout" is the album's finale, "Heart of the Sunrise" which, even at 10 minutes plus, always keeps you interested. All in all, *Fragile* is a musical tour de force. Most importantly, it is one of only a few records that I bought a second copy of, because the first one became so scratched up and warped. A certain sign that I liked it a lot!

6. *Rumours* (1977) – Fleetwood Mac
Good songs often come out of breakups. In the case of *Rumours*, great songs came out of the breakup of John and Christine McVie's marriage as well as the end of the long-running affair between Stevie Nicks and Lindsay Buckingham. This was a great album with emotional and catchy songs by each of the three main artists/songwriters (Nicks, Buckingham and Christine McVie), including the optimistic and happy "Don't Stop" *("thinking about tomorrow")* and "You Make Loving Fun"; angry songs such as "The Chain" *("And if you don't love me now, you'll never love me again, I can still hear you saying you'd never break the chain!")*, "Blue Letter", and "Go Your Own Way" *("you can call it another lonely day")*; and melancholy songs such as "Dreams", "Songbird", and "Never Going Back Again". The album features excellent song melodies,

compositions, guitar playing by Lindsay Buckingham, and a number of beautiful vocals by Christine McVie.

7. *In Search of the Lost Chord* (1968) – Moody Blues
I love The Moody Blues, so I had a hard time choosing among their seven great thematic albums that were released between 1967 and 1972. These include: *Days of Future Passed* (The Day); *In Search of the Lost Chord* (The Inner Self), *On the Threshold of A Dream* (The Subconscious); *To Our Children's Children's Children* (Outer Space); *A Question of Balance* (Nature); *Every Good Boy Deserves Favour* (History and Evolution); and *Seventh Sojourn* (Life's Travels and Travails). *In Search of the Lost Chord* is my close choice because it includes several of my favorite Moody Blues songs, most notably "Legend of a Mind" *("Timothy Leary's dead, no no he's outside looking in")*, "Ride My See-Saw", "Dr. Livingston, I Presume", "Voices in the Sky", "The Actor", "Visions of Paradise", and "The Best Way to Travel". It is the songwriting of Hayward, Lodge, Thomas and Pinder, the vocals of Hayward, and the rich instrumentation, including flute and sitar, that makes this album just a little better than the other six.

8. *Bookends* (1968) – Simon and Garfunkel
Simon and Garfunkel had four great albums, so it was hard to pick one. However, *Bookends* has many of my favorite songs by them, including most notably "America", "Mrs. Robinson", "Fakin' It", "Hazy Shade of Winter", and "At the Zoo". Further, the other songs on the album are also quite good: "Save the Life of My Child", "Old Friends", "Overs", "Punky's Dilemma", and the "Bookends Theme". The songwriting is excellent, both music and lyrics, and the singing and harmonies are exquisite.

9. *Goodbye Yellow Brick Road* (1973) – Elton John
Elton John has had many good albums but none of them matched the consistent excellence of *Goodbye Yellow Brick Road*. There is little question that this album was Elton's best with a nice blend of slow rock ballads and up-tempo rockers and Elton's excellent use of piano, organ and synthesizer. Most memorable songs to this day include all of Side 1 ("Funeral for a Friend/Love Lies Bleeding", "Candle in the Wind", and "Bennie and the Jets") as well as "Saturday's Alright for Fighting",

"Goodbye Yellow Brick Road", "All the Girls Love Alice", "I've Seen that Movie Too", and "Harmony".

10. *Sittin' In* (1971) – Loggins and Messina

There aren't many groups that came together solely by accident, but that was the case with Loggins and Messina. Kenny Loggins wanted to record his first solo album and his friend Jim Messina from Poco agreed to "sit in" on the sessions. The result was one of pop/folk/rock's enduring duos that recorded five albums and toured together until 1978. *Sittin' In* is clearly their best album. There is not a single "weak" track on the album and there are several that became folk-rock classics, including the only single, "Vahevala", the beautiful slow ballads and often covered "House at Pooh Corner" and "Danny's Song", and the great up-tempo "Back to Georgia" and "Nobody But You". The album also features one of my favorite album cuts ever: the trilogy "Lovin' Me/To Make a Woman Feel Wanted/Peace of Mind". While the songwriting on the album is mostly Loggins, Messina did pen the excellent political protest song "Same Old Wine", which is eerily prescient regarding Watergate and its fallout that came to light only a year or so later.

*****

In addition to the albums above, there are many other artists/albums that are very close to my top 10. Here are the honorable mentions:

1. *Dark Side of the Moon* (1973) – Pink Floyd
This is a groundbreaking progressive rock album and one that I played constantly.

2. *Led Zeppelin IV* (1971) – Led Zeppelin
By far their best, with "Stairway to Heaven", "Black Dog", Rock and Roll", and "Going to California".

3. *Tapestry* (1971) – Carole King
A great collection of songs including her early compositions written for others, such as "Will You Love Me Tomorrow" and "A Natural Woman" and her more recent hit songs such as "It's Too Late", "Where You Lead", and "I Feel the Earth Move".

4. *Sweet Baby James* (1970) – James Taylor
This is my favorite James Taylor album with two of his best songs, "Fire and Rain" and "Country Road".

5. *Disraeli Gears* (1967) – Cream
This includes Cream's three best songs: "Strange Brew", "Tales of Brave Ulysses" and "Sunshine of Your Love".

6. *Innervisions* (1973) – Stevie Wonder
This is Stevie's best featuring "Higher Ground", "Don't You Worry 'Bout a Thing", and "Living for the City".

7. *Blind Faith* (1969) – Blind Faith
This includes the rock classics "Presence of the Lord" and "Sea of Joy" and the excellent "Had to Cry Today", "Can't Find My Way Home", and "Well All Right". Only the overly long and meandering "Do What You Like" keeps it off the island.

8. *The Captain and Me* (1973) – The Doobie Brothers
Their best album with "South City Midnight Lady", "China Grove", "Long Train Runnin'", "Rockin' Down the Highway", and "Cold Rain and Snow".

Best Album Sides of the 1960s "With Tangerine Trees and Marmalade Skies"

I got to thinking the other day (always dangerous when I do that!) that an interesting music list would be my favorite album "sides" of the rock "vinyl" era (mid-1960s through the end of the 1970s). A little explanation is in order, particularly for some of those born after the 1970s that may have no concept of what a record album is. Back when I was young (sounding a bit like my dad who used to say "when I was a boy"), I would often play only one side of a record album when listening (given the effort to get up and turn the record over). This was particularly true when listening with headphones while lying in bed in my college dorm room (often at 3am in the morning). Thus, many of us commonly played the better of the two sides of an album much more often.

However, I have a few ground rules. First, in order to avoid having my list dominated by just a few groups (e.g., The Beatles, The Rolling Stones, The Who, Moody Blues, etc.), I have self-imposed a limit of no more than one album side per artist. Of course, I had to make an exception in a couple of cases where I just couldn't decide which album side was best, so I have a couple of Beatles and Stones sides across the lists. Also, I did NOT include greatest hits albums, since these aren't original record albums but compilations that came out much later. Lastly, my album sides leaned heavily in favor of sides that had no weak or subpar tracks. Remember: when lying in bed, no one wants to get up to move the needle in order to skip a bad song.

This chapter includes my ten favorite album sides from the 1960s in chronological order (I had a hard-enough time picking them, so ranking them was a virtual impossibility). I will include my favorites of the 1970s in the next chapter. So herewith my list:

The Doors – **The Doors (Jan. 1967) Side 1** – Break on Through, Soul Kitchen, Crystal Ship, 20th Century Fox, Alabama Song, Light My Fire

This is one of the greatest rock albums ever, but Side 1 is extraordinary. The album starts with the Doors' first single, the lively and tuneful "Break on Through". This is our first indication of the Doors' musical style, almost always dominated by Morrison's energetic vocals, Robbie Krieger's superb guitar playing and Ray Manzarek's interesting keyboards. Another good song, "Soul Kitchen" has an interesting bluesy sound led by Manzarek's organ playing. "Crystal Ship" is a beautiful, soulful ballad that shows off Morrison's excellent vocals. I knew this song first as the B-side of "Light My Fire" (the 3-minute, 45 rpm, single version of the song), before I smartly bought the album. "Twentieth Century Fox" is a more upbeat and lustful rock song, followed by "Alabama Song", a rock drinking song if ever there was one. Last by not least, Side 1 ends with seven minutes of one of the greatest rock anthems ever, "Light My Fire".

Are You Experienced? – **The Jimi Hendrix Experience (May 1967) Side 2** – The Wind Cries Mary, Fire, Third Stone from the Sun, Foxey Lady, Are You Experienced?

I loved Jimi Hendrix's debut album (thank you, Robbie Carey, for introducing me to it!) and particularly Side 2. With the exception of "Purple Haze" and "Hey Joe" on Side 1, all of my favorite tracks are on Side 2 and there is enormous variety across all five songs. "The Wind Cries Mary", a great soft bluesy-style ballad, starts the side perfectly. "Fire" is a much more up-tempo, guitar-infused rocker and remains one of Hendrix's standards. "Third Stone from the Sun" is maybe the album's most interesting song. It is an instrumental with a jazzy guitar melody and spoken lyrics about a space alien viewing earth from his ship (the lyrics are unintelligible on the record as they are slowed down, though my friend Robbie and I naturally played the record at 45 rpm instead of 33 rpm to understand them). "Foxey Lady" is another great Hendrix rock song, perhaps his most famous and certainly one of my favorites. The side ends with the psychedelic "Are You Experienced?" which features unique backwards guitar and drumming at the beginning and during the song. This is a vintage Hendrix song, extremely different and interesting and a fitting conclusion to Side 2.

Sgt. Pepper's Lonely Hearts Club Band **– The Beatles (June 1967)**
Side 1 – Sgt. Pepper's Lonely Hearts Club Band, With A Little Help From My Friends, Lucy in the Sky With Diamonds, Getting Better, Fixing A Hole, She's Leaving Home, Being for the Benefit of Mr. Kite

While the whole *Sgt. Pepper's* album is extraordinary and precedent setting in many respects, it is Side 1 that is consistently the best. Don't get me wrong; Side 2 is excellent as well, particularly "Lovely Rita", "Good Morning Good Morning" and "Sgt. Pepper's Lonely Hearts Club Band (Reprise)" and "A Day in the Life" but it suffers with a too long and only okay Harrison composition "Within You Without You" that starts Side 2. Side 1 begins with the opening "Sgt. Pepper's Lonely Hearts Club Band" setting the tone for the album. This is the first truly thematic rock album ever, about a fictitious band doing a concert. "Sgt. Pepper's" heralds the beginning and the pattern throughout the album, the seamless blending of rock instruments and rock vocals with orchestration produced brilliantly by George Martin. It quickly segues into "With a Little Help From My Friends" as the fictitious Billy Shears (a.k.a. Ringo) delivers an excellent, upbeat song, definitely the best Ringo lead vocal during his Beatles career. The mood shifts suddenly as we move from the first two songs (composed by Paul), to John's first entry, the psychedelic "Lucy in the Sky with Diamonds", arguably the best track on the album. The psychedelic mood is altered quickly as Paul takes over with another great song, the lively "Getting Better", where his optimism *("It's getting better all the time")* is somewhat countered by John's sarcasm and pessimism *("can't get no worse")*. "Fixing a Hole" is ushered in with harpsichord and is another very good composition. "She's Leaving Home", about a teenage runaway, uses orchestration to help cement its somber and sad mood and is one of Paul's better vocals. The mood shifts suddenly as John (with an assist from Paul) finishes the side with a much more upbeat and superb entry, the psychedelic/carnival-like "Being for the Benefit of Mr. Kite". Lacking a manually playable calliope, George Martin assembled a sixty-foot tape loop of steam organs, cut it in one-foot lengths and randomly reassembled them to get the calliope sound that dominates the song. It works extremely well and provides a fitting conclusion to Side 1.[31]

Days of Future Passed – **Moody Blues (Nov. 1967) Side 2** – The Afternoon: Forever Afternoon (Tuesday?); Evening: The Sun Set: Twilight Time; The Night: Nights in White Satin

As an unabashed Moody Blues fan, I had a hard time choosing only one album side for the group. However, if pressed, I would conclude that Side 2 of *Days of Future Passed* is probably their best. The album is The Moody Blues' first thematic work (a single "day"), no doubt partly inspired by The Beatles' *Sgt. Pepper's*. Side 2 is the second half of the day with all songs relating to the late afternoon, early evening and nighttime. It is anchored by two of The Moody Blues' best songs ever: "Tuesday Afternoon" to start and "Nights in White Satin" at the finish. "Tuesday Afternoon" starts with Justin Hayward's soaring vocals and a beautiful melody, integrated with orchestration and sets the tone as a contemplative but lively, late afternoon song. After an orchestral bridge, "Evening" slows the pace down a bit as the day's toils are contemplated and ambiguity sets in *("Evening time to get away...so they say")*. "The Sun Set" creates an excellent musical and lyrical mood *("I can feel the sun slipping out of sight...and the world still goes on through the night")*. The pace quickens with the catchy and more frenetic "Twilight Time". Last, but not least, the album ends with Hayward's emotionally bare and mournful "Nights in White Satin", which beautifully integrates orchestration and rock music. Side 2 of *Days of Future Passed* is perfect to listen to in the late afternoon near sunset and if you time it just right, carries you through the mood of the sunset, twilight and the beginning of the night.

Disraeli Gears – **Cream (Nov. 1967) Side 1** – Strange Brew, Sunshine of Your Love, World of Pain, Dance the Night Away, Blue Condition

This is one of the first non-Beatles albums that I bought. Side 1 is definitely the stronger side (though I love "Tales of Brave Ulysses" on Side 2), and starts with the electric rock-blues of "Strange Brew", one of Cream's best songs featuring Clapton's outstanding electric guitar and Jack Bruce's equally good bass guitar and excellent vocals by both (lead by Clapton, backing by Bruce). But "Sunshine of Your Love" surpasses it and remains one of the most deservedly famous songs in the history of rock music. Though generally associated with Eric Clapton, Jack Bruce shared writing credit as well as lead vocals with Clapton. While difficult to duplicate the energy and high-caliber of the first two tracks, "World of Pain" and "Dance the Night Away" maintain much of the musical energy, the great bluesy rock sound and wonderful vocal harmonies. (e.g., "Dance the Night Away" was sung entirely in two-part harmony by Bruce and Clapton). "Blue Condition" (Ginger Baker's sole contribution to the album) is only okay. But even here, the contrast of the musical inventiveness, rock-blues energy from the first four songs with a simple blues melody and an "I'm in the doldrums" mood actually makes the track more interesting and provides a fitting conclusion to Side 1.

Bookends **– Simon and Garfunkel (Apr. 1968) Side 2** – Fakin' It, Punky's Dilemma, Mrs. Robinson, Hazy Shade of Winter, At the Zoo

Side 2 is my favorite album side of the duo's short (i.e., five albums in five years) but very illustrious career. Four of the five songs are among the best songs the group ever did. "Fakin' It" starts Side 2 with an interesting rhythm, an upbeat chorus and a great tune, and unforgettable lyrics about being on the wrong side of a one-sided relationship *("Girl does what she wants to do...I've just been fakin' it, not really makin' it")*. "Punky's Dilemma" is a daydream muse by Simon *("Wish I was a Kellogg's cornflake, floating in my bowl taking movies...I'm a citizen for boysenberry jam fan")*, which is accurately cast with a simple, lazy but good melody and vocal by Simon. "Mrs. Robinson", the big hit single from the album, has a great acoustic guitar intro and wonderful music and lyrics about the loss of heroes *("Where have you gone, Joe Dimaggio, our nation turns its lonely eyes to you")*. In contrast, "Hazy Shade of Winter" is a more ambiguous but powerful song, both musically and lyrically and was covered very successfully by the Bangles in the 1980s. The side ends with the utter joy of "At the Zoo", which always reminds me of my days as a young child going to the Central Park Zoo. Side 2 of *Bookends* is a wonderful collection of songs that explore a variety of emotions but ends on a happy note.

Blind Faith – **Blind Faith (Aug. 1969) Side 1** – Had to Cry Today, Can't Find My Way home, Well Alright, Presence of the Lord

What happens when you combine Steve Winwood (on temporary hiatus from Traffic) and Eric Clapton (formerly of Cream) in a super-group along with renowned Cream drummer Ginger Baker and bass player Ric Grech from Family? You get the group Blind Faith and one superb album (the group disbanded after six months!). While Side 2 suffers from the overly long, 15-minute "Do What You Like", Side 1 has four great songs. (I had the pleasure of hearing Clapton and Winwood perform all four of these songs live in Columbus almost seven-eight years ago.) "Had to Cry Today" features the dueling rock guitars of Clapton and Steve Winwood, who wrote and sang the almost nine-minute song. The playing is superb, featuring an excellent repeating guitar riff that unifies and makes the song infectious and seem much shorter than it is. The sound and pace change dramatically with Winwood's beautiful "Can't Find My Way Home", featuring Winwood's great tenor voice, keyboards, and Clapton's acoustic guitar. "Well Alright" is a Buddy Holly cover featuring Clapton's usual guitar brilliance, and great organ from Winwood as well as powerful vocals from both. Side 1 finishes and climaxes with Clapton's "Presence of the Lord", which features palatial-sounding organ from Winwood, and great vocals from Winwood, but Clapton's guitar again dominates. And you wonder why I seldom played Side 2!

Abbey Road – **Beatles (Oct. 1969) Side 2** – Here Comes the Sun, Because, You Never Give Me Your Money, Sun King, Mean Mr. Mustard, Polythene Pam, She Came in Through the Bathroom Window, Golden Slumbers, Carry the Weight, The End, Her Majesty

Side 2 of *Abbey Road* is the most cohesive and brilliant piece of music The Beatles ever did from start to finish. Producer George Martin had a lot to do with that as he had "for some time past...been urging that John and Paul to take their music to a higher level by writing in symphonies and movements..." Now for Side 2, "he suggested they each root out fragments of unfinished and unrecorded songs from their bottom drawers, to be arranged in a classical style suite".[32] This organization is evident and seamless on Side 2.

It begins with George Harrison's best song (and the best song on the album), the uplifting "Here Comes the Sun". John Lennon's "Because" is an interesting albeit short respite as John expresses his love for Yoko *("love is all, love is you")*. Paul's piano introduces the next song, "You Never Give Me Your Money", a great McCartney composition with excellent melody and musical bridge. It also includes great guitar work by George, particularly as the song fades out *("one, two, three, four, five, six, seven, all good children go to heaven")* into the sounds of crickets, birds and the beginning bass guitar chords of "Sun King", a religious chant, another short and simple but very effective Lennon song. This is suddenly interrupted by Ringo's drumming and the start of the more moderately paced "Mean Mr. Mustard", the first of a merged trilogy of Lennon-McCartney songs that also includes the frenetic, excellent rock song "Polythene Pam" and finishes with "She Came in Through the Bathroom Window" featuring McCartney's great vocals. There is a brief rest as the band seems to be catching its breath, as Paul's piano introduces another soulful rocker "Golden Slumbers" (which, though different, sounds much like the "reprise" of "You Never Give Me Your Money"), which through Ringo's drum bridge leads to the sonorous chant of "Carry the Weight".

Unofficially, Side 2 ends fittingly and compellingly with "The End", which is musically a Beatles rarity in that it includes a short drum solo by Ringo, and a fantastic dueling guitar jam of McCartney, Harrison and Lennon. (Allegedly, Eric Clapton was part of this jam in an uncredited role, but there is no evidence to support this.) It is almost as if The Beatles have pulled out all the stops since this was the last song on the last album they would record together. (The *Let It Be* album was recorded before *Abbey Road*, but fighting over the final production delayed the release until early 1970.) Technically, the very short ditty "Her Majesty" is actually the last track of the album but it starts a full 10-20 seconds after "The End" and is easily missed. Side 1 is almost as good with the two-sided hit single "Come Together" and "Something" starting the album and the side finishing with the infectious and electric "I Want You (She's So Heavy)" but it is the unusual and wonderful Side 2 that is the best.[33]

In the Court of the Crimson King – **King Crimson (Oct. 1969) Side 1** – 21st Century Schizoid Man, I Talk to the Wind, Epitaph

This album may be best known for its colorful cover, but many consider it one of the first and best progressive rock albums. And Side 1 is by far the best, beginning with the explosive electric guitar of Robert Fripp, Ian McDonald's wailing saxophone and the rough-edged, almost screeching vocals from Greg Lake (a rarity for him) of "21st Century Schizoid Man". The song includes lengthy, syncopated solos between Fripp and McDonald and excellent use of Mellotron and Lake's bass and Michael Giles' drumming throughout. Musically, this was hard rock heaven! And lyrically, it was unforgettable: *"Cat's foot iron claw. Neuro-surgeons scream for more. At paranoia's poison door. Twenty first century schizoid man...Blood rack barbed wire. Politicians' funeral pyre. Innocents raped with napalm fire. Twenty first century schizoid man."* How can you not love this song!

In direct contrast to "Schizoid Man", "I Talk to the Wind" is a soft, almost ethereal song headlined by McDonald's great flute playing and Lake's excellent, mournful vocals. Lyrically, it is simply about disillusionment and isolation, a theme that would be repeated many times in progressive rock over the years *("I talk to the wind, my words are all carried away...the wind cannot hear")*. However, the soft respite was to be short-lived as "Epitaph" crashes to a start with a crescendo of drums and Mellotron. Lake sings, *"The wall on which the prophets wrote is cracking at the seams"* and the song builds through a slow march and some excellent drumming, Mellotron and guitar work. This is a song about ultimate chaos *("Confusion will be my epitaph")* and it is a brilliant close to Side 1. While King Crimson released many more albums, this was the first and only with Greg Lake (who shortly thereafter departed for Emerson, Lake and Palmer) and it is by far their best.

Let It Bleed – **Rolling Stones (Dec. 1969) Side 2** – Midnight Rambler, You Got the Silver, Monkey Man, You Can't Always Get What You Want

Side 2 of *Let It Bleed* is bookended by two of the Stones' greatest long jam-style songs: "Midnight Rambler" *("don't do that")* to start the side and one of their best songs ever, "You Can't Always Get What You Want" to end the side – both with seven minutes of pure rock heaven. In between, you have the slow, bluesy "You Got Silver" and one of the Stones' best album cuts ever, "Monkey Man", which features a great piano introduction to start, fine guitar work throughout and wonderful rock melody and lyrics throughout *("I've a cold Italian pizza, I could use a lemon squeezer...My friends are all junkies")* that spoke to being on concert tours as a rock star in 1969. Side 1 is good, too (e.g., "Gimme Shelter", "Let It Bleed", and "Live with Me") but Side 2 is outstanding.

Best Album Sides of the 1970s
"Blue Jean Baby, L.A. Lady, Seamstress for the Band"

Part 2 of my favorite record album sides was a lot more difficult to compile than I imagined. I started out trying to pick my ten favorite album sides of the 1970s, but ended up with 20. (And even that was difficult; see my honorable mention list.) After all, I was dealing with about twice as many years than the mid-late 1960s. Interesting fact about this list: half the picks were from 1970-71 and only three after 1976. This either says something about disco and its negative impact on quality rock music by the late 1970s or the fact that after college (I graduated in June 1976), I didn't listen to as much new music.

Chicago (II) – **Chicago (Jan. 1970) Side 2** – Wake Up Sunshine, Make Me Smile, So Much to Say, So Much to Give, West Virginia Fantasies, Anxiety's Moment, Colour My World, To Be Free, Now More Than Ever

Chicago's second album (another double album) features their best individual side, "Wake Up Sunshine", and the superlative 13-minute "Ballet for a Girl in Buchannon" written by trombonist James Pankow. This latter composition was actually a compendium of seven songs that flowed smoothly together – "Make Me Smile", "So Much to Say, So Much to Give", two instrumentals ("West Virginia Fantasies" and "Anxiety's Moment"), "Colour My World" (later to become a hit single), "To Be Free" (another short instrumental), and the finale "Now More Than Ever", which was the last verse of the single version of "Make Me Smile". Chicago, which I have since seen live in concert four times (twice in a fairly intimate nightclub setting in Las Vegas), did a wonderful job playing the "Ballet for a Girl in Buchannon" to open one of these concerts. This is not only an excellent side of Chicago songs; it is the most cohesive album side that they ever recorded.

John Barleycorn Must Die – **Traffic (July 1970) Side 1** – Glad, Freedom Rider, Empty Pages

Steve Winwood formed Traffic in late 1967, when his earlier group, Spencer Davis Group (e.g., "Gimme Some Lovin'" and "I'm a Man"), didn't want to experiment with more musical styles. (Steve Winwood was all of 19 years old at the time!) "Barleycorn" is Traffic's best album and features the unique rock, blues and jazz-fusion sound that made them famous. As with all Traffic albums, Steve Winwood wrote or co-wrote all the music and played all keyboards and bass guitar. While Side 2 is good, it is Side 1 that has the three best songs on the album, beginning with the seven-minute instrumental "Glad", which features Winwood's superb piano playing along with excellent saxophone work of Chris Wood. "Freedom Rider" is a great vocal and instrumental song featuring Wood's wonderful saxophone and flute mixed pleasingly with Winwood's ever-present keyboards. The organ fanfare begins "Empty Pages" and Winwood dominates throughout – vocally, musically and lyrically. Winwood's emotional, blue-eyed soul voice belts out *"staring at empty pages"* and you know it isn't just writer's block that he is challenged with but girlfriend troubles as well. In between, Winwood fills in with a very jazzy electric piano, organ and bass. And then the song and the side ends, fading out with Winwood's last few organ notes.

Tapestry – **Carole King (Feb. 1971) Side 1** – I Feel the Earth Move, So Far Away, It's Too Late, Home Again, Beautiful, Way Over Yonder

This is truly a case of an album with two outstanding sides of music and no weak tracks. I picked Side 1 rather than Side 2 largely on the strength of Carole's newer solo hit songs (e.g., "It's Too Late", "I Feel the Earth Move", "So Far Away") versus her old 1960s standards made famous by Aretha Franklin ("A Natural Woman"), the Shirelles ("Will You Love Me Tomorrow") and her friend James Taylor ("You've Got A Friend"). I also like the last three tracks a lot, particularly the uplifting "Beautiful", a song that I still find very inspiring on depressing days *("You've got to get up every morning with a smile on your face and show the world all the love in your heart, and people gonna treat you better, they're gonna find...that you're as beautiful as you feel")*.

The Yes Album – **Yes (Feb. 1971) Side 1** – Yours is No Disgrace, The Clap, Starship Trooper

Like my other favorite groups, Yes posed a difficult decision for me. Yes has three fantastic albums and six excellent album sides on *The Yes Album*, *Fragile*, and *Close to the Edge*, but if I had to choose just one, it would be Side 1 of *The Yes Album*. Both "Yours is No Disgrace" and "Starship Trooper" are lengthy Yes songs, both nearly ten minutes long, showcasing their musical strengths: Steve Howe's guitar, Chris Squire's bass guitar, Bill Bruford's drums, Tony Kaye's keyboards, and Jon Anderson's vocals. Sandwiched in between the two long songs is "The Clap", a short yet excellent acoustic guitar solo by Steve Howe. In listening to this album side MANY MANY times, I am fascinated not just by the great basic melodies, verses and bridges but by the intricacy of the different musical lines of the songs from Howe's multiple guitar chord progressions and Chris Squire's very distinctive bass lines. Both long songs are incredibly catchy. I defy anyone to listen to them several times and not get sucked into the music. And for that reason, every time I listen, I find myself wishing the songs would never end. Now that is the sign of a great album side!

Sticky Fingers – **Rolling Stones (Apr. 1971) Side 1** – Brown Sugar, Sway, Wild Horses, Can't You Hear Me Knocking, You Gotta Move

It's hard to beat Side 1 of *Sticky Fingers* when it comes to Stones albums. Not only does it have the two excellent Stones singles "Brown Sugar" and the often underrated and rock-'n'-bluesy "Wild Horses" *("couldn't drag me away")*, but you have the slow rocker "Sway" and one of the best Stones album cuts EVER, "Can't You Hear Me Knocking", a six-minute tour de force, which ends with a wonderful saxophone solo. The side ends fittingly with the wonderfully slow blues number "You Gotta Move" (one of the few albums that I can remember that is effectively telling you that you have to get up and flip the record to the other side). Side 2 is good, but not nearly as great as Side 1 with only two songs, "Bitch" and "Dead Flowers", among my favorites by the Stones.

Every Picture Tells a Story – **Rod Stewart (May 1971) Side 2** – Maggie Mae, Mandolin Wind, I'm Losing You, Reason to Believe

Rod Stewart's first album was by far his best. Released in May, it peaked in popularity in October 1971 (at the same time "Maggie Mae" was #1 on the charts). It seemed like everyone I knew at boarding school in September owned this album. Side 2 was superb. It featured the mega hit "Maggie Mae" complete with a nice Renaissance-style guitar intro, and Rod's wonderful singing and lyrics *("you turned into a lover, but mother what a lover, you wore me out...you laughed at all of my jokes")*. This was followed by a nice, slow ballad "Mandolin Wind", featuring Ron Wood's mandolin and guitar playing. The third track was the up-tempo, rock-'n'-roll extraordinaire version of the Temps' "I'm Losing You". The final track, "Reason to Believe", featured Stewart's great vocals on this Tim Hardin song *("...knowing you lied straight-faced while I cried, still I love to find a reason to believe...")*. Wow. I don't think I flipped this album over to Side 1 for weeks after I bought it.

Who's Next – **The Who (Aug. 1971) Side 2** – Gettin' in Tune, Goin' Mobile, Behind Blue Eyes, Won't Get Fooled Again

With The Who, the challenge wasn't determining which of their albums was best. This is clearly *Who's Next*. However, the problem was which side to choose. Both are outstanding. However, I gave the slight edge to Side 2 on the strength of "Won't Get Fooled Again" (my favorite Who song ever!) and "Behind Blue Eyes" (my third favorite on the album after "Baba O'Riley" on Side 1). But the first two tracks, "Gettin' in Tune" and "Goin' Mobile", are great songs as well. The musical quality is unbelievably good, including seamless use of synthesizer, keyboards, and other instruments in addition to Townshend's usual fine guitar work, John Entwistle's great bass playing, Keith Moon's always energetic drumming and, of course, Daltrey's excellent vocals. But I'll admit that this was one album that I always got up to flip over. Side 1 is great too, with "Baba O'Riley", "Bargain" and Entwistle's amusing "My Wife" as particular highlights.

Madman Across the Water – **Elton John (Nov. 1971) Side 1** – Tiny Dancer, Levon, Razor Face, Madman Across the Water

While Elton John's *Goodbye Yellow Brick Road* is a better overall album and Side 1 with "Funeral for a Friend", "Candle in the Wind" and "Bennie and the Jets" has three great songs, Side 1 of "Madman Across the Water" is ever so slightly better because it is more integrated as a single side with songs that flow from one to another. It doesn't hurt either that "Tiny Dancer" *("blue jean baby, L.A. lady, seamstress for the band")* and "Levon" are arguably two of John's best song compositions ever. What makes this album and particularly Side 1 so great is the great use and integration of orchestration along with Elton's piano and backing guitar and bass. This is probably most evident with the final cut on Side 1, "Madman Across the Water", an excellent song made even better with the sweeping feel of a full orchestra and Elton's great emotionally charged vocals. The album *Madman Across the Water* was a Christmas Day 1971 gift along with a pair of new headphones. I played Side 1 for weeks before I ever flipped the record over to Side 2.

Led Zeppelin IV (untitled) – **Led Zeppelin (Nov. 1971) Side 1** – Black Dog, Rock and Roll, Battle of Evermore, Stairway to Heaven

Led Zeppelin recorded a lot of great rock songs, something I have grown to appreciate even more over the years. But there was one album that I bought in early 1972 because of only ONE SONG: "Stairway to Heaven". Though overplayed over the years by progressive rock stations, this song still stands the test of time as one of the greatest rock songs ever. It is not surprising that Side 1 of *Led Zeppelin IV* (actually untitled) (which includes the eight-minute plus "Stairway to Heaven") is my favorite Led Zeppelin album side. But it turns out that Side 1 also has some other great songs including, most notably, two hard rockers that are among Zeppelin's all time best: "Black Dog" and "Rock and Roll" *("Been a long time since I rock n' rolled")*. And "Battle of Evermore", which is the weakest cut on the side, grew on me after constant playings and fits nicely between the first two rockers and "Stairway". Not surprisingly, this album was almost never flipped, though Side 2 also has several good tracks, most notably "Going to California".

Sittin' In – **Loggins and Messina (Nov. 1971) Side 1** – Nobody But You, Danny's Song, Vahevala, Trilogy (Lovin' Me/To Make a Women Feel Wanted/Peace of Mind)

A popular duo by accident, Jim Messina had just planned to "sit in" with Kenny Loggins in recording this session. *Sittin' In* was their best album. And though Side 2 is very good with the beautiful "House at Pooh Corner" as the highlight, Side 1 is by far the best on this or any other Loggins and Messina album. It begins with the lively rock-'n'-roll song and great tune "Nobody But You" *("I don't want nobody but you")*, which not only features the excellent vocals of both Loggins and Messina but a brass sound that would characterize much of the rest of the album. This is followed by a respite with Loggins' solo on the slow love ballad "Danny's Song", a song that would later be covered as a successful single by Anne Murray. The Caribbean-inspired "Vahevala", complete with metal drums and great orchestration, is another excellent song, perhaps the best single song on the album. Finally, the album ends with the brilliant 11-minute "Trilogy", which merges three songs together so successfully that they seem as one. It starts with the slow-paced Loggins-Messina duet "Lovin' Me", a great cuddling song, if ever there was one. The pace builds at the end of the song and then moves to a lively guitar/horns/organ bridge to another great tune, the up-tempo "To Make a Woman Feel Wanted" *("...you don't need change in your pocket...soles on your shoes...")* and lastly bridges to the solo slow ballad "Peace of Mind" *("...give me some peace of mind")*. Wow. I loved this album side so much that I literally wore it out and had to replace the album in the mid-1970s.

Harvest – **Neil Young (Feb. 1972) Side 1** – Out on the Weekend, Harvest, A Man Needs a Maid, Heart of Gold, Are You Ready for the Country

My favorite of Neil Young's albums was *Harvest*. It was unique sounding (arguably one of the first country rock albums) and had great song compositions. While both sides are good, it is Side 1 that was my favorite. It begins with the very folksy, slow tempo "Out on the Weekend", a great mood setter for much of the rest of the album, complete with acoustic guitar and harmonica and Young's mournful lyrics *("See the lonely boy out on the weekend, trying to make it pay...")*. "Harvest" is also an excellent song and continues in a similar vein but relies a bit more on twangy electric guitar. "A Man Needs a Maid" is a complete shift – musically dominated by the London Symphony Orchestra, beginning and ending with Young's solo piano. But the theme is familiar, love lost or love on the rocks as Neil sadly ends the song with *"when will I see you again?"*. "Heart of Gold" provides a welcome change, with a much more upbeat and very catchy song, which still ranks as Young's most popular single ever and made even better by backing vocals from Linda Ronstadt and James Taylor. The side ends with the much more rockin' sound of "Are You Ready for the Country", a great finale to Side 1, featuring backing vocals from Graham Nash and David Crosby. Side 2 is very good, including most notably "Old Man" and "Alabama", but Side 1 is still my favorite.

Dark Side of the Moon **– Pink Floyd (Mar. 1973) Side 2** – Money, Us and Them, Any Colour You Like, Brain Damage, Eclipse

It is hard to have been a college student in late 1973-early 1974 and NOT own *Dark Side of the Moon*. This was their most critically acclaimed and by far their most popular album and certainly one that I played constantly at college. In fact, my first copy of the record was inadvertently left out on our dorm room's radiator and became permanently warped. After a few failed attempts to get it to play on the turntable, which were interesting to say the least, we hung the record by a string from the ceiling to give us – voila! – instant dorm room art. And of course, within 24 hours I had bought a new record. Not surprisingly, the whole album is great with songs/tracks almost indistinguishable from each other. Side 1 was excellent with, if you will excuse the pun, the timeless "Time", a particularly outstanding track. The improvised, wordless vocals and outstanding singing of session singer Clare Torey on "The Great Gig in the Sky" is another highly unusual feature of Side 1. But Side 2 was my favorite, starting with the extraordinary guitar work of David Gilmour and bass guitar Roger Waters providing the driving sound behind Pink Floyd's best rock song "Money". Session sax player Dick Parry adds his great sound to "Money" but his work on "Us and Them" is particularly noteworthy. The excellent blended harmony of singers Gilmour and

Richard Wright along with Wright's great work on keyboards provides the ethereal and relaxing quality of "Us and Them" and makes this my favorite track on the album. It's hard to know upon early listening where "Any Colour You Like" begins or when "Us and Them" ends, but it provides a nice musical interlude featuring great organ playing from Wright and guitar work from Gilmour. "Brain Damage" and "Eclipse" are two excellent songs that finish out Side 2 nicely and are the clearest reference to former Pink Floyd member Syd Barrett's mental breakdown *("and if the band you're in starts playing different tunes")*.

The Captain and Me – **Doobie Brothers (Mar. 1973) Side 1** – Natural Thing, Long Train Running, China Grove, Dark Eyed Cajun Woman, Clear As the Driven Snow

The Doobie Brothers recorded a lot of great music but nothing beats Side 1 of *The Captain and Me*. It starts with the guitar/organ fanfare of "Natural Thing" *("...We all got to be loved, it's a natural thing don't you know...")*, then moves to two great rocking singles: "Long Train Running" *("without love where would you be now")* and, of course, "China Grove" *("...they're people just looking to the East")*. "Dark Eyed Cajun Woman" is an enjoyable, albeit slower, country-blues inspired tune. However, the respite is short-lived with the best "non-single" cut on the album, "Clear As the Driven Snow" finishing up the side. It starts as a slow folk-rock song and then builds into a great up-tempo rocker that nicely ends Side 1. Side 2 is good, too, with the rocking "Without You" and the beautiful "South City Midnight Lady", but Side 1 is hard to top.

Innervisions – **Stevie Wonder (Aug. 1973) Side 2** – Higher Ground, Jesus Children of America, All in Love is Fair, Don't You Worry 'Bout a Thing, He's Misstra Know It All

Stevie Wonder's best album was easy to select for me. *Innervisions* was played constantly in my dorm room in college. The hard part was deciding which side to play. Side 1 features the long version of the mega-hit "Living for the City" and three other excellent tracks: "Too High", "Visions", and "Golden Lady". However, Side 2 is slightly better. It begins with Stevie Wonder's great rocker, "Higher Ground", featuring

Stevie's great playing of the Hohner clavinet keyboard (which he originally used most distinctively in "Superstition"). The song morphs into the second track, the beautifully soulful R&B tune "Jesus Children" and next moves to the gorgeous but mournful ballad "All in Love is Fair". The style changes abruptly with "Don't You Worry 'Bout a Thing", an excellent Hispanic-style, up-tempo love song. Lastly, Stevie ends with "He's Misstra Know It All", a nice soul R&B ending to the side. Did I also mention that Stevie Wonder played almost all of the instruments on the album?

Band on the Run **– McCartney/Wings (Dec. 1973) Side 1** – Band on the Run, Jet, Bluebird, Mrs. Vanderbilt, Let Me Roll It

My favorite album of 1974 (though technically a December 1973 release) was Paul McCartney's *Band on the Run* and Side 1 is also McCartney's best album side. The side begins with "Band on the Run", perhaps McCartney's best single of his career ("Band on the Run" set an unofficial record in my quad at Brown for being played the most times in a row – 28 times! – out from the window of my dorm room, much to the great consternation of those living nearby). Side 1 continues with the lively rocker "Jet", followed by the pleasant and slower love ballad "Bluebird", which was one of the rare love songs that features both Paul AND Linda in good form. The pace quickens with the lively "Mrs. Vanderbilt", a great tune (and another single, at least in Europe). The side ends with the excellent guitar-led, slow rocker, "Let Me Roll It", one of McCartney's best compositions. To be clear, Side 2 of the album was also filled with very good songs, notably "Picasso's Last Words (Drink to Me)" and my favorite, "1985", which highlights some mean piano playing by Paul. But Side 1 gets the nod from McCartney's best non-Beatles album.

Born to Run **– Bruce Springsteen (Aug. 1975) Side 2** – Born to Run, She's the One, Meeting Across the River, Jungleland

Springsteen's third album, *Born to Run,* was what hooked me to Springsteen's music. It became his most popular effort to date and created an entire new legion of Springsteen fans. Lyrically and musically, the album was outstanding with not a single weak track. Some compared Springsteen to an electric Dylan (à la "Like a Rolling Stone") but Springsteen took the music further with more complex arrangements, many multiple tracks and more orchestration than Dylan ever contemplated (some critics likened it to the Phil Spector "wall of sound"). And he had a great backup band featuring Clarence Clemons on sax and Stevie Van Zandt on guitar, (though Van Zandt only appeared on "Tenth Avenue Freeze Out" on Side 1).

Side 1 is excellent featuring "Thunder Road" which begins the album with optimistic lovers and early morning harmonica but by the end of Side 1 there is the "broken friendships" of "Backstreets". But it is Side 2 that is my favorite, beginning with the rousing and "wide-screen" drama of "Born to Run", my favorite single of Springsteen's long and illustrious career. Musically, it was wonderful with an unforgettable sound and lyric *("Highways jammed with broken heroes on a last chance power drive")*. The rocking "She's the One" barely tempers the intensity of Springsteen's music. The intensity ebbs with the slow, jazzy horn introduction to the mournful, darker "Meeting Across the River". This song serves as a musical and lyrical bridge to the drama that unfolds in Harlem in "Jungleland", a brilliant nine-and-a-half-minute epic Springsteen song *("The Rangers had a homecoming in Harlem late last night")*. The drama ends badly though *"but they wind up wounded, not even dead, tonight in Jungleland"*. The early optimism of the lovers from Thunder Road is gone and they are "left in fate's hands, in a land where ambivalence reigns and tomorrow is unknown".[34]

Boston **– Boston (Aug. 1976) Side 1** – More Than a Feeling, Peace of Mind, Foreplay/Long Time

Boston's first album was the complete brainchild of Tom Scholz, who wrote all the music and played all the instruments except drums. Scholz's guitar and keyboard work were distinctive and created the unique sound for the group. But it was Brad Delp's soaring tenor vocals that made the Boston sound famous. Side 2 includes two excellent songs ("Something About You" and "Hitch a Ride"), but it is Side 1 that gets the nod on the power of three superb songs. "More Than a Feeling" became Boston's first and biggest hit song with its guitar riffs and Delp's excellent vocals. "Peace of Mind" is almost a match and is similarly styled. But it is the last, almost eight-minute track "Foreplay/Long Time" that is my favorite, beginning with the great musical, almost three-minute intro "Foreplay" which features dueling guitars, organ and bass guitar. This leads seamlessly through a great building drum sequence into the wonderfully guitar-laden "Long Time". Delp's vocals soar, hitting high notes in tune with the guitars. A pièce de résistance! Perhaps I loved Side 1 so much because it was full of uplifting rock music and vocals that I sorely needed in late 1976 and 1977.

Rumours **– Fleetwood Mac (Feb. 1977) Side 1** – Second Hand News, Dreams, Never Going Back Again, Don't Stop, Go Your Own Way, Songbird

I found it difficult to pick my favorite album side for Fleetwood Mac, with Side 1 of *Fleetwood Mac* a close second (i.e., "Monday Morning", "Warm Ways", "Blue Letter", "Rhiannon", "Over My Head", and "Crystal"). However, Side 1 of *Rumours* is truly outstanding. The album has no pretenses; it is very clearly about the breakup of Lindsay Buckingham and Stevie Nicks AND the end of the marriage of Christine and John McVie. "Second Hand News" is Buckingham's upbeat rock lament *("someone has taken my place...I'm just second-hand news")*. This is followed by the beautiful, slow ballad "Dreams", Stevie Nicks' own lament over love lost *("Thunder only crashes when it's raining, players only love you when they're playing...In the stillness of remembering what you had and what you lost")*. This is followed by Buckingham's short song "Never Going Back Again", which the group joins to sing with him and which quickly segues into the brilliantly upbeat rocker and wonderfully optimistic "Don't Stop" *("don't stop thinking about tomorrow, it'll be here better than before, yesterday's gone.")*. While "Don't Stop" might be Fleetwood Mac's best song ever, arguably "Go Your Own Way" might be even better, both musically (great guitar work by Buckingham and a wonderfully lively tune) and lyrically (the simple optimism of "Don't Stop" is replaced by resignation and even anger in *"You can go your own way, you can call it another lonely day"*). The album finishes with Christine McVie's "Songbird", a slow, beautiful ballad that features her lovely vocals and her personal lament of marriage's end *("for you there will be no more crying...and the songbirds are singing like they know the score")*. This album had great personal meaning as I listened to it during the course of my long-distance relationship with my girlfriend during 1977, both the highs and the lows, and the ultimate breakup.

***Aja* – Steely Dan (Sep. 1977) Side 1** – Black Cow, Aja, Deacon Blues

While there are many songs and albums that Steely Dan has recorded that I like a great deal, there is only one record side where I enjoyed ALL the tracks: Side 1 of *Aja*. *Aja* is Steely Dan at their jazziest, though still fundamentally a rock-jazz fusion group. And I can remember listening to this album frequently in the months before heading west to California and Stanford Business School in the summer of 1978. The album starts with "Black Cow", a wonderful song about rocky relationships *("I can't cry anymore while you run around. Break away. Just when it seems so clear that it's over now, drink your big black cow and get out of here")*. The song features great saxophone, keyboards and guitar that fit the mood of the song brilliantly. Next, the title track "Aja" has a distinctly different Asian character, albeit with equally jazzy instrumentation, a lengthy musical interlude in the middle and an extremely relaxed feel to it. Lastly, the album ends with "Deacon Blues", another excellent song and the third lengthy track on the side. Side 2 is quite good as well, but it is Side 1 that is the more consistent.

***The Cars* – The Cars (June 1978) Side 2** – You're All I've Got Tonight, Bye Bye Love, Moving in Stereo, All Mixed Up

The debut album by this Boston area group is without question their best and perhaps the best album of the entire "new wave" of the late 1970s-early 1980s. Energetic and edgy, the Cars had many of their best songs on this one album. It was my first purchase upon arriving in California prior to my first year at Stanford Business School. I played it incessantly and both sides almost equally though ultimately I preferred Side 2 because I liked ALL four songs immensely. In fact, all four tracks flow together musically and lyrically which adds to their overall appeal. "You're All I've Got Tonight" features a great new edgy techno-rock sound primarily using guitars and keyboards. Ironically, it ends lyrically with *"I need you tonight"* and then a six-note musical/lyrical reversal into the second track, "Bye Bye Love", as Ric Ocasek sings *"always with some other guy, it's just a broken lullaby"*, another great techno rocker. (I confess that for years I thought Ocasek was saying *"always with some other guy, it's just a fucking alibi"*, which would have been a better line, but might NOT have been approved by the record company in the 1970s.) The crescendo of techno-rock ends with the same six-note sequence and moves more softly into "Moving in Stereo", another great song that lyrically belies classification *("life's the same I'm moving in stereo, except for my shoes")*. The last song, another great tune, "All Mixed Up" fittingly provides at least some resolution of the tenuous, tempestuous relationship begun with "You're All I've Got Tonight" *("she's always out the window, when it comes to making dreams. It's all mixed up")* but then it finishes *("she says to leave it to me, everything'll be all right")* and the song fades away. This is a brilliant and cohesive album side. Nonetheless, it is only somewhat better than Side 1 and its three excellent singles: "Good Times Roll", "My Best Friend's Girl" and "Just What I Needed".

Appendix of Lyric Attributions

Section I

Book Title: "I've Got the Music in Me" – The Kiki Dee Band

Section I: "Reelin' in the Years" – Steely Dan

1963: "Only the Beginning" – "Beginnings" – Chicago

1964: "I'm Feelin' Glad All Over" – "Glad All Over" – Dave Clark Five

1965 Pt. 1: "I Believe in Yesterday" – "Yesterday" – The Beatles

1965 Pt. 2: "I've Got Sunshine on a Cloudy Day" – "My Girl" – The Temptations

1966 Pt. 1: "Beep Beep Yeah" – "Drive My Car" – The Beatles

1966 Pt. 2: "My Empty Cup Tastes as Sweet as the Punch" – "Along Comes Mary" – The Association

1967: "All You Need Is Love" – The Beatles

1968: "Born to Be Wild" – Steppenwolf

1969: "It's the Time of the Season for Loving" – "Time of the Season" – The Zombies

1970: "I've Seen Sunny Days That I Thought Would Never End" – "Fire and Rain" – James Taylor

1971 Pt. 1: "Listen to the Tide Slowly Turning, Wash All Our Heartaches Away" – "The Story in Your Eyes" – The Moody Blues

1971 Pt. 2: "All You've Got to Do Is Call" – "You've Got a Friend" – Carole King

1972: "It Was a Very Good Year" – Frank Sinatra

1973: "We're An American Band" – Grand Funk Railroad

1974: "You Ain't Seen Nothing Yet" – Bachman-Turner Overdrive

1975: "Thank God My Music's Still Alive" – "Someone Saved My Life Tonight" – Elton John

1976: "Don't Go Breaking My Heart" – Elton John and Kiki Dee

Section II – The Lists

Part 1 – Song Lists

Best Summer Songs: "There Is Danger in the Summer Moon Above" – "See You in September" – The Happenings

Best Rain Songs: "Listen to the Rhythm of the Falling Rain" – "Rhythm of the Rain" – The Cascades

Best Christmas Songs: "Santa Claus Is Coming to Town"- Bruce Springsteen

Best Comedy Singles: "Please Mr. Custer, I Don't Want to Go" – "Mr. Custer" – Larry Verne

Best B-Sides (ex. The Beatles): "Wham Bam Thank You Ma'am" – "Suffragette City" – David Bowie

Best Beatles B-Sides: "Don't You Know It's Gonna Be Alright" – "Revolution" – The Beatles

Best Long Songs: "Take a Sad Song and Make It Better" – "Hey Jude" – The Beatles

Best Rockin' Love Songs: "And You Know You Should Be Glad" – "She Loves You" – The Beatles

Best Number or Alphanumeric Songs: "1-2-3" – Len Barry

Best Originals/Cover Pairs: "It Takes Two, Baby, Me and You" – "It Takes Two" – Marvin Gaye and Kim Weston

Part 2 – Favorite Artists and Album Lists

My Favorite Concerts: "Get Back to Where You Once Belonged" – "Get Back" – The Beatles

Best Family Groups: "It's a Family Affair" – "Family Affair" – Sly and the Family Stone

Best Rock Albums: "It's Only Teenage Wasteland" – "Baba O'Riley" – The Who

Best Album Sides of the 1960s: "With Tangerine Trees and Marmalade Skies" – "Lucy in the Sky With Diamonds" – The Beatles

Best Album Sides of the 1970s: "Blue Jean Baby, L.A. Lady, Seamstress for the Band" – "Tiny Dancer" – Elton John

Bibliography

It would have been impossible to write this book without excellent source material.

Bronson, Fred. ***The Billboard Book of Number One Hits.*** Billboard Publications, 1988. – *Great source of information and trivia about all artists to hit #1 on the Billboard charts.*

Clapton, Eric. ***Clapton: The Autobiography.*** Three Rivers Press, 2007.

Davies, Hunter. ***The Beatles Lyrics.*** Little Brown and Company, September 2014.

DeCurtis, Henke and George Warren. ***The Rolling Stone Album Guide***. Random House, 1992. – *Source of album release dates and rock album reviews.*

Dolenz, Micky and Mark Bego. ***I'm A Believer: My Life of Monkees, Music and Madness.*** Cooper Square Press, 2004.

Fogerty, John. ***Fortunate Son: My Life, My Music.*** Little Brown and Company, October 2015.

Isbell, Dann. ***Ranking the '60s: A Comprehensive Listing of the Top Songs and Acts from Pop's Golden Decade.*** Jefrian Books, 2013. – *Source of top 10 most popular songs by year in Part 1 of my book from 1963-69. Note: this ranking is based on the Billboard charts.*

Isbell, Dann and Bill Carroll. ***Ranking the '70s: A Complete Compilation of the Chart Songs and Acts from Pop's Eclectic Decade.*** Jefrian Books, 2015. – *Source of top 10 most popular songs by year in Part 1 of my book from 1970-76. Note: this ranking is based on Cash Box charts.*

Jovanovic, Rob. ***God Save the Kinks: A Biography***. Aurum Press, 2013.

Norman, Philip. ***Paul McCartney: The Life.*** Little, Brown and Company, 2016.

Pink Floyd: The Story of Wish You Were Here. Documentary Film. Eagle Rock Entertainment, 2012.

Posner, Gerald. ***Motown: Music, Money, Sex and Power.*** Random House, 2005.

Richards, Keith (with James Fox). ***Life.*** Little, Brown and Company, 2010.

Rogan, Johnny. ***The Byrds: Timeless Flight Revisited*** (2nd ed.). Rogan House, 1998.

Simon, Lou. ***'60s Satellite Survey - Sirius XM Radio*** and personal communications.

Spignesi and Lewis. ***100 Best Beatles Songs: An Informed Fan's Guide.*** Tess Press, 2004. – *Excellent source of info on 100 of The Beatles songs. Ranking used on my favorite Beatles B-sides list.*

Spitz, Bob. ***The Beatles: The Biography.*** Little, Brown and Company, 2005.

Springsteen, Bruce. ***Born to Run.*** Simon & Schuster, 2016.

Townshend, Pete. ***Who I Am: A Memoir.*** HarperCollins Publishers, 2012.

Whitburn, Joel. ***Joel Whitburn's Top Pop Singles 1955-2002.*** Record Research Inc., 2003. – *Source of basic information about the artists and songs, including basic biographical info and other trivia, date record debuted and peak position on Billboard Pop Singles chart.*

Whitburn, Joel. ***Joel Whitburn's Top Pop Singles 1955-1978.*** Record Research Inc., 1979. – *Source of peak chart position and date of peak chart position.*

Young, Neil. ***Waging Heavy Peace.*** Penguin Group, 2012.

About the Author

Bruce Braine has been a fan of rock and popular music since the early 1960s. He is an avid collector of music from the 1960s and 1970s. *I've Got the Music in Me* is his first published book. Bruce has a blog on music and economic public policy (thebrainetrust.com) and currently works as a part-time consultant in energy and environmental analysis (brucebraine.com) and as lecturer in policy and economics at The Ohio State University. His full-time work career (1980-2016) includes senior positions at American Electric Power and ICF Consulting.

End Notes

[1] Lou Simon, *'60s Satellite Survey - Sirius XM Radio*.

[2] Hunter Davies, *The Beatles Lyrics* (Boston: Little Brown and Company, 2014), p. 118.

[3] Keith Richards with James Fox, *Life* (Boston: Little, Brown and Company, 2010), pp. 176-177.

[4] Eric Clapton, *Clapton: The Autobiography* (New York: Three Rivers Press, 2007), p. 53.

[5] Stephen J. Spignesi and Michael Lewis, *100 Best Beatles Songs: An Informed Fan's Guide* (New York: Tess Press, 2004), pp. 94-95.

[6] Davies, *The Beatles Lyrics*, p. 174.

[7] Spignesi and Lewis, *100 Best Beatles Songs: An Informed Fan's Guide,* pp. 130-31.

[8] Rob Jovanovic, *God Save the Kinks: A Biography* (London: Aurum Press), pp. 110-111.

[9] Fred Bronson, *The Billboard Book of Number One Hits* (New York: Billboard Publications, 1988), p. 190.

[10] Micky Dolenz and Mark Bego, *I'm A Believer: My Life of Monkees, Music and Madness* (New York: Cooper Square Press, 2004), pp. 90-92.

[11] Bronson, *The Billboard Book of Number One Hits*, p. 215.

[12] Spignesi and Lewis, *100 Best Beatles Songs: An Informed Fan's Guide,* pp. 16-17.

[13] Richards with Fox, *Life*, pp. 184-187.

[14] Johnny Rogan, *The Byrds: Timeless Flight Revisited* (2nd ed.) (UK: Rogan House, 1998), pp. 232-234.

[15] Spignesi and Lewis, *100 Best Beatles Songs: An Informed Fan's*

Guide, pp. 43-45.

[16] Gerald Posner, *Motown: Music, Money, Sex and Power* (New York: Random House, 2005), pp. 184-185.

[17] Tommy James and the Shondells, *Tommy James and the Shondells: Anthology* (Los Angeles: Rhino Records Inc., 1989) R2 70920. Media Notes, pp. 8, 12.

[18] Neil Young, *Waging Heavy Peace* (London: Penguin Group, 2012), pp. 114-15.

[19] Bob Spitz, *The Beatles: The Biography* (Boston: Little, Brown and Company, 2005), p. 851.

[20] Simon, *'60s Satellite Survey - Sirius XM Radio.*

[21] Clapton, *Clapton: The Autobiography,* pp. 126-27.

[22] Philip Norman, *Paul McCartney: The Life* (Boston: Little, Brown and Company, 2016), pp. 437-439.

[23] Henke DeCurtis and George Warren, *The Rolling Stone Album Guide* (New York: Random House, 1992), pp. 310-311.

[24] Pete Townshend, *Who I Am: A Memoir* (New York: HarperCollins Publishers, 2012), pp. 248-258.

[25] Clapton, *Clapton: The Autobiography,* pp. 151-153.

[26] *Pink Floyd: The Story of Wish You Were Here,* Documentary Film (London: Eagle Rock Entertainment, 2012).

[27] Bronson, *The Billboard Book of Number One Hits*, p. 466.

[28] Townshend, *Who I Am: A Memoir*, pp. 279-289.

[29] Bruce Springsteen, *Born to Run* (New York: Simon & Schuster, 2016), pp. 168-169 and pp. 246-260.

[30] Townshend, *Who I Am: A Memoir*, pp. 210-224.

[31] Spignesi and Lewis, *100 Best Beatles Songs: An Informed Fan's Guide,* p. 167.

[32] Norman, *Paul McCartney: The Life*, p. 394.

[33] Spignesi and Lewis, *100 Best Beatles Songs: An Informed Fan's Guide,* pp. 118-121.

[34] Springsteen, *Born to Run*, pp. 219-222.

Made in the USA
Middletown, DE
28 November 2017